Great British Dishes
the Healthy Way

Great British
the Healthy Way

Dishes

PUBLISHED BY THE READER'S DIGEST ASSOCIATION LIMITED
LONDON • NEW YORK • SYDNEY • MONTREAL

BREAKFASTS, SNACKS AND SAVOURIES

STARTERS, SOUPS AND SALADS

EGGS AND CHEESE

Contents

PUDDINGS

BAKING

VEGETABLE DISHES

FISH AND SHELLFISH

POULTRY AND GAME

BEEF, LAMB AND PORK

PRESERVES AND DRINKS

FEASTS AND FESTIVALS

Introduction

The rich, generous style of traditional British dishes makes them tempting and satisfying. Now they can be healthy too.

When a full English breakfast, or fish and chips, or a Sunday roast with all the trimmings, or a sherry trifle tempts you, do you sometimes feel pangs of guilt and retreat reluctantly on grounds of health? These and so many other great British dishes – including toad-in-the-hole, spotted dick and Dundee cake – are widely perceived as 'forbidden foods', when viewed against the latest advice on healthy eating.

Now *Great British Dishes the Healthy Way* sets a new standard for British cooking by showing you how all your favourite dishes can still be enjoyed without guilt or risk of ill health.

There are more than 250 recipes to enjoy. Some are traditional dishes in their original form as they are perfectly in line with today's nutritional guidelines. Others have been adapted as required – by adding fibre, reducing salt or sugar, cutting down on fat or making simple changes to the cooking methods, for example – to provide healthier versions of old favourites. There is also a selection of exciting new ways to prepare the best of British produce, such as Smoked eel risotto or Twice-baked courgette and goat's cheese puffs (see pages 94 and 80-81), all of which reflect the current enthusiasm for 'modern British' cuisine.

Here, at last, is a new kitchen bible for anyone who wishes to savour the nation's gastronomic delights in all their diversity, while still helping themselves to a long, active life by eating a nutritious, well-balanced diet. The clear message of *Great British Dishes the Healthy Way* is that British food can be both good to eat and good for you.

HOW TO USE THIS BOOK

Using the recipes
• Ingredients are given in both metric and imperial measures. These are not exact equivalents: use either measure, but do not mix the two.
• All spoon measures are level, unless otherwise stated; 1 level teaspoon equals 5ml and 1 level tablespoon equals 15ml.
• All eggs are medium unless otherwise specified.
• Many recipes specify black pepper; for the best flavour this should be freshly ground.

Nutritional analyses
• These figures are intended only as a guide as results may vary depending on a number of factors, including the time of year and method of cooking.
• Figures given for each recipe are for average portions. Main course meat recipes such as roast turkey are based on servings of 150g (6oz) of meat.
• The nutritional figures do not include accompaniments, unless they are part of the dish.
• Vitamins present in significant amounts are listed from highest to lowest.

7

Healthy British food

BEEF AND VEGETABLE FILO PIE

W hat we regard as quintessential British food owes much of its character to the climate of these islands. In times past, when work was in the fields and draughty homes were the only protection against cold, damp weather, a hearty diet was required. For many, that simply meant what was readily available; life was hard and short, and no one worried whether a dish was too high in calories or too rich in fat to be truly healthy.

It was not, perhaps, a diet for the more sedentary lives that people lead today, but it has left behind a varied culinary tradition. This is based on an abundance of native plants and animals and also reflects the influences of many other nations whose tastes have been enjoyed and embraced across the centuries.

Foreign influences

The Romans, who ruled the British Isles for some 400 years, introduced many now typical British foods, such as venison, pheasant, chestnuts, apples, cabbage, parsley and turnips. Our passion for piquant savoury condiments, such as Worcestershire and anchovy sauces, is rooted in their love of intensely flavoured seasonings. They also introduced the idea of eating as an aesthetic experience rather than simply as a means of survival.

When the Saxons, Angles and Vikings arrived, we were exposed to new culinary practices. After the Conquest of 1066, the Normans brought with them not only French ideas, but also the vast array of foods and flavours that had taken their fancy while moving through southern Europe and countries bordering the Mediterranean Sea.

Returning Crusaders also brought back flavours from the Middle East, and North African and Arabian ingredients subsequently filtered through into British cooking. Their use became firmly established in the Middle Ages, when saffron, cloves, dried fruits and almonds were all regularly included in sweet-sour savoury dishes and in desserts and baking. These left a lasting impression

on British cuisine and evolved into the traditional range of cakes, pastries, pickles and relishes we still enjoy. It is hardly surprising that during the days of the Raj in India, the British took so readily to the curries and chutneys of Asia – we already had a deeply ingrained, centuries-old taste for spiced dishes.

Many of the foods that we now regard as very ordinary staples were also once seen as exotic curiosities – most notably the potato and the tomato. Both were adopted only after excursions to the Americas in the 1600s. Indeed, the New World has provided us with quite a number of imports that are now commonplace ingredients in British cookery, including coffee, chillies, peppers, maize, turkey and vanilla.

Using culinary ingredients and flavours from around the world has long been a trend in British cookery.

Simple fare

Plain food would have been most familiar to the rural poor, who did not have the money to purchase expensive spices and exotic luxury goods. Periodically, plain food was the order of the day, especially during the Puritan movement of the mid 1600s, because some believed that spices and exotic vegetables inflamed passions, leading to immoderate and lecherous behaviour!

Our most traditional plain foods are the simple pottages, soups or porridges that could be produced by cooking a handful of vegetables or grain in a pot of water, and serving it with fresh bread on the side, or tipped over stale bread. Such dishes are the origin of Britain's famous bread sauce. When fresh game and meat were available, it would be roasted, and being of fine quality, needed nothing but such a basic sauce to make it delicious.

Food and industrialisation

From the 17th to the 19th centuries, many foods now familiar on British tables arrived here for the first time, including broccoli, brussels sprouts, rhubarb, runner beans and swedes. But it took the impact of the Industrial Revolution to really change the diet of

most Britons. With the shift away from living off the land, many now spent their days working in factories rather than in the fields and the focus was on feeding them cheaply. More and more businesses were set up to sell inexpensive, ready-made meals, including pie and mash, and fish and chips. Meanwhile, the wealthy imported French chefs to produce their more refined cuisine – a key influence still evident in our restaurants today.

The World Wars

In the 20th century, two World Wars heralded sweeping social changes, which to some degree levelled out the vast discrepancies in the quantity and quality of foods enjoyed by the rich compared to what was eaten by the poor. It is often said that all Britons were at their fittest during the Second World War, when imported goods were limited and difficult to obtain, even for those who could afford the high prices. Meat, dairy produce, sugar and luxury foods were strictly rationed, which meant that high-fat and sugary items were scarce and the national diet was based largely on fresh fruit and vegetables, and the starchy carbohydrates in potatoes and bread. Everyone was encouraged to 'Dig for Victory' by growing their own food, in a bid to make families more self-sufficient.

The new millennium has brought renewed interest in traditional fare, and exciting new ways to use the best local produce.

Into the future

In the decades following the Second World War, technical advances in processing and preserving made it easier to transport food safely over vast distances. A huge variety is now widely available all year round at affordable prices. Yet, the national diet has not become healthier – largely as a result of social changes. As men and women, too, are increasingly employed full-time outside the home, people have become more inclined to eat out, buy a take-away meal, or pick a ready-prepared gourmet treat from the

Traditional beverages

Ale was brewed in Britain long before the Romans introduced wine, and remained the nation's favoured beverage, for both adults and children, well into the 20th century. Originally a brew flavoured with herbs or spices, the modern, bitter-tasting, hopped style reached these shores from Germany only in the 15th century.

The Anglo-Saxons also had a passion for fermented honey drinks, such as mead, and the Normans made cider-making popular in England after 1066. The late 20th-century interest in traditional foods has spurred a revival in the popularity of both drinks. At the start of the 21st century, there are nearly 150 traditional cider presses in England and a handful of companies producing mead.

supermarket shelf. But in recent years, scientists have warned that a diet of convenience foods is not good for health as many contain high levels of salt and fat, which if consumed to excess can lead to heart disease and stroke, the two major killers in modern Britain.

The news, however, is not all bad. In the 21st century, in response to these concerns, many people are beginning to rediscover good food and recognise that it is at its most tasty and healthy when fresh and in season. In towns and cities across Britain, farmers' markets, selling produce grown or made locally, have become increasingly popular.

All this has been accompanied by a rekindled interest in cooking and a backward glance to old family favourites, the recipes our grandmothers prepared. You will find many of the tastiest in this book – adapted and streamlined to suit modern tastes and dietary guidelines. *Great British Dishes the Healthy Way* bridges the gap between guilt and desire, showing how the best British ingredients can still be combined to create an outstanding national cuisine.

Healthy cooking techniques

Taking the best of British produce and using simple techniques to turn it into healthy, mouth-watering dishes is what this book is all about. Whether you want to create a streamlined version of an old favourite or a new 'modern British' gourmet treat, this book will be an excellent guide.

Where possible, use the best quality ingredients you can afford, preferably in season. This will make both cooking and eating more enjoyable, as good quality ingredients usually work better in recipes and are more easily transformed into delicious meals.

Age-old techniques

Many traditional methods, such as roasting and stewing, are perfectly healthy ways of cooking. For healthy roasts or stews, you may need only to adjust the ratio of ingredients to fit in with current advice on balanced eating. You can do this very easily by simply increasing the amount of starch and vegetables included in the meal, for example, and by limiting the use of saturated fats and trimming any visible fat from the meat.

There are many easy ways to cook food and keep the fat content healthily low:

Searing and dry-frying

You can fry food and still enjoy a low-fat diet. For searing or frying, a good quality nonstick pan is ideal but not essential; more importantly the pan should have a heavy base.

If adding any oil or fat, apply only a very light mist of it to the pan or the food to be cooked; a bottle of vegetable oil spray is useful for this. Heat the pan until it is very hot before putting food in it, and then leave the food, without moving

or turning it, until a light crust has formed. This will prevent it from sticking, while using only the minimum of fat or oil for greasing.

Stir-frying and sautéing

These are similarly speedy cooking methods that help to preserve nutrients, especially in vegetables, and require little or no added oil or fat. Again a nonstick pan would be helpful, but the essential thing is to keep the food moving in the pan, so that it does not get a chance to stick or burn. Both work best if the meat, fish or vegetables are

Marinating meat and poultry

1 Put the meat or poultry in a shallow dish and pour over a marinade made from a savoury liquid, such as wine, soy sauce or citrus juice, flavoured with herbs or spices and seasoning to taste.

2 Leave for at least 30 minutes, but preferably for 1 to 2 hours or overnight. Spoon the marinade over the meat from time to time to keep it well coated.

3 Cook on a very hot grill. With moist marinated meat, the grill pan should not need any oiling.

Low-fat grilling

1 Choose tender slices of prime meat or poultry fillets for grilling. Pull the skin off the poultry and use a sharp knife to cut any visible fat off the meat before cooking.

2 With a meat mallet or rolling pin, flatten the meat or poultry fillets, so that they are an even thickness. Place them in a marinade (see left) or season lightly with salt and black pepper.

3 If not using a marinade, spray or smear a fine film of oil over the surface of the grill pan. Heat the pan over a high heat, until it is very hot and you can see a haze rising up from it.

4 Put the meat in the pan, leave for 1-2 minutes until browned and slightly crusty on the underside. Turn and cook the other side. Brief cooking on a high heat keeps meat tender and juicy.

For no-fat cooking, the oil can be replaced with stock, soy sauce, vegetable juice, wine or any other tasty liquid that goes well with the mix of ingredients that are being prepared.

Grilling

To make sure that food does not sit in fat as it cooks under an overhead grill, lay it on a rack so that the fat can drip away, or use a ridged grill pan or griddle. Marinating food before grilling adds flavour and helps to tenderise and moisten meat. Barbecuing is a form of grilling that also imparts a delicious smoky flavour.

Roasting and baking

Roasting or baking are suitable for meat, poultry, game, fish, vegetables or fruit. A joint of meat or a whole bird may need no extra fat, and using a trivet in the base of the pan will allow fat to drain away during cooking. If roasting vegetables, brush first with a little oil mixed with a sweet balsamic or sherry vinegar for extra flavour.

cut into ready-to-cook, bite-sized pieces before you start, so they can easily be added to the pan at the right time, and also to ensure that they cook quickly and evenly. It is important to use a pan or wok that is quite a

bit larger than the volume of food you are cooking. If the pan is filled to the brim, the food will stew rather than stir-fry. This will make any meat tough and produce soggy, overdone vegetables.

Stewing and braising

These two methods involve food being cooked slowly in a small quantity of flavoured liquid, such as a stock or wine, in a sealed pot or casserole. Both are slow-cooking methods, but they

Succulent steaming

1 Ensure that the base pan is at least a third full of water. If you wish, you can boil firm food, such as potatoes or grains, in this.

2 Place food in successive perforated steaming baskets on top, according to density or firmness – root vegetables are likely to go next, with softer leafy vegetables and fish fillets sitting on top.

produce tender, succulent meals and help to maximise the health benefits of the food being prepared, as nutrients that leach into the cooking liquid can be eaten as part of a tasty sauce. To add extra flavour, meat and poultry are often lightly seared before being placed in the casserole dish.

Poaching
A highly underrated form of cooking, poaching can be used to produce an entire meal of meat or fish and vegetables, without the need for any additional fat. The food is cooked very gently, at just below simmering point until tender, in water or a liquid flavoured with herbs and spices, lemon juice,

vinegar or wine. For best results, do not let the liquid boil as the food may become tough and lose flavour.

Steaming
By cooking food in the hot vapour given off by boiling water rather than in the water itself, its nutrients, colour and texture are better preserved. Add herbs, spices or citrus zest to the liquid to impart a subtle flavouring.

Cooking en papillote
A form of steaming where the food, plus a little liquid such as stock, wine or lemon juice, is wrapped in well-sealed parcels of paper or foil. These are then cooked in the oven.

RECOMMENDED EQUIPMENT

Measuring spoons and scales
It is not always vital to measure ingredients precisely, but do not use more fats and oils than required, and always measure accurately when baking.

Brushes
A good quality heat-resistant brush allows you to coat hot pans or food with an extremely light film of oil or other fat, or with a tasty baste or marinade. Rolled-up kitchen paper can be used instead to grease pans, unless they are very hot.

Zester or fine grater
The quickest way to remove fine strips of zest from citrus fruit is to use a zester. You can also use a fine grater. Zest gives zing to both sweet and savoury dishes without adding fat.

Ridged grill pan or griddle
Any fat melting off the hot food in a ridged pan will collect in the hollows between the ridges, so the food does not sit in the fat. A cast-iron pan or griddle usually has a longer life than a nonstick one. Heat the pan over

a very high heat until it is really hot before adding food. This helps a crust to form quickly, preventing the food sticking.

Nonstick frying pan or wok

With a nonstick frying pan or wok, you can prepare fried food using the minimum possible amount of fat. Durability is the key factor to consider when buying any kind of nonstick cookware. Always buy the best quality that you can afford, preferably a brand that features an extremely tough nonstick lining that will stand up to the occasional accidental use of metal implements for stirring or lifting the food.

It is also a good idea to choose a pan with a handle that can be placed in a hot oven or under a hot grill, as this will allow you to use the pan for preparing the widest possible range of dishes, including thick vegetable-filled omelettes or frittatas.

Steamer

A multi-layered steamer cleverly allows you to cook an entire meal on one hob. For example, a pan of water, rapidly boiling potatoes or rice at the base, gives off steam that will cook successive layers of vegetables,

fish or meat sat above it in perforated steaming baskets. If at all possible, invest in a heavy-based, stainless steel steaming set. The base pan can double as a useful soup pot or casserole. A cheaper alternative is to buy a couple of perforated metal

steamers with a lid, or a set of Chinese bamboo steamers, that can sit on top of your regular saucepans. Avoid the small expanding, perforated metal steamers that fit in the base of saucepans, as they tend to make the pot boil dry before the food is properly cooked.

Salad spinner

The quickest and easiest way to wash and dry fresh salad leaves, so that they stay really crisp, is to use a salad spinner.

Mandolin

This little tool is a well-kept secret of many top chefs when preparing mouth-watering salads. It will cut myriad firm fresh vegetables into juicy paper-thin slices that are both appetising and elegant.

Food processor or blender

Puréeing ingredients using a food processor or blender when you make soups and sauces gives them a creamy texture, but without adding any fat. A hand-held stick blender is especially useful, as it can be used to purée food directly in the saucepan in which it was cooked. Some stick blenders also have a whisk attachment.

Balanced diet

The old adage 'moderation in all things' is proving to be particularly sound dietary advice. As scientists discover more about nutrition and guidelines for healthy eating are revised, it is clear that, unless eaten to excess, many different foods can be enjoyed. And some once thought to be detrimental to health, such as chocolate, eggs and red wine, are now perceived as beneficial if taken in moderation.

A varied diet

Variety is the most important element of balanced eating. To obtain a full range of essential nutrients – carbohydrates, fats and protein, as well as vitamins, minerals and fibre – it is necessary to incorporate a broad range of different foods into your diet. Wherever possible, try to avoid eating the same ingredients for two meals, or even two days, in a row. If, for instance, lunch is a chicken sandwich, enjoy fish with salad and potatoes for dinner.

Eating a wider variety of foods does not mean eating more of them. If you consume more calories than you expend, you will start to put on weight. What is right for you will depend on your age, sex, health and level of activity. This is why advice on daily nutritional requirements always gives a range of desirable daily quantities. On average, between the ages of 20 and 45, men require an intake of about 2500 calories a day and women about 2000 calories.

Fuel for life

Current health guidelines indicate that around 55 to 60 per cent of your daily intake of calories should be in the form of carbohydrates, which provide energy. Even if you lead a fairly sedentary lifestyle, you still need the energy just to stay alive.

Starchy foods, such as bread, cereals and potatoes should be the body's main sources of carbohydrate. They release their energy gradually, so help to keep you going over a long period of time. They also supply

Water

About two-thirds of human body weight is made up by water, which is crucial to all bodily functions. Even slight dehydration can have a big effect on physical and mental well-being, because the body needs a supply of water in order to absorb other life-fuelling nutrients from food. Most adults should drink 2-3 litres (3½-5¼ pints) a day. Some of this can be in the form of fruit juice and hot and soft drinks, but as these may contain stimulants such as caffeine and large amounts of sugar, pure water is best and is certainly the most effective thirst quencher. If you start to drink the recommended amount every day, you will soon be amazed how well and alert you feel.

Bread, potatoes and cereals

6-11 SERVINGS DAILY

important vitamins, minerals and fibre. Sugar is an energy-rich carbohydrate too, but it is absorbed very quickly, so is good for fuelling bursts of high activity but not for longer-term stamina. Pure sugar contributes calories but no nutrients.

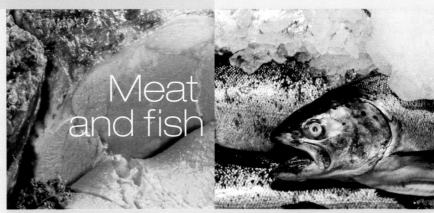

Meat and fish

2-3 SERVINGS DAILY

Body-building protein

Protein is needed for growth, repair and maintenance of the body. But it is required in only quite small amounts – about 55g (2oz) a day for men and about 45g (1½oz) for women, or roughly 10-15 per cent of your daily calories. People who are especially active should try to consume about 1 gram of protein for every kilogram of their body weight.

There are plenty of protein-rich foods to choose from – lean portions of meat, poultry and game, fish and shellfish, and eggs and cheese, as well as beans, pulses and modest quantities of nuts and seeds.

Good and bad fats

We are constantly being urged to reduce our fat intake, but appropriate amounts – about 30-35g (1⅛-1¼oz) per day – are essential for good health. Fats

supply the vital fat-soluble vitamins, A, D, E and K, and also enable the body to absorb them.

Many protein-rich foods are also high in fat, which, like starch is a rich source of calories for energy. Fats of the saturated kind found in meats, such as beef, pork and lamb, and in dairy produce are dangerous if eaten to excess. Medical research has revealed that high

intakes can increase the risk of heart disease and certain cancers of the breast, bowel and pancreas. Nutritionists suggest that no more than 10 per cent of the your daily calories should come from saturated fats.

But while it may be advisable for adults to limit their fat intake, the diets of children under five should not be similarly restricted.

Fats and sugars

0-2 SERVINGS DAILY

VITAMINS FOR HEALTH		
Vitamin	Necessary for	Good sources
Vitamin A	Good vision, growth, healthy skin and hair, healthy tooth enamel	Liver, kidneys, oily fish, milk, cheese, butter, egg yolk As beta carotene*: orange, yellow and green fruit and vegetables
Vitamin B complex	Growth, healthy nervous system, RNA and DNA production, red blood cell formation (folate)	Liver, kidneys, yeast extract, meat, milk, yoghurt, cheese, eggs, fish, brown rice, pulses, wholegrain cereals, green vegetables
Vitamin C	Growth, healthy body tissue, healing of wounds, iron absorption, reduction in severity of colds	Rosehips, blackcurrants, green peppers, kiwi fruit, citrus fruits, strawberries, cabbage, spinach, broccoli
Vitamin D	Healthy bones and teeth	Oily fish, cod liver oil, eggs, liver, butter, margarine, cheese, milk, yoghurt; also made by skin in the presence of sunlight
Vitamin E	Decreased risk of heart disease and some cancers, strong cells, especially in blood	Avocados, blackberries, vegetable oils, lettuce, nuts and seeds, wheatgerm oil, wholegrain cereal
Vitamin K	Blood coagulation, strong bones	Leafy vegetables, especially spinach, wholegrain cereals

* Beta carotene is a substance that is converted into vitamin A in the digestive system

There is now evidence to suggest that some types of fat may even help to reduce blood cholesterol levels, to lower blood pressure and to slow or prevent the growth of cancerous tumours. These are the unsaturated fats that are present in certain kinds of fish and vegetables. They come in two forms – monounsaturated and polyunsaturated.

Monounsaturated fats include olive and rapeseed oils, both of which are excellent for cooking, while sunflower and corn oil can offer vital polyunsaturated fat – you need about 4g (⅙oz) of it a day to stay really healthy. An especially good form of polyunsaturated fat – omega-3 fatty acids – is found in leafy, dark green vegetables, some nuts and oils, and in oily fish, which you should try to eat at least twice a week.

Fruit and vegetables

Nutritionists currently advise us to eat at least five portions (or 400g/14oz) of vegetables and fruit each day, and there is much evidence to suggest that this figure should be higher.

This should not be difficult as there are so many contrasting tastes and textures to enjoy within this group of foods that they can be included in many different meals. Eating fruit can also help to stave off cravings for unhealthy sugary snacks.

Most fresh produce is very low in calories and fat, while being packed with beneficial vitamins and minerals (see charts above and right), antioxidants, which help to guard against certain cancers and heart disease, and fibre (see below).

In general, the richer a fruit or vegetable is in vitamins and antioxidants, the brighter its colouring. So there is every reason to create a colourful selection, which will also look more appetising.

Fibre

All fruit and vegetables, cereals, pulses, nuts and seeds are good sources of fibre, which is essential for the elimination of

Fruit and vegetables

AT LEAST 5 SERVINGS DAILY

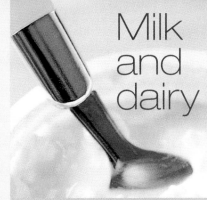

Milk and dairy

2-4 SERVINGS DAILY

potentially toxic waste from the body. It helps bowel function, and also contributes other helpful nutrients, such as phyto-oestrogens that protect against some forms of cancer and heart disease.

To increase the fibre content in your diet, eat as much fresh, rather than processed, produce as possible and avoid too many highly refined foods, such as white flour and sugar.

Include wholegrain foods in your daily menu – wholemeal bread, brown rice and oatmeal – and a grain, such as pot barley or spelt, a few times a week. The tasty skin of scrubbed potatoes and other root vegetables, such as carrots and parsnips, is also fibre-rich and can help you to reach an optimum target of 18g (¾oz) fibre each day.

Happy eating

Remember too that good health is linked to factors other than food. Exercise, relaxation and a feeling of social connection also contribute. Stress encourages the onset of various illnesses, as well as weight gain; the antidote is leisurely eating with friends and family – something this book should help you to do.

MINERALS FOR HEALTH		
Mineral	Necessary for	Good sources
Calcium	Strong bones and teeth, blood coagulation	Dairy produce (milk and cheese), bread, sesame seeds, bones of canned fish, hard water, green vegetables
Iron	Healthy blood and muscles	Liver, kidney, corned beef, cocoa, plain chocolate, offal, watercress, oily fish, lean meat, dried fruit, pulses
Magnesium	Release of energy from food, strong bones, teeth and muscles, regulating body heat	Wholegrain cereal products, wholewheat pasta, brown rice, nuts and seeds, green leafy vegetables, courgettes, milk, yoghurt, lean meat, bananas, dried figs, apricots and raisins
Phosphorus	Strong bones and teeth, absorption of nutrients	All natural foods
Selenium	Healthy liver	Fruit, vegetables, nuts, seeds, lean meat, eggs, wholewheat bread, milk, hard and crumbly cheeses, fish, shellfish
Sodium and potassium	Body's water balance, heart rhythm, nerve impulses, muscle function	Fish, meat, bananas, potatoes, manufactured savoury snacks; as sodium chloride or potassium chloride in food
Zinc	Healthy immune system	Shellfish, canned sardines, lean meats turkey, duck, goose, liver and kidneys, cheese, egg

Breakfasts, snacks

and savouries

Breakfasts, snacks and savouries
the healthy way

Breakfast – the most important meal of the day – boosts energy levels so that the body performs well from the outset.

Breakfast is good for you. It is good for the brain, refuelling it with glucose after the night's fast when blood glucose levels become low. While those who are active may enjoy the protein-packed eggs and bacon meal we call the 'great British breakfast', many now prefer a lighter start to the day. Both can be healthy if you avoid too much sugar and fat.

Proven benefits
Research has revealed that people who skip breakfast generally function less well in the morning and often experience frequent lapses of concentration.

Breakfast-eaters have been shown to be more resilient, to suffer less from colds and flu, and to be less susceptible to depression and stress than those who skip the first meal of the day.

Missing breakfast because you are watching your weight is also a false economy as you are much more likely to get hungry in the middle of the morning and grab a snack that is high in calories and fat, but low in nutrients and fibre.

Carbohydrates
The best breakfasts include wholemeal bread, wholegrain cereal, oats, or fresh fruit, which are rich in carbohydrates and fibre, and will boost your energy levels at a regular rate, avoiding the rapid rise and fall associated with a sugar rush. Healthy snacks and savoury nibbles can also be good sources of carbohydrate.
• At least 50 per cent of calories in a healthy diet should come from carbohydrates – especially from starchy foods such as bread, potatoes, cereals, rice and some types of vegetables. Depending on age and size, you should eat 6-11 portions of carbohydrate daily.
• Starchy carbohydrate foods, such as grains, are best for energy and also provide proteins, essential vitamins – especially B vitamins – and minerals.
• Wholegrain wheat-based cereals are high in insoluble fibre, which helps to prevent constipation and keeps the digestive system in good working order.
• Cereals with a high sugar content should be avoided as the added sugar contributes little nutritionally. It is better to add a little dried fruit.

Dairy products
Dairy foods, in moderation, also make a natural healthy start to the day. Butter, cheese, milk and yoghurt offer nutrients that are essential for overall health and are the best source of calcium, which is vital for strong bones and teeth and also important for the nervous system. Young children especially should include dairy produce in their diet and need full-fat versions until they are two years old. Adults, who may need to limit fat intake, can choose lower-fat alternatives, such as semi-skimmed milk or low-fat yogurt.
• Dairy foods provide protein for growth and repair, and vitamins A and B_{12}.
• They are especially important for women, who are more prone to osteoporisis in later life than men.
• You should eat 2-4 portions daily; portion examples include 1 medium-sized glass of milk, a small pot of yoghurt, 125g (4½ oz) cottage cheese, or a 40g (1½ oz) piece Cheddar cheese.

Oats
Hot porridge in the morning will also set you up for the day with a reserve of energy, especially in the depths of winter. This is because oats are an excellent source of fibre – the type that helps to reduce high blood cholesterol levels. They also help to keep blood sugar levels stable. Instant oatmeal contains fewer nutrients than oat flakes or rolled oats.

Grilling bacon, the low-fat way

1 Bacon is essentially a fatty meat and owes much of its mouth-watering flavour to its fat content. However, by grilling it, the unhealthy fat content can be greatly reduced. This applies to other fatty meats as well. Cut off any large areas of excess fat with a pair of scissors before placing in the grill pan.

2 Always grill the bacon on a rack in the grill pan. Any fat that melts off during cooking will then drip down into the pan. Putting bacon directly into the pan or on foil prevents fat from draining away.

3 Any fat lost during cooking will remain in the pan.

• Yoghurt contains bacteria that will help to keep the digestive system healthy and strengthen the immune system. It is also high in phosphorus and vitamins B_2 and B_{12}, and one small pot can provide as much as a third of the recommended daily allowance (RDA) of calcium.

• 'Bio' yoghurts are made with a strain of bacteria called bifida bacteria, which research suggests help to preserve a healthy bacterial balance in the gut.

The British fry-up

Delicious, but not altogether healthy, a traditional fry-up can have as many as 61g (2¼oz) of fat and 750 calories, which is too high on a regular basis. However, if you grill the bacon, poach the eggs and eat reduced-fat sausages, you will cut the fat and calories to an acceptable level without compromising on taste.

Healthy kippers

Kippers, a traditional British breakfast food, are also a healthy choice. They are a good source of protein and also of omega-3 fatty acids, as smoking does not destroy the nutrients in the fish. A diet containing omega-3 fatty acids can help

to reduce the risk of heart disease and stroke by lowering cholesterol levels and making the blood less likely to clot.

A regular intake of omega-3 fatty acids can also help to ease the pain associated with rheumatoid arthritis, as they have an anti-inflammatory effect.

High-energy breakfasts

'Breakfast like a king, lunch like a knave and dine like a pauper', so the saying goes but, in fact, breakfast does not have to mean a full-blown meal – ideally you should aim to consume about 20 per cent of your daily calories. For a man eating 2500 calories a day this is about 500 calories, for a woman eating 2000 calories a day, it is about 400 calories.

Breakfasts that supply slow-release carbohydrates, such as overnight porridge (see page 25) and muesli with dried fruit (see page 26), are ideal choices for avoiding mid-morning energy dips, as the carbohydrate is converted slowly into sugar, which helps to keep blood-sugar levels stable, staving off hunger pangs.

Breakfast stacks

PREPARATION TIME: 5 MINUTES
COOKING TIME: 10 MINUTES
SERVES 4

4 low-fat herby sausages, skinned
1 tablespoon plain flour
2 slices of rindless smoked back bacon
4 large mushrooms, stalks removed
Olive oil for brushing
1 teaspoon vinegar
4 eggs
Black pepper

1 Heat the grill to moderately hot. With lightly floured hands, shape the sausage meat into four rounds. Place the rounds on the grill rack with the bacon and mushrooms. Brush the mushrooms lightly with oil and cook everything under the grill: the mushrooms and sausage rounds need 3-4 minutes on each side and the bacon about 5 minutes on each side.

2 Meanwhile, add the vinegar to a frying pan of water and heat to simmering point. Break each egg into a cup and gently slide each, one at a time, into the water. Keep the water at a steady temperature, spooning a little water over the yolks as they cook, until the eggs are cooked to your liking. Chop the bacon finely.

3 To serve, put each mushroom, rounded-side down, onto a warm plate. Top with a sausage round. With a slotted spoon, lift each egg from the water, place the spoon on kitchen paper to remove excess water and put an egg on top of each sausage. Sprinkle with bacon and pepper, and serve with grilled tomatoes.

Nutrients per serving
- Calories 170
- Carbohydrate 5g (including sugars 0g)
- Protein 14g
- Fat 11g (including saturated fat 3g)
- Fibre 0.5g
- Vitamins B_{12}, B_6

A **healthy** way to enjoy the **traditional** British breakfast, **grilled** not fried, but with all the **flavour** of the original.

Overnight porridge

Nutrients per serving
- Calories 140
- Carbohydrate 25g (of which sugars 0g)
- Protein 4g
- Fat 3g (of which saturated fat 0g)
- Fibre 3g

PREPARATION TIME: 5 MINUTES, PLUS OVERNIGHT SOAKING
COOKING TIME: 10-20 MINUTES
SERVES 4

140g (5oz) oatmeal
Pinch of salt

To serve:
Semi-skimmed milk
Brown sugar or honey
Stewed plums, rhubarb or apples (optional)

1 Put the oatmeal in a saucepan with 900ml (1 pint 12fl oz) cold water. Stir, then cover and leave somewhere cool overnight.

2 The next day, add the salt and bring slowly to the boil over a medium heat, stirring often. Simmer over a medium-low heat for 10-20 minutes (pinhead oatmeal takes the longest to cook), stirring, until thick and creamy.

3 Serve in warm bowls with a little milk and a sprinkling of brown sugar or a drizzle of honey. Alternatively, serve with stewed fruit.

Soaking oatmeal overnight makes it more digestible, and saves time on busy mornings. Porridge makes a perfect, healthy start to the day – it is high in fibre and packed with complex carbohydrates, a good source of slow-release energy.

Mixed grain muesli with dried fruit salad

PREPARATION TIME: 5 MINUTES,
PLUS 36 HOURS SOAKING
MAKES 12 PORTIONS MUESLI,
4 PORTIONS DRIED FRUIT SALAD

85g (3oz) barley flakes
85g (3oz) rye flakes
85g (3oz) millet flakes
85g (3oz) jumbo oats
20g (¾oz) wheat bran
1 teaspoon ground cinnamon
3 tablespoons plain pumpkin seeds

For the dried fruit salad:
175g (6oz) mixed dried fruit, such as
    apricots, pears, apples, figs and prunes
½ teaspoon almond essence
1 small orange, peeled and segmented
1 small, ripe pear, cored and chopped

1 Put the barley, rye and millet flakes, oats, bran, cinnamon and pumpkin seeds in a large bowl and mix. Transfer to an airtight container to store.

2 To make the dried fruit salad, put the dried fruits in a bowl. Add the almond essence and 225ml (8fl oz) water. Cover and refrigerate overnight, or preferably for 36 hours, stirring occasionally and adding a little more water if necessary.

3 Add the orange and pear to the dried fruit just before serving.

4 Serve in bowls with low-fat natural yoghurt or semi-skimmed milk, topped with the dried fruit salad.

Nutrients per serving
- Calories 155
- Carbohydrate 30g (of which sugars 7g)
- Protein 4g
- Fat 2.5g (of which saturated fat 0g)
- Fibre 3g
- Vitamins B_1, B_6

Making your own muesli avoids the added sugar and salt often found in commercial brands, and also guarantees a much better texture and flavour.

Poached kippers

PREPARATION TIME: 5 MINUTES
COOKING TIME: 5 MINUTES
SERVES 4

300ml (½ pint) semi-skimmed milk
2 kippers, about 300g (10½oz) each
25g (1oz) butter
4 eggs, beaten
Salt and black pepper

Traditional Craster kippers have firmer flesh and a far better flavour than pre-packed kipper fillets, and are worth finding for this high-protein breakfast.

1 Heat the milk in a frying pan to simmering point. Add the kippers. If the milk does not quite cover them, add boiling water. Adjust the heat so the liquid is barely bubbling, cover the pan and poach for about 4 minutes.

2 Meanwhile, heat the butter in a nonstick saucepan, add the beaten eggs and cook over a very low heat, stirring, for about 3-4 minutes until creamy. Add a pinch of salt and stir.

3 Transfer the poached kippers to warmed plates. Spoon on the eggs and grind over some black pepper. Serve with wholemeal toast.

Nutrients per serving
- Calories 412
- Carbohydrate 4g (of which sugars 4g)
- Protein 29g
- Fat 31g (of which saturated fat 9g)
- Fibre 0g
- Vitamins B_2, niacin, B_{12}, B_6

Ham and haddie

PREPARATION TIME: 5 MINUTES
COOKING TIME: 10 MINUTES
SERVES 2

250g (9oz) smoked haddock fillet,
   skinned and halved
100ml (3½fl oz) semi-skimmed milk
15g (½oz) butter
2 slices of dry-cure bacon
2 tablespoons half-fat crème fraîche
Salt and black pepper

Nutrients per serving
- Calories 232
- Carbohydrate 3g (of which sugars 3g)
- Protein 28g
- Fat 11g (of which saturated fat 7g)
- Fibre 0g
- Vitamins niacin, B_6, B_{12}

1 Put the haddock in a saucepan and add the milk and half the butter. Bring slowly to the boil, then cover and simmer gently for about 3 minutes or until just cooked. Carefully remove the fish to two warmed serving plates, reserving the poaching liquid in a bowl.

2 Meanwhile, dry-fry or grill the bacon until crispy.

3 Melt the remaining butter in a clean pan, add 2 tablespoons of the reserved poaching liquid and the crème fraîche and let it bubble for 1-2 minutes to thicken. Add salt and pepper to taste.

4 To serve, pour half the sauce over each piece of haddock and top with a slice of crisp bacon. For an even more substantial dish, serve with a poached egg.

A classic Scottish breakfast dish of smoked haddock (haddie), traditionally Finnan haddock, and bacon (ham). This recipe is lighter than the original, cooked with only a little butter and some half-fat crème fraîche.

Cottage cheese pancakes with berry fruit compote

Nutrients per serving
- Calories 237
- Carbohydrate 32g (of which sugars 16g)
- Protein 15g
- Fat 6g (of which saturated fat 2g)
- Fibre 2g
- Vitamins B_{12}, C, B_2

PREPARATION TIME: 10 MINUTES
COOKING TIME: 6 MINUTES
SERVES 4

225g (8oz) low-fat cottage cheese, drained through a sieve
2 large eggs, separated
40g (1½oz) caster sugar
85g (3oz) self-raising flour
About 3 tablespoons milk
Vegetable oil for cooking

For the berry compote:
280g (10oz) raspberries, or a mixture of raspberries, strawberries and blueberries
2 teaspoons rosewater
Caster sugar (optional)
Low-fat crème fraîche to serve

1. To make the compote, purée 115g (4oz) of the raspberries or mixed berries in a blender or food processor. Stir in the rosewater and remaining berries, with sugar to taste, if desired. Set aside.

2. Beat together the cottage cheese, egg yolks and sugar, then stir in the flour. Whisk the egg whites until stiff. Stir a tablespoonful into the pancake mixture, then gently fold in the remaining egg white in two batches, adding enough milk to make a mixture that falls off the spoon when given a light shake.

3. Lightly brush or spray a nonstick frying pan with oil and heat. When hot, add large tablespoonfuls of the pancake mixture to the pan and spread them out gently with the back of the spoon. Cook for 2-3 minutes until just golden underneath, then turn them over and cook for another 2 minutes, or until golden.

4. Remove the pancakes to a plate and serve with the berry compote and crème fraîche.

Cottage cheese adds unusual lightness to the pancakes. The berries lend a natural sweetness as well as fibre and vitamin C to this fruity breakfast or brunch dish.

Kedgeree

PREPARATION TIME: 10 MINUTES
COOKING TIME: 1 HOUR
SERVES 4

350g (12oz) undyed smoked haddock
3 tablespoons olive oil
2 small onions, finely chopped
2 teaspoons curry powder
½ teaspoon turmeric
175g (6oz) brown rice, rinsed
1 tablespoon tomato purée
250g (9oz) spinach leaves
4 tablespoons low-fat Greek-style yoghurt
Salt and black pepper
4 hard-boiled eggs, quartered

Nutrients per serving
- Calories 428
- Carbohydrate 42g (of which sugars 6g)
- Protein 28g
- Fat 17g (of which saturated fat 4g)
- Fibre 3g
- Vitamins B_1, B_2, niacin, B_6, B_{12}

1 Bring 600ml (1 pint) water to the boil in a large frying pan. Reduce the heat, add the smoked haddock and simmer for 3-4 minutes, until just cooked. Remove the fish, strain the cooking liquid into a bowl and set aside.

2 Heat the oil in a pan, add the onions and cook over a medium heat for 2-3 minutes, then add the curry powder and turmeric and cook for 2 minutes.

3 Add the rice and tomato purée and stir to mix. Add the reserved cooking liquid and bring to the boil. Cover and simmer for 40-50 minutes until the rice is tender, stirring in the spinach just before the rice is cooked.

4 Meanwhile, remove and discard the skin and any bones from the haddock and separate into flakes.

5 Stir the yoghurt into the rice, with salt and pepper to taste, then gently mix in the flaked haddock. Spoon onto a warm serving dish, arrange the eggs on the rice and serve.

Traditionally served for breakfast, kedgeree – a dish dating back to the Raj – is ideal for brunch or a light supper. This recipe uses brown rice and yoghurt, for extra health benefits.

Developed as a necessary means of preserving, smoked

Smoked fish

Britain has a long tradition of smoking fish and other seafood, dating back to around 2000 BC. But the styles of smoked fish that are generally familiar today did not emerge until the 19th century. Originally, smoking was combined with salt-curing to help to preserve fresh fish, and the result was harder and drier than would now be appreciated. Efficient refrigeration and good transport have made preservation less important so that smoking is used these days mainly as a means of flavouring fish.

Methods of smoking

In the past, it was usual in English smokehouses to employ a technique known as cold-smoking, in which food was imbued with smoke at a temperature no higher than 29°C (85°F). Both white fish, such as haddock, and oily fish, such as salmon, were once cold-smoked. Modern smokers are increasingly using hot-smoking

techniques, where temperatures may be above boiling point, so that the fish is partly cooked and its texture is firm and pale, rather than translucent.

From Arbroath to Salcombe

Kippers, a form of hot-smoked herring, were the invention of a Northumberland man called John Woodger in 1843. Originally referred to as the 'Newcastle kipper', they were produced to give a lighter flavour than the hard, salty and heavily smoked herrings so ubiquitous in the Middle Ages. Woodger adopted methods similar for those used for smoking salmon since the 1300s, and the results quickly became popular. During the food shortages of the First World War, some fish-smokers, trying to minimise costs, added

fish is now widely produced and enjoyed for its distinctive taste alone.

commercial dye and reduced the smoking time. These inferior kippers continued to be produced after the war, but the efforts of a small group of fish-smokers dedicated to the original concept mean that undyed kippers are being produced once again.

Another oily fish to benefit from hot-smoking over oak chips is mackerel. The flesh spoils quickly when fresh, and smoking gives a rich taste and texture. A large smoking industry developed in Cornwall, where some of the best mackerel catches were made. And up the coast, Devon has produced its own speciality, the Salcombe smokie, very lightly hot-smoked mackerel.

Smoked eel is another very richly flavoured fish with a high oil content. Eel is traditionally produced in Scotland, where the fish are caught in rivers – notably the Tweed – as they return to the sea after feeding each autumn. There are now also dedicated eel farms.

Haddock, a white fish, became popular as a smoked fish in the 1800s. Finnan haddie, from a village near Aberdeen, refers to a lightly salted, delicately smoked whole fish, originally dry-salted and smoked over peat for some eight hours. Arbroath smokies, which are hot-smoked haddock, originated in Auchmithie rather than Arbroath, but the latter village became the major producer. They were smoked over domestic fires until production increased so significantly that large smoke-pits had to be set up along the cliff edges.

Salmon, the king of smoked fish

Two key British styles of smoked salmon exist, one Scottish, the other known as 'London cure'. European immigrants, particularly Jewish, arriving in East London at the end of the 19th century brought with them the custom of light smoking, to enhance the flavour rather than preserve the fish. However, the less oily, heavier smoked Scottish version is often considered to be the finer cure.

Smoked salmon and melon

PREPARATION TIME: 10 MINUTES
SERVES 4

1½ chilled ripe Charentais, Galia or
    Cantaloupe melons, seeds
    removed, sliced
Juice of ½ lime
½ teaspoon preserved ginger, finely
    chopped
2 tablespoons extra virgin olive oil
Salt and black pepper
115g (4oz) smoked salmon slices
Lemon and lime wedges to serve

1 Arrange the melon slices on
four plates.

2 Whisk together the lime juice,
ginger, olive oil, and salt and
pepper to taste. Spoon over the melon.

3 Arrange the smoked salmon on
the plates with the melon. Serve
with lemon and lime wedges.

Nutrients per serving
- Calories 115
- Carbohydrate 5g (of which sugars 5g)
- Protein 8g
- Fat 7g (of which saturated fat 1g)
- Fibre 1g
- Vitamins C, A, B_1

Fruit and oily fish combine to provide a balanced boost of vitamins and minerals. As well as being sweet and refreshing, melons contain beta carotene and lycopene.

Cullen skink omelette

PREPARATION TIME: 10 MINUTES
COOKING TIME: 12 MINUTES
SERVES 4

450g (1lb) potatoes, peeled and cut into
    2.5cm (1in) chunks
300g (10½oz) smoked haddock fillet
Vegetable oil for brushing
1 onion, finely chopped
5 eggs, beaten
Salt and black pepper
2 tablespoons chopped fresh chives

Nutrients per serving
- Calories 250
- Carbohydrate 19g (of which sugars 2g)
- Protein 24g
- Fat 11g (of which saturated fat 3g)
- Fibre 1.5g
- Vitamins A, B_6, B_{12}

The ingredients for cullen skink – a traditional Scottish soup based on smoked haddock and potatoes – are here turned into an omelette. For the best flavour, use traditional smoked haddock, which is free from artificial yellow dye.

1 Cook the potatoes in boiling, lightly
salted water for about 7 minutes
until tender. Add the haddock to the
water after 2-3 minutes.

2 Meanwhile, brush a nonstick frying
pan with oil and heat. Add the
onion and fry until tender.

3 Drain the potatoes and fish. When
cool enough to handle, flake the
fish into chunks, discarding any skin and
bones. Put the eggs in a large bowl, add
salt and pepper to taste, then add the
chives, potatoes and fish.

4 Transfer the egg mixture to the
frying pan and stir to mix. Cook
over a medium-low heat, without
stirring, for about 4 minutes until lightly
set. Slide the omelette onto a large
warm plate, cut into wedges and serve.

Stilton rarebit with pears and walnuts

PREPARATION TIME: 5 MINUTES
COOKING TIME: 10 MINUTES
SERVES 4

4 slices of wholemeal bread

25g (1oz) unsalted butter

175g (6oz) Stilton cheese,
   finely crumbled

1 tablespoon milk or beer

1½ teaspoons wholegrain mustard

Black pepper

1 small egg yolk

2 ripe pears, halved, cored and sliced

3 tablespoons finely chopped walnuts

1 Heat the grill and toast the bread on both sides. Meanwhile, melt the butter in a small, nonstick saucepan, then stir in the Stilton, milk or beer and mustard, with pepper to taste. Heat gently, stirring, until the cheese has melted, being careful not to overheat it.

2 Remove the pan from the heat and stir in the egg yolk. Spread the cheese mixture on the toast and place under the hot grill for 2-3 minutes, to brown. Reduce the grill to medium and arrange the pear slices on top of the cheese. Sprinkle over the walnuts.

3 Grill for 2-3 minutes to crisp the nuts. Serve at once.

A classic combination of nutty and sweet flavours transforms this dish into a delicious snack for almost any time of day.

Nutrients per serving
- Calories 420
- Carbohydrate 21g (of which sugars 7g)
- Protein 16g
- Fat 30g (of which saturated fat 15g)
- Fibre 4g
- Vitamins B_{12}, B_1, B_6

Crushed beans on toast

PREPARATION TIME: 5 MINUTES
COOKING TIME: 10 MINUTES
SERVES 2

4 cloves garlic
5 tablespoons olive oil
Handful of flat-leaved parsley
Salt and black pepper
400g (14oz) canned butter beans,
    drained and rinsed
1 small onion, finely chopped
1 bay leaf
2-3 teaspoons fresh thyme leaves
2 slices of bread, tomato flavoured
    (optional), toasted

A sophisticated, fresh-flavoured version of the canned snack, using butter beans – an excellent source of protein and fibre.

1 Put the garlic into a small saucepan, cover with water and simmer for 5 minutes. Drain and put into a small blender with 4 tablespoons of the oil and the parsley. Blend to a purée, add salt and pepper to taste and set aside.

2 Meanwhile, heat the remaining oil in a saucepan. Add the beans, onion, bay leaf and thyme and cook for 2-3 minutes, crushing the beans coarsely with a fork, until warmed through. Discard the bay leaf.

3 Add salt and pepper to taste and pile the beans onto the toast. Top with the parsley sauce and serve.

Nutrients per serving
- Calories 500
- Carbohydrate 47g (of which sugars 6g)
- Protein 15g
- Fat 29g (of which saturated fat 4g)
- Fibre 10g
- Vitamins B_6

Oven-baked corned beef hash

PREPARATION TIME: 10 MINUTES
COOKING TIME: 45 MINUTES
SERVES 4

700g (1lb 9oz) waxy potatoes, scrubbed
Olive oil for brushing
1 onion, finely chopped
Salt
225g (8oz) mushrooms, chopped
350g (12oz) canned corned beef, diced
1½ tablespoons Worcestershire sauce
2 tablespoons chopped parsley

A classic snack, with no extra fat, and the addition of mushrooms to increase the fibre content.

1 Cook the potatoes in boiling, salted water for 20-25 minutes until tender, then drain and chop. Meanwhile, heat the oven to 200°C (400°F, gas mark 6).

2 Lightly oil a large, nonstick frying pan, add the onion and sprinkle with salt. Cover and cook gently, stirring occasionally, until golden. Increase the heat, add the mushrooms and cook, uncovered, for 2-3 minutes, stirring often.

3 Stir in the corned beef, potatoes and Worcestershire sauce. Transfer to an ovenproof dish and bake for about 25 minutes, until browned. Sprinkle with parsley and serve.

Nutrients per serving
- Calories 360
- Carbohydrate 31g (of which sugars 2g)
- Protein 28g
- Fat 14g (of which saturated fat 6g)
- Fibre 3g
- Vitamins B_6, B_{12}, B_1

Spiced vegetable wedges

PREPARATION TIME: 10 MINUTES
COOKING TIME: 25 MINUTES
SERVES 4

About 700g (1lb 9oz) mixed vegetables, such as
    celeriac, parsnips, sweet potatoes and squash,
    cut into chunks
4-5 tablespoons curry paste
Chopped coriander leaves to garnish
Low-fat Greek-style yoghurt to serve

Check the label: choose a curry
paste with a strong flavour and
low fat content.

1 Heat the oven to 220°C (425°F, gas mark 7).
Cook all the vegetables in boiling water:
carrots and celeriac for 4-5 minutes, parsnips,
sweet potatoes and squash for 3 minutes. Drain
the vegetables well and put into a large bowl.

2 Stir the curry paste gently into the
vegetables, until coated.

3 Spread the vegetables in a shallow baking
dish and bake for about 20 minutes, or until
tender. Stir once or twice during cooking
to ensure even browning.

4 Sprinkle over the coriander. Serve the
wedges with the yoghurt in a separate
bowl for dipping.

Nutrients per serving
- Calories 140
- Carbohydrate 21g
  (of which sugars 7g)
- Protein 3g
- Fat 5g (of which
  saturated fat 1g)
- Fibre 6g
- Vitamins B_1, B_{12}, B_2

Champ is an Irish dish of mashed potatoes and leeks, and here the tomato dressing adds colour as well as vitamins. Potatoes, in this dish unpeeled, contain their best source of fibre and nutrients in and just under the skin.

Champ cakes with cherry tomato dressing

PREPARATION TIME: 10 MINUTES,
PLUS 1 HOUR CHILLING
COOKING TIME: 30 MINUTES
SERVES 4

550g (1lb 4oz) unpeeled floury potatoes,
    washed and roughly chopped
225g (8oz) leeks, thinly sliced
200ml (7fl oz) semi-skimmed milk
1 egg, beaten
Salt and black pepper
Plain flour for shaping
Olive oil for brushing

For the tomato dressing:
225g (8oz) cherry tomatoes, halved
1 tablespoon olive oil
1 tablespoon sherry vinegar
2-3 teaspoons fresh thyme leaves
Salt and black pepper

1 Steam the potatoes for about 15 minutes or until tender. Transfer them to a dry saucepan.

2 Meanwhile, put the leeks and milk into another saucepan. Cover and cook over a low heat for 5-8 minutes until tender. Drain, reserving the liquid.

3 Heat the potatoes gently for a couple of minutes, shaking the pan, then mash.

4 Add the leeks and egg to the potatoes. Stir to mix, then add 2-3 tablespoons of the reserved liquid, until soft but not sloppy. Add salt and pepper to taste, spread on a plate and leave to cool. Chill for at least 1 hour.

5 Meanwhile, make the tomato dressing. Put the tomatoes, oil, vinegar and thyme in a small saucepan and heat, stirring occasionally, until the tomatoes are beginning to collapse. Using kitchen scissors, chop the tomatoes in the pan. Add salt and pepper to taste and set aside.

6 With floured hands, form the potato and leek mixture into eight flat cakes. Brush lightly with oil and preheat the grill to high. Grill for 2-3 minutes on each side until golden and heated through. Heat the dressing for 2 minutes and serve with the cakes.

Nutrients per serving
- Calories 240
- Carbohydrate 34g (of which sugars 6g)
- Protein 8g
- Fat 8g (of which saturated fat 2g)
- Fibre 4g
- Vitamins B_6, C, B_1

Cauliflower cheese puffs

PREPARATION TIME: 15 MINUTES
COOKING TIME: 25 MINUTES
SERVES 4

Vegetable oil for greasing
550g (1lb 4oz) cauliflower florets
4 large eggs, separated
2 tablespoons semi-skimmed milk
1 teaspoon wholegrain mustard
115g (4oz) mature Cheddar cheese
Salt and black pepper

Nutrients per serving
- Calories 258
- Carbohydrate 5g (of which sugars 4g)
- Protein 20g
- Fat 18g (of which saturated fat 8g)
- Fibre 3g
- Vitamins C, B_{12}, B_6

A low-fat, easy variation of popular cauliflower cheese. Because mature Cheddar cheese has a strong flavour, you do not need to use as much, so cutting down on fat.

1 Heat the oven to 180°C (350°F, gas mark 4) and lightly grease four large ramekin dishes. Steam or boil the cauliflower until tender and drain if necessary.

2 Transfer the cooked cauliflower to a blender or food processor and add the egg yolks, milk and mustard. Crumble the cheese in and blend the mixture to a purée. Add salt and pepper to taste.

3 Whisk the egg whites until stiff. Stir about a quarter of the egg whites into the cauliflower mixture. Then, in three batches, gently fold in the remaining whites.

4 Divide the mixture between the prepared ramekins. Bake for about 20 minutes until just set, puffed and a light golden colour. Eat from the dishes, or unmould the puffs onto warmed plates. Serve with wholemeal or granary bread and a crisp salad.

Celeriac cakes with ham and apple

PREPARATION TIME: 10 MINUTES
COOKING TIME: 20 MINUTES
SERVES 4

550g (1lb 4oz) celeriac, peeled
   and quartered
2 teaspoons wholegrain mustard
1 large egg, beaten
Salt and black pepper
Vegetable oil for brushing
400g (14oz) Bramley cooking apples,
   peeled, cored and chopped
225g (8oz) thick-cut ham

The tart taste of Bramley apples complements celeriac's mild flavour.

Nutrients per serving
- Calories 240
- Carbohydrate 13g
  (of which sugars 11g)
- Protein 12g
- Fat 15g (of which saturated fat 11g)
- Fibre 7g
- Vitamins B_6, B_{12}, C, B_1

1 Cook the celeriac in lightly salted, boiling water for about 10 minutes until just tender. Drain, leave until cool, then grate coarsely with a grater or in a food processor. Mix with the mustard, egg and salt and pepper to taste.

2 Lightly brush a nonstick frying pan with oil and heat. When hot, put 2-3 tablespoons of the celeriac mixture at a time in the pan and press each down to a cake about 7.5cm (3in) in diameter. Cook for about 3 minutes until set and browned underneath. Turn the cakes over and cook on the other side for 2-3 minutes.

3 Meanwhile, put the apple into a saucepan with 2 tablespoons water, cover and cook gently, shaking the pan occasionally, until beginning to collapse but not disintegrate.

4 Put the ham onto serving plates, top with the celeriac cakes and serve with the apple.

Glamorgan sausages

PREPARATION TIME: 10 MINUTES
COOKING TIME: 5 MINUTES
SERVES 4

2 thin celery sticks, white part only,
     very finely chopped
175g (6oz) fresh wholemeal breadcrumbs
115g (4oz) Caerphilly cheese, finely grated
1 tablespoon chopped parsley
Black pepper
1 large egg, beaten
About 2 tablespoons milk
Plain flour for shaping
Olive oil for brushing

For the watercress sauce:
70g (2½oz) watercress
175g (6oz) low-fat fromage frais
Salt and black pepper

Instead of meat, Glamorgan sausages are made with cheese, which, as the Welsh name suggests, should be Caerphilly. Celery has been added for lighter results.

1 For the watercress sauce, bring a saucepan of water to the boil, add the watercress and return to the boil. Drain at once, pressing out excess moisture with the back of a spoon. Chop finely, then put in a bowl. Add the fromage frais and mix well. Add salt and pepper to taste and set aside.

2 Put the celery, breadcrumbs, cheese and parsley in a bowl, add black pepper and stir to mix. Using a fork, quickly mix in the egg and just enough milk to bind the mixture.

3 Divide the mixture into eight. Using floured hands, lightly roll each piece into a sausage shape about 10cm (4in) long.

4 Heat the grill and lightly brush the sausages with oil. Grill the sausages for about 5 minutes until golden, turning them occasionally. Serve with the watercress sauce and a leafy salad.

Nutrients per serving
* Calories 320
* Carbohydrate 21g (of which sugars 1g)
* Protein 17g
* Fat 20g (of which saturated fat 10g)
* Fibre 3g
* Vitamins B$_{12}$

Prawn and tomato new potatoes

PREPARATION TIME: 10 MINUTES
COOKING TIME: 30 MINUTES
SERVES 4

English goat's cheese, especially the fresh variety, has a beautiful, mild flavour that complements the prawns.

8 large new potatoes, about 85g (3oz) each, scrubbed
Olive oil for brushing
350g (12oz) tomatoes, chopped
5 spring onions, finely chopped
¾ teaspoon paprika
Salt and black pepper
1-2 teaspoons tomato purée (optional)
85g (3oz) fresh goat's cheese
2½ tablespoons low-fat Greek-style yoghurt
175g (6oz) peeled, cooked prawns, defrosted if frozen

1 Heat the oven to 220°C (425°F, gas mark 7). Cook the potatoes in boiling, salted water for 12-15 minutes until tender, then drain. Brush the skins lightly with oil and cut a deep cross through each potato without cutting all the way through. Place, cut side up, in a shallow baking dish.

2 While the potatoes are cooking, brush a saucepan lightly with oil and add the tomatoes, spring onions and paprika. Stir and cook over a medium heat for 5-10 minutes until reduced but still chunky. Add salt and pepper to taste, and tomato purée if the flavour needs a boost.

3 Put the goat's cheese and yoghurt in a bowl and beat. Stir the prawns into the tomato mixture and spoon into the potatoes. Top with the cheese mixture. Sprinkle with pepper and bake for about 7 minutes until the cheese is hot and beginning to brown, then serve at once.

Nutrients per serving
- Calories 270
- Carbohydrate 32g (of which sugars 7g)
- Protein 17g
- Fat 9g (of which saturated fat 3g)
- Fibre 3g
- Vitamins B₆, C

Prawns in coffins

PREPARATION TIME: 5 MINUTES
COOKING TIME: 5-7 MINUTES
SERVES 4

4 large, crisp bread rolls
150g (5½oz) small spinach leaves
175g (6oz) peeled, cooked prawns, defrosted if frozen
Salt and black pepper
125g (4½oz) low-fat mayonnaise
3 tablespoons low-fat Greek-style yoghurt
Squeeze of lemon juice

1 Cut a slice from the top of each bread roll, reserving the slice, and scoop out the bread from the middle, leaving a thin shell. (Save this bread to make crumbs for future use.)

2 Pack the spinach into a saucepan and heat, stirring frequently, until beginning to wilt. Remove from the heat and set aside. Heat the prawns gently in a covered saucepan and add salt and pepper to taste.

3 Heat the mayonnaise gently in a small pan over a low heat. Add the yoghurt and stir until warmed through. Add the lemon juice.

4 Divide the spinach between the rolls, spoon in the seafood and top with the sauce. Replace the lids and serve.

Nutrients per serving
- Calories 280
- Carbohydrate 28g (of which sugars 4g)
- Protein 16g
- Fat 11g (of which saturated fat 1g)
- Fibre 1g

The origins of this recipe lie in the Victorian dish, 'Oysters in coffins', popular at a time when oysters were affordable, everyday fare.

Starters,

soups and salads

Starters, soups and salads
the healthy way

Preparing delicious soups and salads is a great way to ensure that everyone enjoys a variety of nutrient-rich vegetables.

One of the quickest and easiest routes to good health is to eat five or more portions of fruit and vegetables a day. An excellent way to boost your intake is to enjoy a varied selection of soups and salads made from fresh produce.

All the goodness
Satisfying, homemade soups can make an important contribution to the overall nutritional balance of your diet. Recent research from the Institute of Food and

Nutrition in Paris also suggests that people who regularly eat soup are more likely to be within the ideal weight range than those who do not.
• Homemade soups contain none of the additives and emulsifiers that are in canned varieties and taste quite different.
• A good stock contributes flavour and nutrients, while natural thickeners, such as potato, pasta or rice, add healthy starchy carbohydrates, and extra fish or meat provides additional protein.

• Soup is also a varied dish. Light soups such as Mussel and fennel broth (page 50) are ideal as a starter, while more substantial soups like Winter vegetable soup (page 56) make a satisfying lunch.
• Packed with nutritious vegetables, a soup can be wonderfully satisfying and filling without being hugely calorific.

Salad variations
The dictionary definition of salad is 'a dish of raw leafy green vegetables', but in recent years salads have become much more varied and colourful dishes. A salad can be simple or exotic, hot or cold,

Puréed soups

1 Sweat some chopped onion in a little oil over a medium heat until it is soft. Add any diced vegetables you wish, ideally including a root vegetable, and let them sweat for 3-4 minutes until they also soften.

served as a side dish or a substantial main meal and prepared from a vast array of ingredients – vegetables, pulses, pasta, rice, nuts, seeds, fruit or even flowers. As a result, today's salads can make an even more important contribution to a healthy diet.

• Most salad leaves and vegetables are very low in calories and virtually fat free.

• Although salad leaves are more than 90 per cent water, they provide many nutrients, including vitamin C, beta carotene, folate, calcium and iron.

• Watercress is very high in vitamin C and beta carotene.

• Raw spinach is high in nutrients, providing vitamin C, beta carotene, folate as well as iron. Young leaves are best for salads as older leaves can be tough.

• Darker, more strongly flavoured salad leaves, such as rocket, spinach and watercress, generally have higher levels of vitamins and phytochemicals than the paler, sweeter leaves. The dark outer

Salad dressing

3 tablespoons white wine vinegar
2 tablespoons water
1 teaspoon caster sugar
Salt and black pepper
1 heaped teaspoon snipped chives or chopped tarragon

Put the vinegar, water and sugar in a bowl and whisk until the sugar dissolves. Add salt and pepper to taste, then stir in the herbs. Use to dress a salad at once.

2 Pour enough stock or water into the pan to cover the vegetables and add any seasonings and herbs or other flavourings to taste. Bring gently to the boil, then leave to simmer until all the vegetables are very soft. This should take around 20-30 minutes.

3 Allow to cool slightly, then pour into a blender or food processor and purée until smooth. You can use a hand blender in the pan instead, but this works best with small quantities. If you want a super-smooth soup, push the purée through a fine sieve. Thin with extra liquid if required, then check the seasoning. For a richer soup, add a spoonful of crème fraîche, yoghurt or fromage frais.

leaves of lettuce, for example, can provide as many as 50 times more carotenoids than the inner pale leaves.

• Only avocado pears have a high fat content, which is predominately the healthy monounsaturated variety, and they are also a good source of vitamin E and vitamin B_6.

• Shredded cabbage – an excellent winter salad ingredient – is high in the essential minerals iron and potassium.

Preserving the goodness in salad leaves

Always buy the freshest salad vegetables available, choosing local produce whenever possible, as they are at their most nutritious when they are first harvested. Ready-prepared salad leaves should be used within a day as they begin to lose B and C vitamins from the moment they are cut and stored.

Rinse salad leaves and spin or pat them dry as soaking will also result in the loss of water soluble vitamins such as vitamin C and folate. Do not add a dressing until the salad is ready to serve as acid vinegar will wilt the leaves.

To make salad dressings use good olive oil, sunflower or groundnut oil and any well-flavoured vinegar. Mix yogurt and mayonnaise for a lower-fat creamy dressing or try an oil-free dressing (see above), as an alternative.

Salad facts

• The fresh vegetables and fruit used to prepare salads will provide an excellent range of vitamins, minerals, antioxidants and phytoprotective compounds, all of which play an important role in keeping us healthy.

• Research has shown that people who eat a lot of fresh fruit and vegetables are at less risk of heart disease and stroke.

• The World Cancer Research Fund estimates that a diet rich in a variety of fruit and vegetables could help to prevent 20 per cent of all cancers.

Homemade
herbed curd cheese

PREPARATION TIME: 10 MINUTES,
WITH 2 DAYS TO STAND
SERVES 4

500g (1lb 2oz) thick yoghurt
½ teaspoon salt
3 tablespoons chopped thyme leaves and
    thyme flowers, if available
1 tablespoon chopped fresh parsley
2 teaspoons finely snipped chives
Black pepper
2-3 small sprigs of thyme (preferably in
    flower) to garnish

1 Put a 25cm (10in) square of muslin in a saucepan, add boiling water to cover and return to the boil. Remove from the heat and, when cool enough to handle, squeeze the muslin dry.

2 Mix the yoghurt and salt. Line an unused 13cm (5in) diameter flowerpot with the muslin and spoon in the yoghurt, folding the muslin over to cover the surface.

3 Cut a piece of firm plastic (or the lid from the yoghurt pot) to fit neatly inside the flowerpot, covering the yoghurt, but with enough room for it to be able to sink slightly. Put a 200g (7oz) can of tomatoes or beans on top of the plastic and stand the flowerpot on top of a biscuit cutter inside a small bowl, to allow room for the whey to drain. Refrigerate for 2 days, draining off the whey after about 12 and 24 hours.

4 Turn the cheese out onto a plate and carefully strip off the muslin. (The cheese will keep, wrapped, in the fridge for up to 2 weeks.) When ready to serve, spread the herbs and some pepper out on a sheet of greaseproof paper and gently roll the cheese in them to coat the sides and top.

5 Decorate with thyme sprigs and serve with radishes and Bath Oliver biscuits. Alternatively, serve with lightly cooked broad beans, skinned, and crusty bread.

Nutrients per serving
- Calories 100
- Carbohydrate 10g (of which sugars 10g)
- Protein 7g
- Fat 2g (of which saturated fat 1g)
- Fibre 0g
- Vitamins B$_2$

Making your own cheese may seem a lengthy process, but it is **easy**, enjoyable and very **rewarding**. This **low-fat**, herby cheese is **delicious,** and perfect for summer picnics or lunches.

Asparagus with anchovy eggs

**PREPARATION AND
COOKING TIME:** 30 MINUTES
SERVES 4

4 slices medium-thick white bread
1kg (2 lb 4oz) asparagus, trimmed
4 large eggs
2 teaspoons anchovy essence
2 tablespoons semi-skimmed milk
25g (1oz) butter
Black pepper

Nutrients per serving
* Calories 340
* Carbohydrate 30g (of which sugars 6g)
* Protein 21g
* Fat 16g (of which saturated fat 5g)
* Fibre 5g
* Vitamins B$_6$, C, B$_1$

The **best asparagus** grows nearest home and reaches you without air miles, for a few short weeks in late May and June. It is so good it demands only the simplest of treatments, and is a natural partner to scrambled eggs.

1 Heat the grill and toast the bread on both sides. Using a large, sharp knife, cut off the crusts, then split each slice in two horizontally. Cut each piece diagonally to give 16 triangles. Return the triangles to the grill, untoasted side up, and remove each piece from the heat as soon as it browns and curls. Pile into a napkin-lined dish to cool.

2 Cook the asparagus in boiling, salted water for 8-10 minutes, or until a sharp knife goes in easily just below the tip. Drain.

3 While the asparagus is cooking, put the eggs and anchovy essence into a bowl and beat. Put the milk and butter in a nonstick saucepan and swirl over a low heat until the butter melts. Add the beaten eggs and stir over a low heat until the eggs are lightly cooked but still very soft. Add plenty of black pepper.

4 Spoon the eggs onto warmed plates and arrange the asparagus spears on top. Serve with the toast.

Parsley-coated smoked mackerel pâté

PREPARATION TIME: 10 MINUTES
PLUS 1 HOUR CHILLING
SERVES 4

250g (9oz) smoked mackerel, skinned
2 teaspoons green peppercorns
Grated zest of 1 unwaxed lemon
6 tablespoons low-fat fromage frais
Olive oil for coating
3 tablespoons chopped parsley
Thinly sliced granary toast to serve

Mackerel, fished from **British** waters between April and July, is **naturally healthy**. Rich in **omega-3** fatty acids, it can **protect** against heart disease and **help** in the treatment of skin problems and arthritis.

1 Flake the mackerel into a blender or food processor, discarding any bones. Grind the peppercorns coarsely with a pestle and mortar or with the end of a rolling pin in a bowl. Add to the mackerel with the lemon zest.

2 Add the fromage frais and blend or process briefly to a smooth paste. Turn out onto a plate and shape into a ball, then flatten slightly.

3 Lightly oil the base and sides of a small bowl. Sprinkle the parsley into the bowl to coat evenly. Put the pâté into it and press lightly, then turn it out onto a small plate. Cover loosely with cling film and refrigerate for at least 1 hour. Serve with granary toast.

Nutrients per serving
- Calories 260
- Carbohydrate 2g (of which sugars 2g)
- Protein 14g
- Fat 22g (of which saturated fat 4g)
- Fibre 0.5g
- Vitamins B$_{12}$, C, B$_6$, niacin

Warm potted shrimps on shredded lettuce

PREPARATION TIME: 20 MINUTES
SERVES 4

1 egg
A pinch of dried mustard
1-2 tablespoons lemon juice
300ml (10fl oz) olive oil
4 x 55g (2oz) pots of potted shrimps
4 heads Little Gem lettuce, washed, dried and finely sliced
Petals from 2 marigold flowers (optional)

Potted shrimps have been **popular** in the North of England since the 18th century, and still arrive at the market from **Morecambe Bay** in Lancashire.

Nutrients per serving
- Calories 220
- Carbohydrate 1g (of which sugars 0g)
- Protein 12g
- Fat 18g (of which saturated fat 5g)
- Fibre 0g
- Vitamins B$_{12}$

1 Put the egg in a blender, then add the mustard and lemon juice and blend for a few seconds. With the motor running, start adding the oil through the hole in the lid, drop-by-drop at first, then in a thin stream, until the mixture is thick.

2 About 15 minutes before serving, stand the shrimp pots in an enamel dish or tin. Pour hot water into the dish or tin to about half way up the pots, but not deep enough to float them.

3 Divide the lettuce between four plates. Invert a pot of shrimps onto each serving, allowing the buttery sauce to run into the lettuce. Top with marigold petals, if desired. Serve with a spoonful of the mayonnaise and wholemeal bread (see page 260).

Smoked salmon
on horseradish potato farls

PREPARATION TIME: 15 MINUTES
COOKING TIME: 25 MINUTES
SERVES 4

125g (4½oz) smoked salmon
2 floury potatoes, about 125g (4½oz)
    each, peeled and cut into 2-3 chunks
3 tablespoons buttermilk or low-fat
    yoghurt, plus extra to serve
1-2 teaspoons grated horseradish or
    1-2 tablespoons horseradish sauce
Salt and coarsely ground black pepper
100g (3½oz) self-raising flour
1 tablespoon vegetable oil
15g (½oz) butter
Chopped fresh dill to garnish
Lemon wedges to serve

A farl, a savoury cake usually made with oatmeal, but in this recipe with potato, comes from Scotland. The name, from the word fardel, meaning 'fourth part', refers to the triangular portion produced when the round is cut.

1 Separate the slices of smoked salmon and arrange them in loose folds on a plate to dry off slightly. Cook the potatoes in boiling, salted water until tender. Drain thoroughly, return them to the pan and mash.

2 Add the buttermilk or yoghurt, horseradish and salt to taste and beat until smooth. Gradually work in about two-thirds of the flour. When the mixture begins to break up, knead it with your hands, still adding flour, until it leaves the side of the pan clean.

3 Dust a work surface generously with flour. Turn the dough out and pat out lightly to a round. Turn the round over and, using more flour to prevent sticking, roll out to a round just under 23cm (9in) in diameter. Dust off any surplus flour.

4 Heat the vegetable oil and butter together in a heavy 23cm (9in) frying pan. Swirl to coat the base and lower sides, then pour any surplus into a cup. Using a fish slice or wide spatula, lift the potato cake into the pan. Cook over a low heat for 5-6 minutes until the underside is browned, then turn it over, returning the reserved oil and butter to the pan. Cook for 5 minutes until browned, then slide onto a flat dish and leave to cool slightly.

5 Arrange folds of smoked salmon over the cake and drizzle with buttermilk or yoghurt. Sprinkle with pepper and dill and serve in quarters (farls) with a lemon wedge.

Nutrients per serving
- Calories 233
- Carbohydrate 31g (of which sugars 1g)
- Protein 21g
- Fat 8g (of which saturated fat 3g)
- Fibre 1.5g
- Vitamins B_6, B_{12}, B_1

PREPARATION TIME: 15 MINUTES
COOKING TIME: 3 HOURS, PLUS
6 HOURS COOLING AND SETTING
SERVES 6-8

800g (1lb 12oz) boned shin of beef
1 teaspoon salt
1 large outer celery stick, halved
3-4 sprigs each of parsley and thyme
½ teaspoon black peppercorns
½ teaspoon allspice berries
2 small bay leaves
Handful of onion skins
1-2 tablespoons medium
   Amontillado sherry
2 sachets gelatine, 20g (¾ oz) in total
Mustard and cress to garnish

For the sauce:
4 teaspoons English mustard powder
150ml (5fl oz) sour cream

Potted hough
with mustard sauce

1 Put the beef into a large saucepan or stockpot, about 3 litres (5¼ pints) in capacity. Cover with water, add the salt and bring slowly to the boil. Simmer for 1 hour, skimming the scum off at regular intervals and adding a cup of cold water from time to time to replace lost liquid, until no more scum rises from the beef.

2 Add the celery, parsley, thyme, peppercorns, allspice berries, bay leaves and onion skins. Partially cover and simmer for a further 2 hours until the meat is beginning to fall apart, skimming occasionally.

3 Lift out the meat and set aside to cool. Strain the stock into a deep bowl, discarding the flavourings. Add salt to taste. Leave to cool completely, then skim off any fat from the surface.

4 Strain again, through a sieve lined with muslin and transfer 900ml (1 pint 12fl oz) to a 1.5 litre (2¾ pint) bowl, stirring in sherry to taste. Shred the cooked beef, cover and refrigerate.

5 Measure another 300ml (½ pint) stock into a small bowl (adding water if there is not enough) and sprinkle the gelatine on top. Leave to swell, then stand the bowl in a small pan of boiling water and leave until completely clear, putting the pan over a low heat if necessary. Stir the dissolved gelatine into the strained stock, then add the shredded meat. Chill to set.

6 Up to 1 hour before serving, make the sauce: mix the mustard with 1 tablespoon cold water and leave for 10 minutes. Stir in the sour cream.

7 To serve, dip the bowl briefly into a sinkful of very hot water, to loosen the hough. Put the serving plate over the bowl and invert to unmould the jelly. Garnish with mustard and cress and serve with cherry tomatoes, crusty bread and the mustard sauce.

Nutrients per serving, when serving 8
- Calories 164
- Carbohydrate 0g
- Protein 20g
- Fat 8g (of which saturated fat 4g)
- Fibre 0g
- Vitamins B_{12}, B_6

Seared pigeon breast
on barley pilaf

PREPARATION TIME: 10 MINUTES
COOKING TIME: 1 HOUR
SERVES 4 AS A STARTER OR
2 AS A MAIN COURSE

125g (4½ oz) pearl barley, rinsed
About 500ml (18fl oz) chicken stock
  (see page 120)
5 tablespoons red wine
2 sprigs of thyme
3 tablespoons olive oil
1 small red onion, chopped
100g (3½ oz) chestnut mushrooms, sliced
2 teaspoons redcurrant jelly
2 tablespoons ruby port
4 pigeon breasts
Salt and black pepper
2 tablespoons chopped parsley

It may be easier to buy whole pigeons for this recipe, and to remove the breasts. You can then use the rest to make stock, following the recipe on page 120.

A **Scottish** savoury beef jelly – 'hough' is Scots for shin – this is a **delicious**, nutritional dish. The beef is **lean** and packed with a wide range of **nutrients**, including valuable minerals, particularly **iron and zinc.**

1 Put the barley in a saucepan with plenty of cold water. Bring to the boil and cook for 15 minutes. Drain and return it to the saucepan with 350ml (12fl oz) of the stock, the wine and thyme. Bring to the boil, then cook gently for 40-45 minutes until tender, adding stock to prevent it drying out.

2 When the barley has been cooking for about 25 minutes, heat 2 tablespoons of the oil in a small frying pan, add the onion and cook over a low heat for 2-3 minutes. Add the mushrooms and cook until soft.

3 Gently warm the redcurrant jelly and port in a small saucepan with 4 tablespoons of the remaining stock. Simmer until reduced by about half.

4 Heat a ridged griddle pan until very hot. Brush the pigeon breasts on each side with the remaining oil and sprinkle the skin side with salt and pepper. Place them skin side down on the hot pan and cook for 3-4 minutes. Season the flesh side, turn and cook for 2-3 minutes until browned but still pink inside. Transfer to a warm plate to rest.

5 Add the mushroom and onion mixture and parsley to the cooked barley and mix. Spoon onto plates.

6 Make three diagonal cuts through each pigeon breast and put onto plates. Pour any juices from the pan and the resting plate into the sauce, reheat briefly and drizzle around each serving.

Nutrients per serving
- Calories 325
- Carbohydrate 31g (of which sugars 4g)
- Protein 19g
- Fat 12g (of which saturated fat 2g)
- Fibre 1g
- Vitamins niacin, B_6

Grated courgette and potato soup

PREPARATION TIME: 10 MINUTES
COOKING TIME: 20 MINUTES
SERVES 4

600g (1lb 5oz) floury potatoes, peeled
and cut into 1cm (½ in) slices
2 large cloves garlic, peeled and chopped
Salt and black pepper
1 yellow and 2 green courgettes, each
about 140g (5oz), coarsely grated
Extra virgin olive oil for splashing
4 large mint or basil leaves, torn
Cayenne pepper

This **fast** and **healthy** vegetable soup is flavoured
with **garlic**, which has strong **antifungal** and
antiviral powers and helps to prevent colds and flu.

1 Put the potatoes in a saucepan and cover with 1 litre (1¾ pints) water. Bring to the boil, skimming off the white foam that rises to the surface. Add the garlic and cook at a fast simmer for 10-12 minutes until the potatoes are soft enough to mash.

2 Remove the pan from the heat and mash the potatoes and garlic in their cooking water, adding salt and pepper to taste.

3 Add the grated courgettes and return the soup to the heat. Cook at a low boil for a further 5 minutes until the courgettes are just soft.

4 Ladle the soup into soup plates or bowls and top each with a splash of olive oil. Sprinkle with the torn mint or basil leaves and a little cayenne pepper. Serve at once, with bread.

Nutrients per serving
- Calories 160
- Carbohydrate 27g (of which sugars 3g)
- Protein 5g
- Fat 3g (of which saturated fat 1g)
- Fibre 3g
- Vitamins B_6

Mussel and fennel broth

PREPARATION TIME: 15 MINUTES
COOKING TIME: 10 MINUTES
SERVES 4

4 tablespoons olive oil
1 fennel bulb, chopped
2 leeks, about 200g (7oz), finely sliced
1 large clove garlic, crushed
300ml (½ pint) medium-dry white wine
300ml (½ pint) fish stock (see page 88)
1kg (2lb 4oz) live mussels
150ml (¼ pint) low-fat crème fraîche
Black pepper
2 tablespoons chopped parsley to serve

Nutrients per serving
- Calories 290
- Carbohydrate 4g (of which sugars 2g)
- Protein 15g
- Fat 18g (of which saturated fat 5g)
- Fibre 2g
- Vitamins B_{12}, B_6

The delicate **aniseed** flavour of fennel complements
mineral-rich mussels in this tasty broth.

1 Heat the oil in a large saucepan, add the fennel, leeks and garlic and cook over a low heat for 5 minutes until the leeks wilt. Add the wine and stock, remove from the heat and set aside.

2 Meanwhile, scrub the mussels if necessary, scraping off any barnacles and pulling away the beards. Discard any with damaged shells, and any that do not close when tapped sharply on the edge of the sink.

3 Bring the wine and vegetable mixture to the boil, then add the mussels. Cook, covered, over a high heat for 3-4 minutes, shaking the pan from time to time, until the shells open.

4 Using a slotted spoon, remove the opened mussels to a bowl, discarding any that have not opened.

5 Pick the mussels from the shells, leaving some in for decoration, if desired, and return them to the broth. Heat gently, whisk in the crème fraîche and add black pepper to taste. Transfer to warmed bowls, sprinkle with parsley and serve with homemade soda bread (see page 261).

Chilled trout soup

An elegant,
pale pink dish,
perfect to serve
in summertime.
The fromage
frais makes it
creamy, but
keeps it low
in fat at the
same time.

PREPARATION TIME: 10 MINUTES
COOKING TIME: 40 MINUTES, PLUS
COOLING AND CHILLING
SERVES 6

1 fennel bulb, quartered lengthways
2 slices raw, unpeeled beetroot,
    1cm (½in) thick
2 bay leaves
½ teaspoon black peppercorns
½ teaspoon salt
250ml (9fl oz) medium-dry white wine
2-3 sprigs of tarragon
1 large fresh, cleaned trout,
    about 350g (12oz)
150g (5½oz) low-fat fromage frais
1 tablespoon grated horseradish or
    2 tablespoons horseradish sauce
85g (3oz) smoked trout fillet, flaked

1 Put the fennel into a saucepan large enough to hold the trout. Add the beetroot, bay leaves, peppercorns, salt, wine and 1 litre (1¾ pints) cold water. Pick the leaves off the tarragon and reserve. Add the stems to the pan.

2 Bring to the boil and cook at a slow boil for 10 minutes, then add the whole trout. Bring back to the boil, then reduce the heat and simmer for 7-8 minutes until the flesh is opaque throughout. Remove to a plate.

3 Skin and bone the trout and return the head, tail, skin and bone to the saucepan, reserving the flesh. Bring back to the boil and simmer, partially covered, for 15 minutes, then strain the liquid into a bowl and leave to cool.

4 Put the cooked trout, fromage frais and horseradish in a blender or food processor and purée the mixture. Transfer to a bowl, removing any that remains with a little poaching liquid, then add the remaining strained cooking liquid to the mixture. Add salt and pepper to taste, then chill.

5 When chilled, ladle the soup into cold soup plates. Sprinkle with the flaked smoked trout, reserved tarragon leaves and black pepper. Serve with cucumber sandwiches.

Nutrients per serving
- Calories 131
- Carbohydrate 3g (of which sugars 3g)
- Protein 16g
- Fat 3g (of which saturated fat 0g)
- Fibre 0g

Minted pea soup
with prawns and chives

Peas in the pod are available in summer, and are best soon after picking, while they still have their natural sweetness. The high vitamin and fibre content of peas is also found in the pods, and this healthy soup makes the most of both.

Nutrients per serving
- Calories 280
- Carbohydrate 17g (of which sugars 2g)
- Protein 33g
- Fat 8g (of which saturated fat 2g)
- Fibre 3g
- Vitamins B₁

PREPARATION AND COOKING TIME:
50 MINUTES
SERVES 4

700g (1lb 9oz) peas in pods
500g (1lb 2oz or 2 pints) cooked shell-on prawns
2 tablespoons vegetable oil
5-6 spring onions, trimmed and sliced
1 large clove garlic, roughly chopped
2.5cm (1in) piece of fresh ginger, unpeeled and coarsely grated
2 sprigs of mint
1 teaspoon black peppercorns
1 large floury potato, about 250g (9oz), peeled, grated and rinsed
Salt and black pepper
Sugar (optional)
Small bunch of chives, snipped

1 Pod the peas into a bowl. Reserve and roughly chop the pods. Peel the prawns, reserving their heads, shells and any roe.

2 Heat the oil in a saucepan, add the spring onions and cook over a gentle heat for 1-2 minutes until soft, then add the garlic, pea pods and prawn shells and cook, stirring frequently, for 4-5 minutes until the prawn shells release a powerful aroma.

3 Add the ginger, mint, peppercorns and 1 litre (1¾ pints) water and bring to the boil. Skim, reduce the heat and simmer for 15 minutes. Strain the contents of the pan through a large sieve into a deep bowl, pressing down with the back of a spoon to extract as much liquid as possible. Discard the flavourings.

4 Return the liquid to the rinsed saucepan and add the grated potato and half the peas. Bring to the boil, then cook at a low boil for 5 minutes. Purée, using a hand-held blender. Return to the heat, add the remaining peas and simmer for 3-4 minutes until tender.

5 Add salt, pepper to taste and sugar, if needed, and transfer the soup to warmed soup plates or bowls. Add the shelled prawns, top with chives and serve.

England's horticulturists grow a bounty of aromatic salad herbs and leaves,

Salad leaves, vegetables and herbs

The exciting variety of fresh leaves and herbs we enjoy today – in sharp contrast to the limp lettuces of past decades – is not an entirely new phenomenon, but part of a long tradition dating back to Roman times. The word salad is derived from the Latin *sal* (salt), which was added to oil and vinegar and served on raw vegetables. It appeared in English in the Middle Ages, when green leaves were mixed with flowers to make a 'sallet', or salad. A typical English 16th-century kitchen garden contained a wealth of aromatic herbs and leaves, and by the 17th century the 'grand sallet', containing a multitude of ingredients, was widespread.

Leaves for the bowl

Although lettuce was probably produced for medicinal purposes originally, it has been grown for culinary use since the ancient Greeks discovered its eating qualities. Today, the range of lettuces available is

increasingly impressive, thanks to supermarkets and, in part, to farmers' markets, where demand for lesser known varieties can be tested. Ever-popular Little Gem make crisp, bright salads. Butterhead lettuces, with names such as Big Boston, have soft, rounded leaves. The tightly compact leaves of crisphead lettuces, such as Iceberg, add bite to a salad. The Cos, or Romaine, group of lettuces have long, thin and crisp leaves, while loose-leaved lettuces, which are often a reddish colour and have oak-shaped and frilly leaves, add a decorative element to the salad bowl.

Year-round choice

If the freshest lettuces are available only in the summer months, there are plenty of other salad leaves, vegetables and herbs that can be enjoyed in other

from crisp to soft, and peppery to creamy.

seasons. Vitamin-rich, peppery watercress, for instance, is available all year. Long valued for its medicinal qualities, it was first grown for culinary use only in the early 19th century. Rocket, available in February and March, adds welcome variety too, as do seasonal varieties of cabbage. And many root vegetables, such as beetroot, carrot and celeriac, are delicious finely grated and dressed, as cold-weather salads. They also provide important antioxidants that help the body to combat disease.

Scientists have recently discovered that many herbs, far from acting as mere flavourings, are often higher in antioxidants than fruit or vegetables, with oregano heading the list. Tender herbs, such as chervil, dill, tarragon and parsley, can be combined to make a delicious leafy salad, while the more robust

herbs such as oregano, sage and thyme are best when finely chopped and added to dressings. Their flowers can also be used as flavourings.

Edible flowers

The use of flowers in salads, as both decorative and edible garnishes, appears to be exclusive to Britain and was especially popular during Victorian times, when chrysanthemums, lavender, carnations and scented geraniums were used. Nasturtium leaves, stalks and flowers, which have a peppery flavour, have been used in salads since the 17th century. Sweet cicely – which grows wild in the north of England and Scotland – and marigold, are also part of a long culinary tradition, with the leaves, flowers and even seeds being added to salads.

Winter vegetable soup

PREPARATION TIME: 20 MINUTES
COOKING TIME: 35-40 MINUTES
SERVES 4

1 tablespoon olive oil
25g (1oz) butter
1 large onion, chopped
125g (4½oz) leeks, rinsed and sliced
280g (10oz) parsnips, peeled and chopped
400g (14oz) carrots, peeled and chopped
1 large potato, peeled and chopped
900ml (1 pint 12fl oz) vegetable stock
   (see page 182)
4-5 tablespoons semi-skimmed milk
   (optional)
Salt, black pepper and freshly
   grated nutmeg
2 tablespoons chopped parsley

1 Heat the oil and butter in a large saucepan. Add the onion and leeks and cook, stirring, over a medium heat, for 4-5 minutes until soft. Add the parsnips, carrots and potato and cook, stirring, for 2-3 minutes.

2 Pour in the stock, bring to the boil, then simmer for 20-25 minutes until all the vegetables are tender.

3 Transfer to a blender or food processor and process until smooth. Return to the saucepan and pour in a little milk to thin, if needed. Season with salt, pepper and nutmeg, then stir in the parsley.

4 Reheat gently, then transfer to warmed bowls. Serve with bread.

Nutrients per serving
- Calories 215
- Carbohydrate 29g (of which sugars 13g)
- Protein 5g
- Fat 9g (of which saturated fat 4g)
- Fibre 7g
- Vitamins A, C

Other winter vegetables can be used in this thick, warming soup. Try Jerusalem **artichokes** or **swede** in place of the parsnips or carrots. Garlic sippets (see right) are also very good with this.

Gammon and broad bean soup

PREPARATION TIME: 5 MINUTES
COOKING TIME: 45 MINUTES
SERVES 4

2 tablespoons olive oil
150g (5½oz) gammon steak,
   chopped into 1cm (½in) pieces
1 onion, chopped
2 large, thick leeks, about 400g (14oz)
   in total, sliced
4 sprigs of thyme
2 bay leaves
115g (4oz) pearl barley
1.5 litres (2¾ pints) vegetable stock
   (see page 182)
225g (8oz) podded broad beans
Salt and black pepper
3 tablespoons chopped flat-leafed parsley

1 Heat the oil in a large saucepan and fry the gammon, onion and leeks over a medium-low heat, stirring occasionally, for about 10 minutes or until the vegetables are soft and golden. Add the thyme and bay leaves towards the end of cooking.

2 Add the barley and cook for 1-2 minutes, then pour in the stock. Bring to the boil and simmer, uncovered, for about 30-40 minutes until the barley is tender and the stock reduced to a soupy consistency.

3 Add the broad beans 4-5 minutes before the end of the cooking. Season with salt and pepper and transfer the soup to warmed bowls. Sprinkle with parsley and serve with granary bread.

Nutrients per serving
- Calories 275
- Carbohydrate 31g (of which sugars 5g)
- Protein 19g
- Fat 9g (of which saturated fat 1g)
- Fibre 6g
- Vitamins B_{12}, B_6, B_1

London Particular with garlic sippets

PREPARATION TIME: 10 MINUTES,
PLUS 30 MINUTES SOAKING
COOKING TIME: 45-50 MINUTES
SERVES 4

250g (9oz) split dried green peas
60g (2¼oz) streaky bacon, chopped
1 onion, chopped
1 carrot, chopped
1 celery stick, chopped
1.2 litres (2 pints) chicken stock
   (see page 120)
Salt and black pepper
2 slices white bread, crusts removed
1 clove garlic, crushed
Chopped parsley to serve

Named after the dense **pea-souper fogs** – once a regular occurrence in London – this **thick** pea soup is **sustaining, nutritious** and very **simple** to make.

1 Put the split peas in a bowl, add boiling water to cover and leave to soak for 30 minutes. Drain.

2 Dry-fry the bacon in a heavy-based saucepan for 2-3 minutes, until lightly coloured. Add the onion, carrot and celery and cook, stirring, for 2-3 minutes, without browning.

3 Add the stock and peas, bring to the boil, then cover and simmer for 30-40 minutes until tender. Purée in a blender until smooth. Return to the pan and add salt and pepper to taste.

4 Cut the bread into 1cm (½in) dice and toss with the garlic to coat evenly. Spread on a baking sheet and toast under a hot grill, turning until golden brown. Serve the soup hot, sprinkled with the sippets and parsley.

Nutrients per serving
- Calories 325
- Carbohydrate 48g (of which sugars 5g)
- Protein 18g
- Fat 9g (of which saturated fat 3g)
- Fibre 5g
- Vitamins B_1, A

Jersey potatoes with samphire and quail's eggs

PREPARATION AND COOKING TIME: 35 MINUTES

SERVES 2

12 quail's eggs
400g (14oz) samphire, washed
400g (14oz) small Jersey potatoes,
   washed
55g (2oz) butter
Black pepper

Samphire, available from fishmongers, grows around the British coastline in May and June.

1 Cook the eggs in simmering water for 5 minutes, then plunge them into cold water to cool. Pick over the samphire, discarding any woody or damaged and discoloured stems. Cook the potatoes in boiling, salted water for 8-15 minutes or until tender. Drain.

2 Meanwhile, plunge the samphire into a large saucepan of boiling water, bring back to the boil, then drain immediately. Transfer to a wide dish. Add the butter and the potatoes to the samphire and toss gently to mix.

3 Shell and halve most of the eggs, leaving some in their shells for decoration. Arrange over the samphire and potatoes. Sprinkle with pepper and serve warm.

Nutrients per serving
- Calories 520
- Carbohydrate 36g (of which sugars 6g)
- Protein 21g
- Fat 33g (of which saturated fat 7g)
- Fibre 5g
- Vitamins B_6, B_{12}, C, B_1

Butternut, blue cheese
and walnut salad

An autumnal salad to make the most of the
squash season. Dorset Blue Vinney adds good, sharp
flavour but is lower in fat than most cheeses,
making this a healthy dish all round.

PREPARATION TIME: 15 MINUTES
COOKING TIME: 1 MINUTE
SERVES 4

400g (14oz) butternut squash
1 small frisée lettuce, washed
40g (1½oz) lamb's lettuce, washed
85g (3oz) Blue Vinney cheese, rind removed
55g (2oz) walnuts, roughly chopped
Salt and black pepper
2 tablespoons extra virgin olive oil
2 tablespoons walnut oil
1 tablespoon sherry vinegar

1 Halve the squash lengthways and scoop out
the pith and seeds. Peel each half, then cut
into 3mm (⅛in) slices. Transfer the slices to a
saucepan and add plenty of boiling water.
Bring to the boil for 30 seconds, drain in a
colander, then run cold tap water over to cool.
Set aside to drain.

2 Tear the frisée into a salad bowl. Add the
lamb's lettuce and mix briefly.

3 Crumble the cheese over the salad, then
sprinkle with the walnuts and drained
squash. Add salt and pepper to taste.

4 Put both oils and the vinegar into a small
screw-top jar, cover and shake vigorously
to emulsify. Trickle over the salad, toss gently to
coat, then serve with granary bread.

Nutrients per serving
- Calories 324
- Carbohydrate 10g (of which sugars 2g)
- Protein 8g
- Fat 28g (of which saturated fat 7g)
- Fibre 3g
- Vitamins B_6

Salad of prawns with avocado and pink grapefruit

PREPARATION TIME: 20 MINUTES
SERVES 4

2 large pink grapefruit
Salt
2 tablespoons extra virgin olive oil
1 teaspoon lemon juice
2 avocado pears
85g (3oz) prepared watercress
200g (7oz) shelled Atlantic prawns,
　　thawed if frozen

Nutrients per serving
- Calories 280
- Carbohydrate 8g (of which sugars 7g)
- Protein 14g
- Fat 21g (of which saturated fat 4g)
- Fibre 4g
- Vitamins E, C, B$_6$

1 Peel one grapefruit with a small, sharp knife, removing the white pith and membrane. Holding it on a plate to catch the juice, cut between the membranes of each segment to release the flesh in a neat wedge. Repeat with the other grapefruit, put the juices into a bowl and the segments into a nylon sieve over the bowl.

2 Transfer 2 tablespoons of the grapefruit juice to a small screw-top jar and add a pinch of salt.

With the lid on the jar, shake to dissolve the salt. Add the olive oil and lemon juice to the jar, cover and set aside.

3 Halve, pit and skin the avocados, then slice them thinly. Place in a salad bowl with the grapefruit segments and watercress. Shake the jar of dressing vigorously, then drizzle over the salad. Toss very gently before scattering the prawns over the top. Serve with wholemeal bread.

Pink grapefruit has just the right sharpness to bring out the flavour of Atlantic prawns, and is even higher in vitamin C than the yellow variety.

Winter salad of batavia with pomegranate

PREPARATION TIME: 15 MINUTES
SERVES 4

1 batavia head, leaves washed and dried
1 red pomegranate, quartered
2 spring onions, trimmed
Leaves from 2 bushy sprigs of flat-leaved
　　parsley
3 tablespoons plus 1 teaspoon extra
　　virgin olive oil
1 clove garlic, chopped
Flaky sea salt and black pepper
1½ teaspoons rice white wine vinegar

1 Tear the batavia leaves into a wide salad bowl. Working over a small dish, bend back the skin of each pomegranate quarter, releasing the seeds onto the dish. Pick away all the flimsy yellow membrane.

2 Halve the spring onions lengthways, then slice them finely crossways. Place the parsley leaves on top and chop both finely.

3 Add 1 teaspoon olive oil to the pomegranate, mix, then sprinkle it over the spring onion and parsley mixture. Mix gently, so that the greenery clings to the seeds.

4 Put the chopped garlic on a board, sprinkle with sea salt and, working with the flat of the knife, crush it to a pulp. Scrape it up with the knife and transfer it to a small screw-top jar. Add the vinegar and remaining olive oil, screw the lid on and shake the jar vigorously to emulsify the dressing. Add to the salad leaves and toss gently.

5 Scatter the pomegranate mixture over the dressed leaves and serve at once with crusty bread and duck pâté or cold cuts of meat.

Beetroot salad
with mint dressing

PREPARATION TIME: 5 MINUTES
SERVES 4

450g (1lb) cooked beetroot, sliced
    5mm (¼ in) thick
2 teaspoons sherry vinegar
2 teaspoons white wine vinegar
1 tablespoon olive oil
Salt and black pepper
4 tablespoons fresh mint, shredded
Low-fat Greek-style yoghurt

1 Put the beetroot in a shallow dish. Whisk together the vinegar and oil. Add salt and pepper to taste. Pour over the beetroot and toss to coat.

2 Scatter the mint over and lightly fork it through the beetroot. Top with yoghurt and serve with soda bread (see page 261).

Nutrients per serving
- Calories 100
- Carbohydrate 11g (of which sugars 10g)
- Protein 3g
- Fat 4g (of which saturated fat 1g)
- Fibre 2g

Use fresh **beetroot** and cook as directed on page 186, or buy it vacuum-packed from supermarkets and greengrocers, but do not use beetroot packed in vinegar. **Fresh** mint makes a **delicious** contrast to the **sweetness** of the beetroot.

Nutrients per serving
- Calories 100
- Carbohydrate 4g
  (of which sugars 4g)
- Protein 1g
- Fat 9g (of which
  saturated fat 1g)
- Fibre 1.5g

Batavia is at its **best** in the weeks after Christmas and can come as a welcome, refreshing addition to our **winter** diet.

Chicken and warm potato salad

PREPARATION AND COOKING TIME: 25 MINUTES
SERVES 2 FOR A LIGHT SUPPER

350g (12oz) small new potatoes, washed

1 large shallot or small red onion, halved, peeled and thinly sliced

½ red pepper, seeded and thinly sliced

4 tablespoons olive oil

4 boneless, skinless chicken thighs

Salt and black pepper

1 teaspoon runny honey

1½ teaspoons English mustard

2 teaspoons tarragon vinegar or white wine vinegar

85g (3oz) mixed salad leaves

1 Cook the potatoes in boiling, salted water for about 15 minutes until tender. Add the shallot and red pepper, return to simmering point and drain into a colander.

2 Meanwhile, preheat the grill to hot. Use 1 tablespoon of the oil to brush the chicken thighs and sprinkle both sides with salt and pepper. Transfer them to the rack of the grill pan and grill for 10-12 minutes, turning them once, until cooked through. Remove and set aside.

3 Put the honey, mustard, vinegar and remaining oil into a small screw-top jar with a pinch of salt and shake vigorously to emulsify. Put the drained, cooked vegetables into a wide dish, sprinkle with salt and pepper, then add the dressing and toss.

4 Scatter the salad leaves over the cooked vegetables and toss together gently. Cut each chicken thigh into 3 pieces, add to the salad, toss briefly and serve.

Choose waxy potatoes of good flavour such as Jerseys, Pink Fir Apple, Anya or, if you are in Scotland, Ayrshires.

Warm salad of chicken livers and grapes

Nutrients per serving

- Calories 540
- Carbohydrate 36g
  (of which sugars 10g)
- Protein 35g
- Fat 29g (of which saturated fat 5g)
- Fibre 3g
- Vitamins niacin, B_6, C, B_1

PREPARATION TIME: 10 MINUTES
COOKING TIME: 15 MINUTES
SERVES 4

2 thick or 4 thin rashers streaky bacon,
  cut into batons
1 tablespoon olive oil
6 chicken livers, about 250g (9oz) in total
125g (4½oz) mixed baby spinach and
  trimmed watercress
Salt and black pepper
2 teaspoons red wine vinegar
1 tablespoon walnut or hazelnut oil
150g (5½oz) seedless white grapes

1 Fry the bacon gently in the olive oil for 5-7 minutes until crisp, stirring frequently.

2 Meanwhile, separate each liver into its two lobes, cutting away the white connecting tissue and removing any discoloured areas. Cut each lobe in half. Divide the spinach and watercress between four plates and sprinkle with salt and pepper.

3 Push the crisp bacon to one side of the frying pan and fry the chicken livers for 5-6 minutes over a medium heat, turning often, until brown all over but with a hint of pink in the middle.

4 Divide the liver between the salad plates. Add the vinegar to the pan over the heat and let it sizzle for a few seconds, then remove from the heat and add the nut oil. Add pepper, then spoon the dressing, including bacon bits, over the liver and salad. Sprinkle with grapes and serve with crusty bread.

Nutrients per serving

- Calories 270
- Carbohydrate 7g (of which sugars 6g)
- Protein 16g
- Fat 20g (of which saturated fat 6g)
- Fibre 1g
- Vitamins B_6, B_{12}, C, A

Spinach leaves with peppery watercress make a good base for this iron-rich starter salad. Liver is one of the best sources of vitamin A, zinc and magnesium.

Grilled chicory, Stilton and walnut salad

PREPARATION TIME: 5 MINUTES
COOKING TIME: 8-13 MINUTES
SERVES 4

4 small or 2 large chicory heads, halved
    lengthways and cores removed
Vegetable oil for brushing
1 large Conference or Williams pear,
    peeled, cored and sliced
2 tablespoons walnut oil
Salt and black pepper
100g (3½ oz) Stilton cheese,
    finely crumbled
25g (1oz) walnut halves, lightly toasted

1 Heat the grill to very hot. Brush the chicory lightly with vegetable oil and place on the grill rack, cut side up. Grill as near to the heat as possible for 2-3 minutes for smaller heads (or 3-4 minutes for larger heads) until beginning to soften and char. Turn, then brush lightly with oil and continue to cook for 2-3 minutes (or 3-4 minutes) until softened and lightly charred.

2 Turn the chicory over again to cut side up. Lay the pear slices on the chicory, brush lightly with walnut oil, sprinkle with salt and pepper and return to the grill for 4-5 minutes to warm the pears.

3 Transfer to warmed plates, sprinkle with the Stilton and toasted walnuts and drizzle over the remaining walnut oil. Serve at once.

Nutrients per serving
- Calories 235
- Carbohydrate 4g (of which sugars 3g)
- Protein 7g
- Fat 21g (of which saturated fat 7g)
- Fibre 1g

Warm potato and black pudding with rhubarb relish

Grilling adds a lovely **smoky** flavour to the chicory in a **nutritious** salad that includes the classic **British duo** of Stilton and heart-healthy walnuts

PREPARATION AND COOKING TIME: 25 MINUTES
SERVES 4

400g (14oz) small new potatoes
200g (7oz) young rhubarb, trimmed and cut into 15mm (⅝ in) pieces
3-4 teaspoons granulated sugar
2 teaspoons wholegrain mustard
3 tablespoons olive oil
4 spring onions, trimmed and sliced
150g (5½ oz) cooked, peeled beetroot, cut into 2cm (¾ in) pieces
Salt and black pepper
4 teaspoons vegetable oil
175g (6oz) black pudding, sliced 1cm (½ in) thick
1 teaspoon caraway seeds, toasted

The **British** have always relished **sweet-sour** flavour combinations, and the **vibrant** mixture of beetroot and rhubarb provides just that.

1 Cook the potatoes in boiling, salted water until tender, then drain. Meanwhile, put the rhubarb in a saucepan with 3 teaspoons sugar. Cover and cook over a gentle heat for about 10 minutes, shaking the pan from time to time, until the rhubarb has partially broken down.

2 Remove 1 tablespoon of the cooked rhubarb liquid from the pan and put into a small bowl or cup with the mustard. Mix, then beat in the olive oil. Add the spring onions, stir to mix and set aside.

3 Add the beetroot to the rhubarb, then add salt, black pepper and more sugar, if needed. Toss the drained potatoes with the spring onion and mustard dressing and keep them warm while you cook the black pudding.

4 Heat the vegetable oil in a nonstick frying pan, add the black pudding and cook over a medium heat for about 40 seconds on each side. Put the potatoes and black pudding onto plates and serve with the rhubarb relish, sprinkled with caraway seeds.

Nutrients per serving
- Calories 336
- Carbohydrate 30g (of which sugars 8g)
- Protein 8g
- Fat 21g (of which saturated fat 5g)
- Fibre 2g
- Vitamins B_6, B_{12}, C

Eggs

and cheese

Eggs and cheese
the healthy way

For high-quality protein and many other essential nutrients, there are few foods to beat simple eggs and cheese.

Eggs and cheese are staple foods that people across the world have eaten for thousands of years in the knowledge that they are highly nutritious – a belief that modern science has confirmed.

What eggs can offer
Eggs contain all nine essential amino acids, making them an excellent source of high-quality protein. They are one of the few dietary sources of vitamin D, essential to bone health, and also provide good amounts of vitamins A, E, B_2 and B_{12}. One egg provides almost 100 per cent of the recommended daily intake of vitamin B_{12}, which is vital for the blood, growth and a healthy nervous system.

In addition, they are rich in lecithin and choline, substances that help to keep the brain functioning properly.

The white of an egg is mostly water, plus a little protein, potassium and vitamin B_2. Most of the calories, fat, nutrients – and all of the cholesterol – are in the yolk.

The cholesterol question
Eggs contain relatively high levels of cholesterol, once believed to be directly linked to high blood cholesterol, which can trigger heart disease.

Although the British Heart Foundation still suggests eating no more than four eggs a week, it is now thought that too much saturated fat – rather than dietary cholesterol – is the culprit, causing the liver to manufacture excessive blood

Perfect poached eggs

1 Use a wide, shallow pan and add about 8cm (3in) of water. Add a little vinegar to the boiling water, which helps the eggs to hold their shape. Before adding the eggs, reduce the boiling water to a simmer.

2 Use very fresh eggs. Break them into a measuring cup and then slip carefully into the middle of the simmering water. Cover immediately and turn off the heat.

3 Set a timer for exactly 3 minutes for medium-firm yolks. Remove from the water with a slotted spoon.

cholesterol. So that, although a medium-sized egg (235mg cholesterol, 1.9g saturated fat) contains almost 30 times more cholesterol than 25g of chocolate (8mg cholesterol, 4.4g saturated fat), it is, in fact, less likely to raise blood cholesterol as the chocolate has more than twice as much saturated fat.

Buying and storing eggs

Egg labelling can be misleading and confusing, with terms such as 'farm' implying free-range chickens, but in fact indicating battery-reared chickens. All eggs labelled organic, however, must also be free-range.

Eggshell colour can vary according to the breed of the hen, but this does not affect the quality, flavour, nutritional value, or cooking characteristics of the egg. As a guide when buying and storing:
• Never buy eggs with cracked or blemished shells.
• Check the date stamp to make sure you are buying the freshest eggs.
• Store eggs in the refrigerator with the pointed end down to keep the yolk centred.

Salmonella in eggs is rare – only one egg in every 7000 harbours the bacteria. High temperatures kill the bacteria, but there is a slight risk of infection when eating lightly cooked or raw eggs.

As a result, children, pregnant women and the elderly or the sick should avoid dishes containing eggs that have not been cooked to at least 71°C (160°F), the temperature at which the salmonella bacteria are destroyed.

Cheese for calcium

Cheese supplies protein, vitamin A, phosphorus, vitamin D and vitamin B_2. Like other dairy products, it is also one of the best sources of the mineral calcium, which is vital for strong bones and teeth.

CALORIE AND FAT CONTENT PER 100g (3½oz) CHEESE			
	Kcals	Total fat*	Saturated fat
Brie	319	27	17
Caerphilly	375	31.3	19.6
Cheddar	412	34	22
Half-fat cheddar	261	15	9.4
Cheshire	379	31	19
Cottage cheese	98	4	2.5
Cream cheese	439	47	30
Double Gloucester	405	34	21.3
Feta	250	20	14
Lancashire	373	31	19.4
Mozzarella	289	21	13
Parmesan	452	33	20
Ricotta	144	11	7
Stilton	411	35.5	22.2
Wensleydale	377	31	20

* Total fat content includes fatty compounds and other fatty acids in addition to saturated fat.

Calcium is the most abundant mineral in the human body, accounting for around 2 per cent of total body weight. Although 99 per cent of calcium is found in the bones and teeth, it is also essential for blood clotting, muscle contraction and nerve function.

If diet does not provide enough calcium, the body robs bones of their calcium in order to supply the muscles, heart and nerves. Adults, particularly women, need a regular intake of calcium-rich foods to help to maintain optimum bone density throughout life in order to minimise the effects of osteoporosis – a natural part of ageing involving the loss of protein tissue from bone, which causes it to fracture easily.

Eat in moderation

Most types of cheese, especially those that we consider to be traditionally British, such as Cheddar, Stilton and Double Gloucester, are packed with nutrients but are also high in fat – particularly saturated fat – and so should be eaten in moderation.

In cooking, it is often possible to substitute a small quantity of a cheese with a strong flavour, such as a mature Cheddar or a Stilton, for a larger quantity of a milder-tasting cheese.

Another way to reduce the amounts of high-fat cheese used is to grate it very finely as this makes it go farther in sandwiches or when the cheese is melted as a topping. It is also worth noting that reduced-fat cheeses are not necessarily the healthiest option as they are often highly processed.

Pregnant women are advised to avoid soft and blue-veined cheese such as Stilton, Camembert and Brie, as they may contain the bacteria that produce listeriosis, which can cause miscarriage or damage to the unborn child.

Classic baked eggs

PREPARATION TIME: 10 MINUTES
COOKING TIME: 9 MINUTES
SERVES 4

Unsalted butter for greasing
2 tomatoes, finely chopped
2 tablespoons chopped mixed herbs, such as parsley, basil and chives
2 teaspoons English mustard
1 teaspoon Worcestershire sauce
4 tablespoons half-fat crème fraîche
Salt and black pepper
4 eggs

1 Heat the oven to 200°C (400°F, gas mark 6). Lightly butter four small ramekin dishes and divide the chopped tomatoes and herbs between them. In a bowl, mix the mustard, Worcestershire sauce and crème fraîche. Add salt and pepper to taste and set aside.

2 Break an egg into each dish on top of the tomato-herb mixture and transfer the dishes to a roasting tin half filled with hot water.

3 Bake for 4-5 minutes or until the whites have begun to set. Spoon over the mustard and cream mixture and return them to the oven for a further 3-4 minutes. Serve at once with thick slices of wholegrain toast.

Nutrients per serving
- Calories 122
- Carbohydrate 2g (of which sugars 2g)
- Protein 8g
- Fat 9g (of which saturated fat 3g)
- Fibre 0.5g
- Vitamins B_{12}

This is an easy and fast way of preparing eggs, with finely chopped tomatoes and fresh herbs adding flavour, colour and nutrients.

Crowdie eggs

PREPARATION TIME: 10 MINUTES, PLUS COOLING AND CHILLING
COOKING TIME: 12 MINUTES
SERVES 4

1.2 litres (2 pints) skimmed milk
Juice of ½ lemon
Salt and black pepper
3 large hard-boiled eggs, peeled and finely chopped
Grated zest of 1 unwaxed lemon
1 tablespoon each finely chopped chives and chervil
1 tablespoon low-fat mayonnaise
2 spring onions, finely chopped

1 Put the milk in a jug and add the lemon juice. Leave to stand for 20-30 minutes, until soured. Transfer to a saucepan and place over a very low heat until just warm, but not simmering, and the liquid whey separates from the curds. Remove from the heat and leave to cool, then drain off the whey.

2 Line a colander with a clean tea towel. Pour in the curds and leave until most of the remaining whey has drained. Gather up the corners of the cloth and squeeze out the last of the liquid. Transfer to a bowl – there should be about 140g (5oz). Add a pinch of salt, beat until smooth and set aside.

3 Put the chopped egg in a bowl with the lemon zest, chives and chervil, mayonnaise and pepper.

4 Fold the eggs into the curds until mixed. Spoon into four ramekin dishes and sprinkle with the spring onions. Chill for 30 minutes, then serve with oatcakes (see page 240).

Nutrients per serving
- Calories 90
- Carbohydrate 2.5g (of which sugars 2.5g)
- Protein 6g
- Fat 6g (of which saturated fat 1.5g)
- Fibre 0g
- Vitamins B_{12}

Curried eggs

PREPARATION TIME: 20 MINUTES
COOKING TIME: 25 MINUTES
SERVES 4

15g (½ oz) unsalted butter
1 onion, finely chopped
1 small red chilli, deseeded and finely chopped
2 cloves garlic, crushed
1 tablespoon medium curry powder
1 teaspoon turmeric powder
Lightly crushed seeds of 4 cardamom pods
400g (14oz) canned chopped tomatoes
1 dessert apple, cored and finely chopped
400ml (14fl oz) canned low-fat coconut milk
1 teaspoon soft brown sugar
Salt and black pepper
4 large hard-boiled eggs, shelled and halved
Squeeze of lemon juice
Cooked brown or basmati rice to serve
Parsley or coriander sprigs to garnish

1 Heat the butter in a large frying pan, add the onion and cook until golden. Add the chilli, garlic, curry powder, turmeric and cardamom seeds. Cook, stirring, for 1 minute.

2 Add the tomatoes, apple and 175ml (6fl oz) water, bring to the boil and simmer for 10 minutes. Add the coconut milk and sugar and cook for a further 5 minutes. Add salt and pepper to taste. Transfer to a blender or food processor and purée until smooth.

3 Return the sauce to the pan, add the eggs and gently reheat. Add a squeeze of lemon juice and serve with rice, topped with parsley or coriander sprigs.

One of the many recipes to be adopted by **English** households during the years of the Raj, curried eggs was a **Victorian** favourite.

Nutrients per serving
- Calories 270
- Carbohydrate 13g (of which sugars 11g)
- Protein 10g
- Fat 21g (of which saturated fat 4g)
- Fibre 1.5g
- Vitamins B$_{12}$, B$_6$

Crowdie is a **Scottish** fresh cheese, traditionally made by crofters. The name comes from the Lowland Scots word 'cruds', meaning **curds**.

Vegetarian Scotch eggs

A vegetarian version of a **Scottish speciality**, using kidney beans for **fibre** and a **reduced** fat content.

PREPARATION TIME: 30 MINUTES
COOKING TIME: 15 MINUTES
SERVES 4

1 tablespoon sunflower oil
1 small onion, finely chopped
1 clove garlic, crushed
400g (14oz) canned kidney beans, drained and rinsed
85g (3oz) mature Cheddar cheese, grated
2 teaspoons finely chopped fresh sage
1 teaspoon sesame seeds
1 teaspoon sunflower seeds
Salt and black pepper
4 small eggs, hard-boiled, plus 1 large egg for coating
55g (2oz) dried wholemeal breadcrumbs
Groundnut oil for deep-frying
Mustard sauce (see page 48) to serve

1 Heat the oil in the frying pan, add the onion and cook for 4-5 minutes until soft, then add the garlic and cook for a further minute.

2 Put the kidney beans in a blender or food processor. Add the onion and garlic, cheese, sage, sesame and sunflower seeds, and salt and pepper to taste. Purée until combined.

3 Divide the mixture into four and, using wet hands, mould each portion evenly around an egg.

4 For the coating, crack the raw egg into a small, shallow bowl and beat with a little salt. Put the breadcrumbs in a separate bowl. Toss each coated egg in the beaten egg, then in the breadcrumbs. Transfer to a plate and chill for 10-15 minutes.

5 In a deep-fat fryer, deep-fry the eggs, in 2 batches, for 1-2 minutes until golden. Drain on kitchen paper and serve hot or cold with the mustard sauce and a green salad.

VARIATION

Mix 225g (8oz) pork sausagemeat (see page 174) with 2 teaspoons finely chopped sage, thyme or parsley. Shape the mixture around the hardboiled eggs, coat and chill, then deep-fry for 3-4 minutes until golden.

Nutrients per serving
- Calories 477
- Carbohydrate 26g (of which sugars 14g)
- Protein 24g
- Fat 31g (of which saturated fat 9g)
- Fibre 7g
- Vitamins B_{12}, B_6, B_1, B_2

Good woman's eggs

PREPARATION TIME: 15 MINUTES
COOKING TIME: 45 MINUTES
SERVES 4

450g (1lb) potatoes, peeled and diced
Salt and black pepper
1 teaspoon chopped rosemary
3 tablespoons olive oil, plus extra
    for greasing
1 large onion, finely sliced
450g (1lb) butternut squash, peeled
    and diced
3 large, flat mushrooms, roughly chopped
2 cloves garlic, crushed
3 slices of lean back bacon, roughly
    chopped
6 small eggs
1 tablespoon grated Parmesan cheese

A hearty baked-egg dish traditionally served as a nutritious farmer's breakfast, brought up to date with the addition of Parmesan and squash.

1 Heat the oven to 200°C (400°F, gas mark 6). Put the potatoes in a large, nonstick baking tin. Sprinkle with salt and pepper and add the rosemary and oil. Mix well and cook in the oven for 10 minutes, stirring occasionally.

2 Remove from the oven and add the onion, squash, mushrooms, garlic and bacon. Stir well and return to the oven for a further 20 minutes, stirring occasionally, until golden.

3 Tip into a large ovenproof dish and make six indents. Crack an egg into each indent. Sprinkle with salt, pepper and Parmesan. Bake for 10-12 minutes until the eggs are just set. Serve at once with a mixed salad.

Nutrients per serving
- Calories 383
- Carbohydrate 30g (of which sugars 9g)
- Protein 20g
- Fat 21g (of which saturated fat 5g)
- Fibre 3g
- Vitamins A, B_1, B_2, B_6, B_{12}

Creamed eggs with mushrooms

PREPARATION TIME: 15 MINUTES
COOKING TIME: 15 MINUTES
SERVES 4

25g (1oz) unsalted butter
1 onion, finely chopped
1 clove garlic, crushed
225g (8oz) brown cap mushrooms,
    finely chopped
Pinch of freshly grated nutmeg
1 teaspoon finely chopped thyme leaves
1 tablespoon finely chopped parsley
Salt and black pepper
4 large eggs, beaten
25g (1oz) fresh goat's cheese, crumbled

Ideal for brunch, this dish is best made with really fresh eggs. For a special occasion, use seasonal wild mushrooms, freshly picked if possible.

1 Melt half the butter in a heavy-based, nonstick saucepan. Add the onion and garlic and cook over a medium heat, stirring, until translucent.

2 Add the mushrooms, cover and cook for 5-6 minutes. Add the nutmeg and herbs, and salt and pepper to taste. Remove to a bowl and set aside in a warm place. Wipe the pan.

3 Melt the remaining butter in the pan and add the eggs, with salt and pepper to taste. Cook over a very low heat for 3-4 minutes or until they start

to thicken. Add the mushroom mixture and goat's cheese, then remove from the heat.

4 Continue stirring off the heat until creamy. Serve at once on a bed of mixed leaves or on toast.

Nutrients per serving
- Calories 170
- Carbohydrate 2g (of which sugars 1.5g)
- Protein 10g
- Fat 13g (of which saturated fat 6g)
- Fibre 1g
- Vitamins B_{12}

Cheeses of **Britain**

The best-known British cheese is Cheddar and today it is made in many countries around the world. Named after the famous Cheddar Gorge in Somerset, the pressed cow's milk cheese was first developed over 800 years ago. It quickly became a hit with royalty and Henry II declared Cheddar cheese to be the best in Britain. During the reign of Charles I, the production of Cheddar was monopolised by the royal court.

The best true Cheddars are still made on farms in Somerset, Devon and Dorset, although high-quality Scottish Cheddar has been produced since 1885, when a Somerset farmer was brought to Scotland by the Ayrshire Agricultural Trust to pass on his skills to local farmers and cheese-makers.

Unlike Cheddar, blue Stilton, a world-renowned British cheese, has always had its area of production controlled by law. Any cheese that is labelled Stilton will have been manufactured only within the regions of Nottinghamshire, Derbyshire and Leicestershire. The cheese is made with *Penicillium roquefortii* and then pierced with needles to leave holes that encourage the growth of the mould.

Caerphilly cheese, named after the town, and the only Welsh cheese to become popular outside Wales, is made with cow's milk, traditionally in a wheel shape. Typically produced by small farms, demand for it began to exceed supply in the 1800s, so production spread to Somerset, where it is still made today. The traditional methods of making Caerphilly have recently been revived on a number of farms in south Wales.

Salty, crumbly Cheshire cheese has been made in the border area of Shropshire and Wales since pre-Roman times. Local cattle graze on ground with salt-bearing rock strata, from where the flavour and texture are said to come. Red Cheshire is coloured with annatto, an American plant used for its pigment that was introduced

pre-Roman times, and new varieties of cheese are still being developed.

into Britain in the 17th century. Blue Cheshire is left to develop a blue mould, which gives the cheese a characteristic sharp flavour and nutty aftertaste.

Old and new

The late 20th century saw a renaissance in British cheese-making. Small producers began experimenting with methods that resulted in cheeses other than the regional ones, such as Cheddar and Stilton, for which Britain is famous. Most notable of these are the soft goat's cheeses now being made in the West Country.

Yet while these pioneering artisans may seem to have been mimicking the success of continental European cheeses, they are also exploring authentic British traditions, in many cases reviving cheeses lost through wartime rationing and factory production.

Wensleydale, originally a blue mould ewe's milk cheese similar to French Roquefort, was introduced to Britain after the Norman Conquest of 1066. In recent years, a few small farmhouse cheese-makers have revived this old-style cheese and have been producing mould-ripened sheep's milk Wensleydale.

Meanwhile, cow's milk Wensleydale and white Stilton – mild, firm cheeses that previously received little attention – have emerged as two of Britain's best sellers thanks to the popularity of combining savoury and sweet flavourings. Combining cheese with herbs, nuts, fruits and spices is not a new idea, and sage Derby, with its distinctive and vivid green marbling from the herb, is a long-established flavoured cheese.

Another recently developed cheese, based on a lost 17th-century recipe for 'nettle cheese', is Cornish yarg, a crumbly cheese made from cow's milk and wrapped in nettle leaves. The name, while giving a sense of old rural tradition, in fact comes from the backward spelling of Gray – the surname of the couple who revived the cheese in the 1970s.

The classic British omelette

The most successful omelettes are
always beautifully simple and do
not need an elaborate, rich filling.

PREPARATION TIME: 5 MINUTES
COOKING TIME: 5 MINUTES
SERVES 2

15g (½oz) unsalted butter
3-4 large eggs
Salt and black pepper

Wild mushroom filling
200g (7oz) wild mushrooms, such as chanterelles, sliced and stir-fried in 15g (½oz) butter, mixed with chopped parsley.

Cheese and tomato filling
1 beef tomato, thinly sliced, with 1 tablespoon grated mature Cheddar cheese.

Smoked salmon and chive filling
55g (2oz) smoked salmon and 1-2 tablespoons chopped chives (omit the salt).

Ham and cheese filling
55g (2oz) thinly sliced Wiltshire ham, with 1 tablespoon mature grated Cheddar cheese.

1 Heat a 25cm (10in) omelette pan until just hot and add half the butter. Crack the eggs into a jug and beat very lightly with a fork. Prepare your chosen filling.

2 When the butter is on the point of changing colour, add salt and pepper to the eggs and pour half into the pan. Gently fork through the egg until it begins to set.

3 Leave for 5-10 seconds or until nearly set. Add half of your chosen filling. Using a spatula, fold one side into the centre, then tilt the pan and fold over other side. Slide onto a warmed plate and serve at once. Repeat with the remaining ingredients to make the second omelette.

Nutrients per serving (mushroom filling)
- Calories 270
- Carbohydrate 0g
- Protein 14g
- Fat 23g (of which saturated fat 11g)
- Fibre 1g
- Vitamins B_{12}, B_2, A

Omelette Arnold Bennett

PREPARATION TIME: 10 MINUTES
COOKING TIME: 15 MINUTES
SERVES 2

55g (2oz) unsalted butter, plus extra for greasing
175g (6oz) undyed smoked haddock fillet
3 tablespoons low-fat mayonnaise
1 teaspoon English mustard
3 large eggs
Salt and black pepper
25g (1oz) mature Cheddar cheese, grated
Watercress and rocket leaves to serve

1 Heat the grill and lightly grease a shallow ovenproof dish. Place the haddock fillet in the dish, spread with half the butter, then grill for 4-5 minutes until cooked through. Leave to cool, then remove and discard the skin and separate the flesh into flakes.

2 Put the mayonnaise and mustard in a bowl and beat, then fold in the haddock. Melt the remaining butter in a 25cm (10in) omelette pan. Crack the eggs into a separate bowl and lightly stir with a fork. Add salt and pepper to taste and when the butter begins to bubble, pour the eggs into the butter.

3 Gently fork through the egg until thickened, remove the pan from the heat and spread the smoked haddock mixture evenly over the surface. Sprinkle with the cheese.

4 Place under a hot grill for about 1 minute until the omelette is golden and bubbling. Remove from the grill and cut into four wedges. Top with watercress and rocket leaves and serve at once.

Nutrients per serving
- Calories 520
- Carbohydrate 2g (of which sugars 1g)
- Protein 35g
- Fat 44g (of which saturated fat 20g)
- Fibre 0g
- Vitamins B_{12}, A, B_2, B_6

An omelette immortalised by the English novelist and theatre critic Arnold Bennett, a frequent visitor to the Savoy Hotel Grill in the 1920s. This healthy, modern version uses grated cheese and low-fat mayonnaise instead of rich béchamel and hollandaise sauces.

Cheese pudding

Leeks and
celery moisten
and lighten
this traditional
English dish.

PREPARATION TIME: 15 MINUTES
COOKING TIME: 1 HOUR
SERVES 4

15g (½oz) unsalted butter, plus extra for greasing
1 large leek, trimmed and roughly chopped
2-3 celery sticks, trimmed and roughly chopped
1 glass dry white wine
1 small loaf wholemeal or walnut bread,
   crusts removed, cut into cubes
3 eggs
600ml (1 pint) semi-skimmed milk
Salt and black pepper
2 spring onions, finely chopped
140g (5oz) mature Cheddar cheese, grated
2 tablespoons Parmesan cheese, finely grated

1 Heat the oven to 200°C (400°F, gas mark 6).
Melt the butter in a large saucepan and add
the leek and celery. Stir for 1 minute, then cover
and cook over a medium heat for 3-4 minutes.
Uncover, add the wine and bubble until half the
liquid has evaporated.

2 Meanwhile, put the bread cubes in a
greased ovenproof dish. Put the eggs in a
jug, add the milk and beat. Add salt and pepper
to taste. Pour the mixture over the bread cubes
and sprinkle with the leek and celery mixture.
Top with the spring onions and cheeses.

3 Cook in the oven for about 35 minutes
or until just set, golden and risen. Serve at
once with a crisp green salad.

Vegetable macaroni cheese

Broccoli and
cauliflower add
extra nutrients
to a family
favourite, while
a fat-free sauce
keeps it light.

PREPARATION TIME: 20 MINUTES
COOKING TIME: 35 MINUTES
SERVES 6

600ml (1 pint) skimmed milk
55g (2oz) plain flour
Salt and black pepper
Pinch of dried mustard powder
Pinch of freshly grated nutmeg
280g (10oz) cauliflower, cut into florets
280g (10oz) broccoli, cut into florets
140g (5oz) small macaroni
115g (4oz) mature Cheddar cheese, grated
3 tablespoons fresh white breadcrumbs
2 tablespoons grated Parmesan cheese

1 Put the milk in a small saucepan, add the
flour and cook over a medium heat, whisking
vigorously until the sauce has thickened and is
smooth. Add salt and pepper, the mustard
powder and nutmeg and reduce the heat to
very low. Cook for 5-6 minutes, then remove
from the heat and set aside. Heat the oven to
200°C (400°F, gas mark 6).

2 Cook the cauliflower and broccoli in
boiling, salted water for 3-4 minutes until
just tender, then drain.

3 Meanwhile, cook the macaroni in plenty of
boiling, salted water for 4-6 minutes until
tender. Drain well, then return it to the pan.

4 Add the white sauce and Cheddar, then stir
in the cauliflower and broccoli. Pour the
mixture into a large ovenproof dish. Sprinkle
over the breadcrumbs and Parmesan.

5 Cook in the oven for 10-15 minutes or
until the top is puffy and lightly browned.
Serve at once with a green salad.

VEGETABLE MACARONI CHEESE

Celeriac and Stilton soufflé

Nutrients per serving
- Calories 270
- Carbohydrate 2.5g (of which sugars 2g)
- Protein 16g
- Fat 21g (of which saturated fat 8g)
- Fibre 4g
- Vitamins B$_{12}$

PREPARATION TIME: 20 MINUTES
COOKING TIME: 40 MINUTES
SERVES 4

Unsalted butter for greasing
1 tablespoon grated Parmesan cheese
1 head of celeriac, about 450g (1lb), peeled and cubed
3 tablespoons half-fat crème fraîche
100g (3½ oz) Stilton cheese, crumbled
Black pepper
4 large eggs, separated

Fibre- and potassium-rich celeriac adds a **creamy** flavour to this elegant, **light** dish. The Stilton creates a sharp, tangy contrast.

1. Preheat the oven to 200°C (400°F, gas mark 6). Lightly butter an 18cm (7in) soufflé dish and sprinkle evenly with Parmesan, turning the dish to coat the sides.

2. Put the celeriac in a saucepan, cover with lightly salted water and bring to the boil. Simmer for about 10 minutes until tender, then drain. Return to the pan and mash over a low heat for 1-2 minutes or until the excess liquid has evaporated and the celeriac is smooth.

3. Add the crème fraîche, Stilton and pepper and stir to mix. Add the egg yolks, one at a time, beating well after each addition.

4. In a separate, clean bowl, beat the egg whites until soft peaks form. Using a large metal spoon, lightly fold the egg whites into the celeriac mixture until well combined. Spoon into the prepared dish.

5. Cook in the oven for 20-25 minutes or until risen and golden. Serve at once with a tomato or green salad.

1. Heat the oven to 180°C (350°F, gas mark 4). Lightly butter six ramekin dishes. Heat the oil in a frying pan over a medium heat. Add the courgettes and cook, covered, for 5 minutes or until just tender. Transfer to a sieve and set aside for a few minutes to drain. Transfer to a blender or food processor and work until finely chopped.

2. Melt the butter in a large saucepan, add the flour and cook, stirring, for 1 minute. Whisk in the milk, then stir until the mixture has boiled and thickened. Remove from the heat and mix in 175g (6oz) of the goat's cheese, the thyme, courgettes, egg yolks and some pepper.

3. In a separate, clean bowl, beat the egg whites until soft peaks form. Using a large metal spoon, lightly fold the egg whites into the cheese mixture until well combined, then spoon into the prepared ramekins.

4. Place the filled ramekins in a baking dish and add enough hot water to come halfway up the sides of the ramekins.

5. Bake for 20 minutes or until puffed and set. Remove from the oven and set aside to cool, until needed.

6. When nearly ready to serve, run a sharp knife around the sides of the soufflés and invert onto a deep serving dish. Spoon a tablespoon of crème fraîche over each soufflé. Top with a slice of ham and the remaining goat's cheese.

7. Return to the oven and bake for a further 15 minutes or until puffed and golden. Serve at once with a lightly dressed rocket salad.

Twice-baked courgette and goat's cheese puffs

PREPARATION TIME: 20 MINUTES
COOKING TIME: 40 MINUTES
SERVES 6

Nutrients per serving

- Calories 284
- Carbohydrate 8g (of which sugars 4g)
- Protein 17g
- Fat 20g (of which saturated fat 10g)
- Fibre 0g
- Vitamins B_{12}, B_2, A

25g (1oz) unsalted butter, plus extra
   for greasing
2 tablespoons olive oil
2 courgettes, roughly chopped
35g (1¼oz) plain flour
300ml (½ pint) semi-skimmed milk,
   warmed
200g (7oz) fresh goat's cheese, crumbled
1 tablespoon chopped fresh thyme
3 eggs, separated
Black pepper
6 tablespoons half-fat crème fraîche
6 thin slices of dry-cure ham

These little soufflé puffs are twice-baked, so you can cook them in advance, then simply reheat them when you need them.

Stuffed jacket potatoes

PREPARATION TIME: 10 MINUTES
COOKING TIME: 55-60 MINUTES
SERVES 4

4 large potatoes, about 225g (8oz) each,
    scrubbed
Olive oil for greasing
Coarse sea salt and black pepper
2 slices lean back bacon, cut into strips
4 spring onions, finely chopped
225g (8oz) low-fat cottage cheese
2 tablespoons finely chopped chives
    or parsley
2 tablespoons virgin olive oil
1 egg yolk
40g (1½ oz) mature Cheddar
    cheese, grated

Nutrients per serving

- Calories 365
- Carbohydrate 41g (of which sugars 4g)
- Protein 18g
- Fat 15g (including saturated fat 4g)
- Fibre 3g
- Vitamins B_6, B_{12}, B_1

1 Heat the oven to 200°C (400°F, gas mark 6). Rub the potato skins all over with some oil and salt. Transfer to a baking sheet and cook for about 50 minutes or until cooked through.

2 Meanwhile, heat a frying pan and dry-fry the bacon until golden and crispy. Add the spring onions and cook for a further 2 minutes. Set aside.

3 Prick the potatoes briefly with a fork to let the steam escape. Cut a slice from the longest side of each potato. Scoop the middles into a bowl, leaving enough for the skins to keep some shape. Mash the middles and mix in the bacon and spring onions, cottage cheese, chives, half the oil, the egg yolk, and salt and pepper to taste.

4 Spoon the potato mixture back into the skins. Sprinkle with Cheddar, drizzle with the remaining oil and return to the oven for 5 minutes or until the cheese is golden. Serve at once with a green salad.

Baked potatoes, with their lovely crisp skins, are extremely nutritious, being high in vitamin C, fibre and potassium.

Cheese and mushroom pâté

PREPARATION TIME: 10 MINUTES,
PLUS 1 HOUR CHILLING
COOKING TIME: 10 MINUTES
SERVES 4

This is a **very good** way of using up scraps of cheese, as well as making a **healthy**, satisfying snack or lunch.

15g (½ oz) unsalted butter
5 large, flat mushrooms, about 225g (8oz), roughly chopped
1 large leek, trimmed and finely chopped
5 tablespoons half-fat crème fraîche
1 teaspoon English mustard
Pinch of freshly grated nutmeg
Ground black pepper
125g (4½ oz) Cheddar or Lancashire cheese, crumbled

1 Melt the butter in a large saucepan. Add the mushrooms and leek, cover and cook over a medium heat for 5 minutes, stirring occasionally. Add the crème fraîche, mustard, nutmeg and some black pepper and cook, uncovered, for 5 minutes, until almost all the liquid has evaporated.

2 Transfer the mixture to a blender or food processor, add the cheese, and purée in short bursts until smooth.

3 Scrape the mixture into a bowl or four individual ramekin dishes and chill for at least 1 hour or overnight before serving with oatcakes (see page 240) and mixed crudités.

Nutrients per serving
- Calories 200
- Carbohydrate 2g (of which sugars 1g)
- Protein 10g
- Fat 17g (including saturated fat 10g)
- Fibre 1g

Spinach, cheese and egg filo pie

PREPARATION TIME: 30 MINUTES
COOKING TIME: 35 MINUTES
SERVES 4

125g (4½ oz) filo pastry, about 8 sheets
4 tablespoons olive oil
500g (1lb 2oz) fresh spinach leaves, washed
Salt and black pepper
Freshly grated nutmeg
2 tablespoons chopped fresh parsley
175g (6oz) Wensleydale and Lancashire cheese, crumbled
4 eggs
1 tablespoon sesame seeds

Nutrients per serving
- Calories 516
- Carbohydrate 21g (of which sugars 2g)
- Protein 25g
- Fat 36g (of which saturated fat 13g)
- Fibre 3g
- Vitamins C, B$_{12}$, B$_6$, A, B$_2$

1 Heat the oven to 200°C (400°F, gas mark 6). Lightly brush each sheet of filo with oil and put in a layer, oiled side down, to cover the base and sides of a 20cm (8in) loose-bottomed, deep flan tin, letting the excess hang over the edges. Brush the pastry all over with a little oil.

2 Put the spinach in a large saucepan. Cover and cook over a medium heat for 3-4 minutes, stirring occasionally, until wilted. Drain well, pressing as much liquid from the leaves as possible with the back of a spoon. Roughly chop and add salt, pepper and nutmeg to taste. Mix in the parsley.

3 Place half the spinach in an even layer in the pastry case. Add the cheese and make four hollows with a spoon. Break an egg into each. Top with the remaining spinach and carefully fold over the edges of the filo to cover the spinach and egg. Drizzle with the remaining oil and sprinkle over the sesame seeds.

4 Transfer to the oven and cook for 20-25 minutes until golden. Serve hot or warm with a tomato salad or spring onion and crisp green salad.

Filo pastry is a **good, healthy alternative** to its buttery cousins. This delicious pie includes spinach, which is high in **vitamin C, zinc and potassium**.

Fish

and shellfish

Fish and shellfish
the healthy way

Fresh, frozen, canned or smoked – fish and shellfish are endlessly versatile and packed with nutritional benefits.

Quick and easy to prepare, fish and shellfish are two of the healthiest foods on offer. They are an excellent source of protein and vitamin B_2, which is vital for growth, for making red blood cells and for a healthy nervous system. They also contain iodine, which is involved in regulating the metabolic rate, growth, reproduction and other vital functions.

• Shellfish and white fish – such as cod, haddock and plaice – are very low in fat, making them ideal for anyone counting the calories or following a low-fat diet.

• White fish are also a source of lean protein and are delicate enough for the digestive systems of invalids and children.

Oil-rich fish

Oil-rich fish, such as mackerel, salmon, tuna and sardines, are low in saturated fat but rich in a type of polyunsaturated fat called omega-3 fatty acids, which offer a whole host of health benefits. Nutrition experts currently recommend that we should all aim to eat at least 1-2 portions of oil-rich fish a week.

• Omega-3 fatty acids can help to reduce the risk of heart attack and stroke. They also have an anti-inflammatory effect, which can help to relieve symptoms of rheumatoid arthritis and psoriasis

• Research suggests there may be a link between omega-3 intake and mental health. A low level of omega-3s in the blood may contribute to depression, antisocial behaviour and schizophrenia, and has also been linked to dyslexia.

• Omega-3 fats are not destroyed by cooking, curing or canning – so you can eat your fish as smoked salmon or canned sardines; the exception is tuna, which loses much of its omega-3 fatty acids in the canning process.

• Canned fish, such as salmon, which is eaten with the bones, is also an excellent

Preparing fish to be cooked *en papillote*

1 Once the fish is gutted and cleaned, season with a sprinkling of salt and black pepper, then stuff it with any flavourings, such as citrus peel or fresh herbs.

2 Brush the foil or baking parchment, in which the fish is to be wrapped, lightly with oil to stop the fish sticking to it.

3 Add a little liquid – water or wine – to each parcel to keep the fish moist and to help to steam it.

4 Seal the parcel well to stop the liquid leaking out while cooking.

source of bone-strengthening calcium – one average-sized portion of canned salmon provides almost half the recommended daily intake of calcium.

Shellfish

All shellfish are very low in fat and calories, and high in protein, making them a great choice for healthy eating.

• Shellfish contain useful amounts of B vitamins, particularly B$_{12}$, and zinc, which is vital for normal growth and a healthy reproductive system. B vitamins are also a good source of selenium, an important antioxidant mineral.

• People with high cholesterol levels used to be advised to avoid shellfish because of its high cholesterol content, but research shows that the cholesterol is poorly absorbed from these foods. Some studies even suggest that eating shellfish can lower, rather than raise, blood cholesterol levels.

Healthy cooking methods

Fish and shellfish can be cooked in a variety of delicious and healthy ways.

• Poaching and steaming are quick and leave nutrients intact. These methods are good for delicately flavoured white fish.

• Cooking en papillote is another easy method of steaming (see left).

• Traditional British fish and chips can be an unhealthy dish when deep-fried in batter, which adds large amounts of saturated fat. To lessen the fat content, coat the damp fish in breadcrumbs, then brush it lightly with oil, before baking it in the oven (see page 108).

• Char-grilling oily fish, such as salmon and tuna, on a ridged iron griddle allows fat to drip away from the food as it cooks, and the fish retains its nutrients.

• A quick healthy way of cooking small pieces of fish or shellfish is to stir-fry them, using the merest smear of oil.

FAT CONTENT PER 100g (3½oz) RAW FISH (unless otherwise stated)				
	Kcals	Total fat*	Saturated fat	Omega-3 fats
Cockles (boiled)	48	0.3	0.1	0
Cod (raw)	76	0.7	0.1	0.3
Coley	82	1	0.1	0.2
Crab meat (boiled)	127	5.2	0.7	1.2
Dogfish/rock salmon	154	10	1.4	2.5
Eel	168	11.3	3	1.4
Haddock	73	0.6	0.1	0.3
Halibut	92	2.4	0.3	0.7
Herring	234	18.5	5.3	2.0
Lemon sole	81	1.4	0.2	0.4
Mackerel	223	16.3	3.3	2.0
Mackerel (smoked)	354	31	6	5.0
Monkfish	66	0.1	0	0.1
Mussels (no shell)	74	1.8	0.4	0.5
Oysters (no shell)	65	1.3	0.2	0.4
Plaice (raw)	91	2.2	0.3	0.3
Prawns (no shell)	107	1.8	0.4	0.2
Rainbow trout	125	5.2	1.1	1.6
Salmon	182	12	2.2	2.3
Salmon (canned)	155	8	1.5	1.8
Salmon (smoked)	142	4.5	0.8	1.0
Sardines	165	9	2.7	2.5
Scallops	118	2.4	1.4	0.3
Sea bass	100	2.5	0.4	0.5
Tuna (in brine)	99	0.6	0.2	0.1
Tuna (raw)	136	3.6	1.2	1.6
Turbot	95	2.7	0.7	0.5
Whiting	81	0.7	0.1	0.1

Total fat content includes fatty compounds and other fatty acids in addition to saturated and omega-3 fats.

Fish stock

If you are cooking fresh fish, keep the trimmings and use them to make stock (see page 88), which can be the basis of a sauce or tasty soup (see Trout soup, page 51), or frozen for later use. It will only take about half an hour to prepare.

• Fresh fish stock is low in salt and, unlike stock cubes, is additive-free.

• Fresh stock freezes well and will keep in the refrigerator for up to three days or in the freezer for up to three months.

• Frozen stock retains water-soluble vitamins so is as nutritional as fresh stock.

Homemade stock is very **simple** to prepare and can **transform** all kinds of fish dishes. Once cooled, it will keep in the refrigerator for up to two days, or can be **frozen** for up to one month.

Fish stock

**PREPARATION AND
COOKING TIME:** 30 MINUTES
MAKES ABOUT 1.2 LITRES (2 PINTS)

900g (2lb) trimmings from white fish, including
    skin, bones, and heads without gills
1 onion, thinly sliced
4 sprigs of parsley
2 bay leaves
2 carrots, thinly sliced
2 celery sticks, thinly sliced
4 black peppercorns
1.3 litres (2¼ pints) boiling water

1 Rinse the fish bones and heads well, then place in a large saucepan. Add the onion, parsley, bay leaves, carrots, celery and peppercorns, and pour in the boiling water. Bring back to the boil, then reduce the heat and simmer gently for about 30 minutes, skimming off the froth as it appears on the surface.

2 Remove from the heat and leave to cool for 10 minutes, then strain the stock through a fine sieve into a heatproof bowl. Discard the fish trimmings and vegetables. Use the stock at once, or cool and chill.

VARIATIONS

Use 300ml (½ pint) white wine and 1 litre (1¾ pints) water in place of the water.

Use 400g (14oz) inexpensive white fish fillet, such as pollock, instead of the trimmings.

Make a shellfish stock using prawn, crab, lobster or mussel shells instead of the white fish trimmings.

Plaice with creamy anchovy sauce

Lean, white fish, rich in B vitamins, is flavoured with herbs that are quintessentially British – parsley, sage, rosemary and thyme. The creamy anchovy sauce uses low-fat fromage frais instead of cream or sour cream to add a luxurious texture to the dish.

PREPARATION TIME: 10 MINUTES, PLUS 2 HOURS MARINATING
COOKING TIME: 10 MINUTES
SERVES 4

Grated zest and juice of 1 unwaxed lemon
3 tablespoons vegetable oil
2 tablespoons chopped parsley
½ tablespoon finely chopped thyme
½ tablespoon finely chopped sage
Salt and black pepper
4 plaice fillets, about 175g (6oz) each
1 sprig of rosemary, bruised
Vegetable or olive oil for brushing

For the sauce:
175g (6oz) fromage frais
Grated zest and juice of ½ unwaxed lemon
½ teaspoon anchovy essence, or to taste
2-3 drops of Tabasco sauce (optional)

1 Put the lemon zest and juice, oil and chopped herbs in a large, shallow, glass or china dish. Add a little salt and black pepper and whisk briefly to mix.

2 Lay the cleaned fish fillets in the dish and turn them carefully to coat in the marinade. Nestle the sprig of rosemary between the fillets, then cover and refrigerate for 2 hours, turning them after about 1 hour.

3 Meanwhile, to make the sauce, put the fromage frais, lemon zest and juice and the anchovy essence in a small bowl. Whisk well, adding salt and pepper to taste and Tabasco sauce, if desired. Set aside at room temperature until ready to serve.

4 When ready to cook, remove the fish from the refrigerator. Heat a griddle or heavy-based frying pan over a high heat until very hot. Brush or spray the griddle or pan lightly with oil.

5 Transfer the fish to the hot griddle or pan and reduce the heat to medium-low. Cook for 3 minutes until the fish is charred and lifts away easily from the griddle or pan. Turn the fish and cook for a further 2-3 minutes, until cooked through. Serve immediately with the creamy anchovy sauce and new potatoes.

Nutrients per serving
- Calories 283
- Carbohydrate 2.5g (of which sugars 2.5g)
- Protein 34g
- Fat 15g (of which saturated fat 3g)
- Fibre 0g
- Vitamins B_1, B_2, B_6, B_{12}, niacin

Fish supper
with swede patties

Nutrients per serving

- Calories 500
- Carbohydrate 54g (of which sugars 18g)
- Protein 30g
- Fat 19g (of which saturated fat 2g)
- Fibre 11g
- Vitamins A, B₆, B₁₂, C, niacin

PREPARATION TIME: 10 MINUTES
COOKING TIME: 25 MINUTES
SERVES 2

650g (1lb 7oz) swede, peeled and cut into chunks
100g (3½ oz) medium oatmeal
Salt and black pepper
2½ tablespoons olive oil
100g (3½ oz) mushrooms, sliced
100g (3½ oz) tomatoes, cut in wedges
1 spring onion, finely chopped
225g (8oz) halibut, plaice or sole fillets, skinned
Creamed horseradish or vegetable chutney to serve

Swede is not only cheap and delicious, it is also very nutritious, being rich in cancer-fighting compounds and high in fibre and vitamin C.

1 Cook the swede in boiling, salted water for about 12 minutes until tender, then drain. Mash well and add three-quarters of the oatmeal. Mix, adding salt and pepper to taste and more of the oatmeal as necessary to give a stiff mixture. Shape into four patties and set aside.

2 Heat ½ tablespoon of the olive oil in a small saucepan and add the mushrooms. Sauté over a moderate heat until they release their juices, 3-5 minutes. Add the tomatoes and spring onion and cook for a further 2-3 minutes until the tomatoes are softened and heated through. Season and set aside in a warm place.

3 Meanwhile, heat the remaining olive oil in a large, heavy frying pan. Add the fish fillets and swede patties and cook for 5-8 minutes over a moderate heat, turning once, until nicely browned on each side.

4 Reheat the mushroom mixture if necessary and serve on warmed plates with the swede patties, fish and horseradish or chutney.

VARIATION
If you can find it, laver is excellent in place of the swede in the patties. Mix 100g (3½ oz) prepared laver with the oatmeal and proceed as directed.

Steaming brings out the excellent flavours of turbot, which has always been regarded as a prime fish for special occasions. You could use halibut, plaice or lemon sole instead.

Steamed turbot with cabbage, barley and raisins

PREPARATION TIME: 5 MINUTES
COOKING TIME: 1 HOUR 30 MINUTES
SERVES 4

100g (3½ oz) barley or spelt
1 baby green cabbage, about
    350g (12oz), chopped
1 tablespoon olive or vegetable oil
4 tablespoons pine kernels or almonds
4 tablespoons raisins
1 tablespoon malt vinegar, balsamic
    vinegar or cider vinegar
4 tablespoons chopped parsley
Salt and black pepper
4-6 turbot fillets, about 500g (1lb 2oz)
    in total
1 tablespoon lemon juice
Lemon wedges to serve

1 Put the barley or spelt in a large saucepan and cover generously with water. Bring to the boil and simmer for 45-60 minutes (longer if using spelt) or until tender.

2 Add the chopped cabbage and return to the boil for 1 minute until the cabbage has a vibrant colour. Drain immediately, rinsing well under the cold tap. Set aside to drain.

3 Heat the oil in a large, heavy-based frying pan, add the pine kernels or almonds and toast until fragrant and golden brown. Add the raisins, drained barley or spelt and cabbage. Sauté over a medium heat for 2-3 minutes to warm through.

4 Add the vinegar and cook for a further 2-3 minutes. Stir in 3 tablespoons of the parsley and add salt and pepper to taste. Set aside in a warm place.

5 Meanwhile, prepare a steamer by filling the base with water and bringing it to the boil. Lightly season the fish with salt and pepper and place in the steamer to cook for 6-8 minutes, depending on the thickness of the fillets.

6 Pile the barley or spelt mixture onto warmed serving plates. Top with the steamed fish and sprinkle with the remaining parsley, the lemon juice and some more black pepper. Serve at once with lemon wedges.

Note: Spelt is available in health-food shops and delicatessens.

Nutrients per serving
- Calories 400
- Carbohydrate 35g (of which sugars 10g)
- Protein 28g
- Fat 17g (of which saturated fat 2g)
- Fibre 3g
- Vitamins B_1, B_{12}, C

Baked sea bass with barley pilaf and watercress

PREPARATION TIME: 5 MINUTES
COOKING TIME: 50-60 MINUTES
SERVES 4

2 tablespoons vegetable oil, plus
    extra for brushing
1 small onion, finely chopped
1 celery stick, finely chopped
200g (7oz) pearl barley
125ml (4fl oz) white wine or cider
1 litre (1¾ pints) fish stock (see page 88)
4 fillets sea bass, about 115g (4oz) each
25g (1oz) chopped fresh mixed herbs,
    such as parsley, chervil, chives,
    dill or rocket
Salt and pepper
40g (1½ oz) watercress

1 Heat the oil in a large saucepan. Add the onion and celery and cook for 5 minutes, stirring occasionally. Add the barley and cook, stirring, for a further 2-3 minutes, until fragrant.

2 Add the wine or cider to the pan and simmer until the liquid has evaporated. Add the fish stock, bring to the boil and cook, stirring frequently, for 40-50 minutes, until the barley is tender and the mixture is soupy. Add a little hot water if it is becoming too dry.

3 Shortly before the end of cooking, heat the oven to 200°C (400°F, gas mark 6). Brush an ovenproof skillet lightly with oil and place it over a high heat until very hot. Lightly season the sea bass fillets and place in the pan, skin side down, pressing down with a fish slice to sear the skin. Cook for 1-2 minutes, then transfer the pan to the hot oven and bake for 10 minutes.

4 Add the herbs to the cooked barley and mix, adding salt and pepper to taste. Spoon the barley onto warmed serving plates and top with the roast fish. Serve with the watercress.

VARIATION

In place of sea bass, try gurnard, John Dory, mullet or salmon.

Nutrients per serving
- Calories 390
- Carbohydrate 44g (of which sugars 2g)
- Protein 27g
- Fat 10g (of which saturated fat 1.5g)
- Fibre 1g
- Vitamins B$_{12}$, C

Haddock with parsley and whisky sauce

Barley and celery add **vitamins** and **minerals** to this dish, while their textures **enhance** the delicate flesh and wonderful flavour of sea bass.

Poaching fillets of protein-rich haddock keeps the fish beautifully **moist** and the fat content low.

PREPARATION TIME: 10 MINUTES
COOKING TIME: 10 MINUTES
SERVES 4

4 haddock fillets, skinned, about 115g (4oz) each
1 tablespoon dry white wine
1 blade of mace
2-3 parsley stalks (use leaves in sauce)
2-3 chives
1 bay leaf
½ teaspoon green or black peppercorns

For the sauce:
1 small handful of parsley leaves
1 small handful of spinach leaves
2-3 chives
1 teaspoon capers
1 teaspoon vegetable oil
1 teaspoon whisky
1 teaspoon lemon juice
½ teaspoon mustard
Salt and black pepper
½ teaspoon sugar (optional)

Nutrients per serving
- Calories 110
- Carbohydrate 0g
- Protein 24g
- Fat 2g (of which saturated fat 0g)
- Fibre 0.5g
- Vitamins B$_6$, B$_{12}$, niacin

1 Place the fish fillets in a single layer in a large frying pan. Add cold water just to cover the fish, then add the wine, mace, parsley stalks, chives, bay leaf and peppercorns. Bring to a simmer, then reduce the heat and poach gently for 5-8 minutes, until the flesh is opaque.

2 Meanwhile, put the parsley and spinach leaves, chives, capers, oil, whisky, lemon juice and mustard in the small bowl of a food processor or in a blender. Alternatively, put in a small bowl and use a hand-held blender.

3 Remove 3 tablespoons of hot cooking liquid from the pan and add it to the sauce ingredients. Blend to a smooth purée. Add salt and pepper to taste, and a little sugar if the sauce seems too sharp. Process again briefly.

4 Using a slotted spoon, carefully lift the fish from the cooking liquid and pat dry. Place on warmed serving plates, pour the sauce over the top and serve. (The poaching liquid can be strained and frozen for later use in other fish dishes, soups, sauces and risottos.)

VARIATION
Cod, halibut, sea bass or salmon can be used in place of haddock. Increase the cooking time to account for their size and density.

Smoked eel risotto

Nutrients per
serving
- Calories 480
- Carbohydrate 64g
  (of which sugars 3g)
- Protein 16g
- Fat 17g (of which
  saturated fat 3g)
- Fibre 1.5g
- Vitamins A

**PREPARATION AND
COOKING TIME:** 35 MINUTES
SERVES 2

600ml (1 pint) fish stock (see page 88)
100g (3½ oz) smoked eel fillets
2 tablespoons olive oil
1 small onion, chopped
150g (5½ oz) risotto rice, such as arborio
125ml (4fl oz) dry white wine
Finely grated zest of ¼ unwaxed lemon
1 handful of parsley leaves
1 handful of rocket leaves
Salt and black pepper

This recipe
provides an
excellent
balance of
nutrients.
Rich in
complex
carbohydrates
and **protein,**
the addition of
a side salad
creates a
**deliciously
healthy**
gourmet meal.

1 Put the stock in a small saucepan and slowly bring to simmering point. Meanwhile, trim any skin from the smoked eel. Run your fingers along the fillet to feel for stray bones and cut them away. Chop the fillets into 1cm (½ in) pieces and set aside.

2 Heat the oil in a large, heavy saucepan. Add the onion and cook for 5 minutes, stirring frequently, until translucent. Add the rice and cook, stirring, for 2 minutes until the rice is shiny and fragrant.

3 Add the wine and lemon zest and simmer, stirring, until evaporated. Add a ladle of hot stock and cook, stirring constantly, until the liquid has been absorbed. Add another ladle of stock and continue stirring and cooking until it too has been absorbed. Repeat this process until all or most of the stock has been used and the rice is just cooked, about 17 minutes from the first addition of hot stock to the rice.

4 Remove the pan from the heat and stir in the smoked eel, parsley and rocket, so that the leaves wilt only slightly. Add salt and pepper to taste and serve immediately.

Note: Instead of the white wine and lemon zest, you can add verjuice, a recently revived medieval ingredient available in some supermarkets and independent gourmet stores. It adds a strong fruity flavour to this dish that helps to cut through the richness of the eel.

VARIATION
Stir in 2-3 tablespoons of fresh or defrosted peas during the last 2 minutes of cooking to add healthy variety to this carbohydrate-based dish.

Mackerel, orange and parsley salad

PREPARATION TIME: 10 MINUTES
SERVES 2

2 smoked mackerel fillets, about 175g (6oz) in
    total, skinned and broken into large chunks
1 large orange
1 small red onion, finely sliced
12 pitted black olives, halved or sliced if large
20g (¾oz) parsley sprigs, tough stalks removed
Juice of ½ lemon
1 tablespoon olive oil
Black pepper

Parsley is more than a herb – it
can be used as a **nutritious**
salad leaf as well. Here its strong
iron-rich flavour provides a
perfect counterpoint to the sweet
orange and smoky, oily fish.

1 Put the mackerel in a large bowl. Using a
small serrated knife, peel the skin from the
orange, removing all the white pith. Holding the
orange over the bowl of fish to catch the juices,
segment the orange by cutting down on either
side of each membrane and easing out the
segments. Pick out any seeds. Once the orange
is segmented, squeeze the membrane over the
bowl to remove all the juices, then discard.

2 Scatter the onion and olives into the bowl.
Tear the parsley leaves in from the sprigs,
leaving on tender stems if desired. Add to the
salad bowl and toss carefully.

3 Pour in the lemon juice and olive oil and
season with black pepper. Toss the salad
carefully again and serve with brown bread.

VARIATION
Smoked herring can be used in place of
mackerel and half a bulb of fennel instead
of the onion, if preferred.

**Nutrients per
serving**
- Calories 450
- Carbohydrate 11g
  (of which sugars 10g)
- Protein 17g
- Fat 38g (of which
  saturated fat 7g)
- Fibre 3g
- Vitamins B_1, B_2, niacin,
  B_6, B_{12}, C

Sweet pickled herrings

Herrings are high in **omega-3** fatty acids, which help to **protect** against heart, skin and **circulation** problems. When **fresh**, herrings are susceptible to spoilage, so pickling is an **excellent** way to preserve them.

PREPARATION TIME: 10 MINUTES, PLUS 4 DAYS SALTING AND MARINATING
SERVES 4

6 fresh herrings, cleaned and filleted
Salt
250ml (9fl oz) white malt vinegar
250ml (9fl oz) white wine vinegar
150g (5½ oz) granulated sugar
2 small onions, peeled and cut
    into fine rings
6 cloves
6 allspice berries
Pinch of fennel seeds
Black pepper

1 Divide the filleted herrings in two lengthways and remove any bones, trimming away any small ones at the edge with small scissors.

2 Sprinkle a layer of salt into a deep bowl and place three fillets down in a single layer. Sprinkle again with salt, and continue with layers of salt and fish for the remaining nine fillets, ending with a sprinkling of salt. Cover tightly and refrigerate for 2 days.

3 Take the herrings from the dish and remove the skin. Rinse the dish and put the fillets back with 250ml (8fl oz) water. Set aside for 1-2 hours. Taste the water and replace with fresh if it seems too salty.

4 Mix the vinegars, sugar, onion, cloves, allspice, fennel and pepper in a jug, stirring to dissolve the sugar.

5 Rinse the herrings well in cold water and pat them dry with kitchen paper. Put into a clean bowl and add the vinegar mixture. Cover tightly and refrigerate for 2 days before eating. Serve with brown bread and butter, or chopped and added to a potato salad.

Nutrients per serving
- Calories 390
- Carbohydrate 10g (of which sugars 10g)
- Protein 25g
- Fat 28g (of which saturated fat 8g)
- Fibre 0g
- Vitamins B_6, B_{12}

Herring
in oatmeal

PREPARATION TIME: 5 MINUTES
COOKING TIME: 8 MINUTES
SERVES 4

8 tablespoons fine oatmeal
4 pairs of herring fillets, cleaned
Vegetable oil for frying
Black pepper

1 Spread the oatmeal out on a large dish. Quickly rinse the herring fillets under the cold tap and shake dry. Lay each pair of fillets in the oatmeal, pressing down firmly and turning to coat the fish well.

2 Heat a very fine film of vegetable oil in a large heavy frying pan and cook the fish for 3-4 minutes on each side. Remove to plates, sprinkle with pepper and serve with lemon wedges and mustard or horseradish sauce.

Nutrients per serving
- Calories 480
- Carbohydrate 22g (of which sugars 2g)
- Protein 25g
- Fat 33g (of which saturated fat 8g)
- Fibre 2g
- Vitamins B_6, B_{12}, niacin

This is a **traditional** Scots way with **heart-friendly** herring and oatmeal. Using **fresh** damp fish and fine oatmeal is **healthier** than coating the fish in a heavier mixture of flour, egg and breadcrumbs.

Trout stuffed with herbs

PREPARATION TIME: 10 MINUTES
COOKING TIME: 20 MINUTES, PLUS
5 MINUTES RESTING
SERVES 2

4 trout fillets, about 175g (6oz) each,
    unskinned
60g (2¼oz) low-fat curd cheese
10g (¼oz) mixed herbs such as chives,
    dill, parsley and tarragon, chopped
Grated zest of ½ unwaxed lemon
1 small clove garlic, crushed
Salt and black pepper
Olive oil for brushing

1 Run your fingers over the flesh side
of the fish and, using tweezers,
remove any pin bones still in the fillets.

2 Slowly heat a flat griddle plate or a
large heavy frying pan until the
heat rises from the surface.

3 Meanwhile, put the curd cheese,
herbs, lemon zest, garlic and some
salt and pepper in a small bowl and
mix. Spread the mixture evenly on the
flesh side of two of the fillets.

4 Place the remaining fillets on top,
flesh side down, to make two
parcels. Tie pieces of kitchen string
around both parcels to secure them,
then brush lightly with oil on each side.

5 Transfer the fish to the hot griddle
plate or frying pan and cook for
8-10 minutes on each side, until cooked
and pale pink throughout. Remove the
fish to a plate and let rest for 5 minutes,
then remove the string and serve with
boiled new potatoes and carrots.

VARIATION
You can also use a small whole salmon
in place of trout. For a whole salmon,
simply double the filling mixture and
cook the fish for 15-20 minutes on
each side, then leave to rest for
10 minutes before serving.

Nutrients per serving
- Calories 434
- Carbohydrate 0g
- Protein 61g
- Fat 19g (of which saturated fat 6g)
- Fibre 0g
- Vitamins B$_1$, B$_6$, B$_{12}$, A, niacin

Baked trout
with mushrooms

PREPARATION TIME: 10 MINUTES
COOKING TIME: 35 MINUTES
SERVES 4

400g (14oz) brown, chestnut or field
   mushrooms, wiped and halved or
   quartered, depending on size
2 teaspoons olive or vegetable oil,
   plus extra for brushing
1 small onion or large shallot,
   finely chopped
Salt and black pepper
4 rainbow trout, boned
2-3 sprigs of tarragon, chopped
2-3 sprigs of parsley, chopped

Trout, like salmon
and all other oily
fish, is rich in
omega-3 fatty acids.
Nutritionists
recommend that
we eat at least two
portions of
protein and
vitamin-rich oily
fish per week.

1 Put the mushrooms into a food
   processor or blender and work until
finely minced, scraping large pieces off
the sides of the bowl as necessary.

2 Heat the oil in a nonstick frying
   pan and add the onion or shallot.
Cook, stirring occasionally, for
5 minutes or until tender. Add the
mushrooms and cook for 10 minutes,
stirring occasionally, until the juices have
evaporated and the mixture is dry. Add
salt and pepper to taste.

3 Meanwhile, heat the oven to
   180°C (350°F, gas mark 4). Wipe
the fish dry and trim as necessary. Place
on a large, lightly oiled baking tray.

4 Stir the chopped herbs into the
   mushroom mixture and remove
from the heat. Using two teaspoons,
spoon the mushroom mixture into the
cavity of each fish, pressing it in and
patting the body of the fish back over
the stuffing.

5 Brush the tops of the fish lightly
   with oil and bake for 20 minutes
until cooked through, then serve, with
steamed vegetables and rice.

Nutrients per serving
- Calories 225
- Carbohydrate 2.5g (of which sugars 1.5g)
- Protein 32g
- Fat 10g (of which saturated fat 2g)
- Fibre 1.5g
- Vitamins A, B_1, B_2, B_6, B_{12}, niacin

An island race, we have always enjoyed a close relationship with the sea,

Freshwater fish and seafood

In recent years, the British have begun to rediscover the culinary delights that fish and seafood can offer. The increase in consumption is largely due to a recognition of their highly nutritious oils and vitamins. Although this coincides with a decrease in stocks of the most traditionally popular fish, it does mean that in the future many delicious but as yet unfamiliar types of fish, including regional varieties such as elver from the West Country and char from Lake Windermere, will become widely recognised and incorporated into British cooking.

Rivers and sea

Wild salmon, the king of British fish, is now dangerously low in numbers, yet it is increasingly appreciated for its flavour and low fat levels, compared with the intensively farmed salmon sold cheaply in supermarkets. Organic fish-farming,

notably in Orkney and Ireland, is fast developing to bridge the gap and provide a sustainable source.

Cod, Britain's most prized white fish, is, with haddock, the stock choice for fish and chip vendors throughout the country. Extensive fishing of cod dates back to medieval times, when salt cod was in high demand during Lent, but modern fishing technology has reduced the levels to an all-time low. As with salmon, farmed cod may well hold the key to sustainable supplies in the future.

Dover sole, so named because the Kentish town was the closest supplier to the London market, has long been enjoyed for its fine flavour and texture. Lemon sole, however, is generally accepted as a good alternative, and is far more plentiful. Conger eel and pilchards, or large sardines, feature strongly in traditional Cornish dishes. Pilchards

making use of every edible morsel fished or gathered.

are the main ingredient for Cornish stargazy pie, where the fish are arranged with their heads at the rim of the dish – stargazing. Pilchards are now largely exported, as they tend to be more readily appreciated in the Mediterranean than they are locally, where mackerel has taken over in terms of popularity.

Shellfish

Cockles, once a mainstay in the diet and economy of south Wales, were regarded as a delicacy in London's East End. In the Victorian era, women collected them, as part of a tradition where men went to sea while the women took the cockles, along with the men's catch, inland to sell. Overfishing and pollution have depleted stocks, but a cockle fair is still held in Swansea every September. Mussels enjoyed similar popularity in Scotland, where they were sold as street food.

Scotland also has extensive crab fisheries, and the protein-rich meat was once a staple food for the poor in coastal villages. Crabs are landed at ports all round the country, but Cromer crabs, from Norfolk, which are the smallest, are considered the sweetest.

The Romans liked British oysters so much that they exported them to Rome. By the 15th century, because they were both highly nutritious and plentiful, oysters had become an important food of the poor. Their price was even regulated by the mayor of London to keep it low. It was only in the late 19th century, after a spell of disease and bad weather had significantly reduced the Thames production, that oysters became the expensive, sought-after delicacy they are today.

Foil-baked salmon trout with gooseberry and elderflower sauce

PREPARATION TIME: 30 MINUTES
COOKING TIME: 40 MINUTES, PLUS
1½ HOURS COOLING
SERVES 6-8

1 salmon trout, about 1.3kg (3lb),
   cleaned with head on
Salt and black pepper
2 sprigs of fresh dill
Vegetable oil for brushing
4 tablespoons dry white wine
4 courgettes, trimmed

For the sauce:
5 tablespoons low-fat mayonnaise
5 tablespoons set low-fat yoghurt
5 tablespoons lightly sweetened, cooked
   gooseberries
2-4 teaspoons elderflower cordial
1 tablespoon chopped fresh dill

Gooseberries arrive in **early summer**, just when **elderflower** bushes burst into creamy-white blossom. Together they make a **piquant** sauce for a whole salmon trout, cooked in foil to keep it deliciously **moist** and to ensure **minimal** loss of nutrients.

1 Heat the oven to 180°C (350°F, gas mark 4). Rinse the fish, flushing out any blood left inside it, then pat dry with kitchen paper. Season inside and out with salt and pepper and put 2 sprigs of dill inside the fish.

2 Spread a large sheet of foil on a baking sheet or inside a roasting tin and brush with oil. Put the fish in the middle, splash over the wine and parcel the fish loosely, folding the foil into a tight seam and twisting the ends. Bake in the middle of the oven for 40 minutes, then remove and leave to cool in its foil.

3 Using a vegetable peeler, shave the courgettes lengthways into ribbons, discarding the outer slices. Bring a saucepan of salted water to the boil and add the courgette ribbons. As soon as the water returns to the boil, drain into a colander and run under the cold tap for 2 minutes to cool. Set aside in a bowl of cold water.

4 For the sauce, put the mayonnaise, yoghurt and gooseberries in a bowl and mix, adding elderflower cordial to taste. Season with salt and pepper, and more sugar if needed.

5 To serve, remove the head and skin from the fish, if preferred. Remove the dill sprigs from inside and place the fish on a long, oval platter.

6 Drain the courgette ribbons and pat them dry gently but thoroughly on several changes of kitchen paper. Arrange them around the fish. Add the chopped dill to the sauce and serve separately in a bowl, with the fish, new potatoes and salad.

Nutrients per serving, when serving 8
- Calories 275
- Carbohydrate 5g (of which sugars 5g)
- Protein 40g
- Fat 10g (of which saturated fat 1.5g)
- Fibre 0.5g
- Vitamins B_1, B_6, B_{12}, C, niacin

Marinated salmon
with orange and cloves

PREPARATION TIME: 10 MINUTES,
PLUS 2 HOURS MARINATING
COOKING TIME: 8 MINUTES
SERVES 4

Freshly grated zest and juice of 1 orange
2 tablespoons vegetable oil
3 thin slices of fresh ginger, shredded
½ teaspoon coriander seeds
3 cloves
Salt and black pepper
4 salmon steaks, about 175g (6oz) each
Vegetable or olive oil for brushing

Nutrients per serving
- Calories 390
- Carbohydrate 0g
- Protein 32g
- Fat 29g (of which saturated fat 5g)
- Fibre 0g
- Vitamins B_1, B_6, B_{12}, niacin

Cloves, coriander, ginger and orange are flavours often associated with **medieval England**. Here they add a tang to a contemporary dish of nutritious **salmon** steaks.

1 Put the orange zest and juice, oil, ginger, coriander seeds and cloves in a large, shallow, glass or ceramic dish. Season with a little salt and black pepper and whisk briefly to mix.

2 Add the fish and turn to coat in the marinade. Cover and chill for 2 hours, to marinate, turning the steaks after about 1 hour.

3 When ready to cook, heat a griddle or heavy-based frying pan over a high heat until very hot. Brush or spray the griddle or pan lightly with oil.

4 Lift the fish out of the marinade and remove any flavourings stuck to the flesh. Place the fish on the hot griddle or pan and immediately reduce the heat to medium-low. Cook for 3-5 minutes or until the fish lifts easily away from the griddle or pan. Turn and cook for a further 3 minutes, or until cooked through, and serve at once with wild rice and mangetout peas.

Salmon fish cakes

PREPARATION TIME: 40 MINUTES,
PLUS 1 HOUR CHILLING
COOKING TIME: 1 HOUR
SERVES 4

500g (1lb 2oz) potatoes, peeled and cubed
250g (9oz) swede, peeled and cubed
350g (12oz) salmon fillets
2 tablespoons chopped onion
2 tablespoons chopped carrot
1 tablespoon chopped celery
1 bay leaf
½ teaspoon mustard seeds
300ml (½ pint) skimmed milk
1 tablespoon finely chopped chives
2-3 drops of Worcestershire sauce
Salt and black pepper
1 egg
115g (4oz) fresh white breadcrumbs
Vegetable or olive oil for brushing

Nutrients per serving
- Calories 410
- Carbohydrate 43g (of which sugars 1g)
- Protein 25g
- Fat 16g (of which saturated fat 3g)
- Fibre 3g
- Vitamins B_1, B_6, B_{12}

1 Cook the potatoes and swede in boiling, salted water until tender. Drain, mash well, and set aside.

2 Meanwhile, put the salmon, onion, carrot, celery, bay leaf and mustard seeds in a large frying pan. Add the milk, cover and set over a high heat. Just before it boils, reduce the heat and poach gently for 10 minutes or until the fish is opaque.

3 Lift the fish out of the cooking liquid and set aside. Discard the liquid and flavourings.

4 Remove any skin or bones from the fish and flake the flesh into large chunks. Place in a mixing bowl and gradually stir in the mashed potato and swede, together with the chives. Add Worcestershire sauce, salt and pepper to taste. Shape the mixture into 8 fish cakes and place on a tray. Cover and refrigerate for 1 hour.

5 Meanwhile, heat the oven to 190°C (375°F, gas mark 5). Put the egg and 2 tablespoons of water in a shallow bowl and beat. Put the breadcrumbs in another shallow bowl.

6 Dip the chilled fish cakes in the beaten egg to coat, then in the breadcrumbs. Transfer them to a nonstick baking sheet and brush lightly with oil. Bake for 20-30 minutes or until crisp and lightly browned. Serve with green beans and pea sauce.

To make a pea sauce, blend 150g (5½oz) cooked frozen peas with 150ml (¼ pint) hot vegetable stock until smooth. Add salt and pepper to taste, with 1 tablespoon fromage frais and a few chopped mint leaves, if desired.

For an even healthier version of these fresh salmon fishcakes, coat them in oatmeal instead of breadcrumbs.

Grilled sardines

PREPARATION TIME: 10 MINUTES
COOKING TIME: 10 MINUTES
SERVES 4

6 tablespoons chopped fresh herbs, such
    as parsley, chives and basil
1 tablespoon Dijon mustard
Juice of ½ lemon
12 fresh sardines, about 125g (4½oz)
    each, gutted and cleaned
Salt and black pepper
Olive oil for brushing
Lemon wedges

1 Mix the herbs, mustard and lemon
juice. Rinse the sardines and pat dry.
Sprinkle salt and pepper into the gutted
cavities, then divide the herb mixture
between the sardines, spooning it into
each cavity.

2 Brush the sardines lightly on both
sides with oil. Heat a ridged griddle
pan until very hot, then add the
sardines and cook for 2-3 minutes on
each side to brown. Reduce the heat
and cook for a further 4 minutes or
until cooked through.

3 Remove to plates and sprinkle
with salt and pepper. Squeeze with
lemon and serve with brown bread.

Note: When available, sprats make an
excellent substitute for sardines. You will
need about 650g (1lb 7oz).

Nutrients per serving
- Calories 444
- Carbohydrate 0.5g (of which sugars 0g)
- Protein 52g
- Fat 26g (including saturated fat 7g)
- Fibre 0g
- Vitamins B₁, B₆, B₁₂, niacin

Rich, oily fish, both mackerel and
sardines offer the heart-friendly
benefits of omega-3 fatty acids as well
as being excellent value for money.

Mackerel with rhubarb and orange sauce

PREPARATION TIME: 20 MINUTES
COOKING TIME: 30 MINUTES
SERVES 4

4 whole mackerel, gutted and cleaned
1 large bunch of parsley or thyme stalks
3 tablespoons chopped chervil to garnish

For the sauce:
450g (1lb) rhubarb, chopped
Finely grated zest and juice of ½ orange
15g (½oz) butter
1 tablespoon sugar
1 teaspoon coriander seeds
Salt and black pepper

1 To make the sauce, put the rhubarb
in a saucepan with the orange zest
and juice, butter, sugar and coriander
seeds. Cover and bring slowly to the
boil over a low heat, then uncover and
simmer, stirring frequently, for about
10 minutes, until thick and pulpy.

2 Remove from the heat and
leave to cool for a few minutes.
Using a spoon, pick out and discard
the coriander seeds, then transfer the
sauce to a blender or food processor.
Purée until smooth, then pass through
a sieve back into a clean saucepan.
Add salt and pepper to taste and a
little more sugar if necessary. Warm
the sauce through over a low heat
while you cook the mackerel.

3 Heat the grill to medium. Using a
sharp knife, make three diagonal
slashes on each fish. Generously season
the fish inside and out with salt and
pepper. Put a small bundle of herb
stalks inside each fish, then transfer
them to the grill pan.

4 Grill for 8-10 minutes on each
side. Remove from the heat and
discard the herb stalks from each fish.

5 Make a pool of the warm rhubarb
sauce on each serving plate, top
with the mackerel and sprinkle with the
chervil. Serve with new potatoes and
green beans.

Nutrients per serving
- Calories 450
- Carbohydrate 6g (of which sugars 6g)
- Protein 34g
- Fat 32g (of which saturated fat 8g)
- Fibre 1.5g
- Vitamins B₁, B₂, B₆, B₁₂, niacin

Fisherman's pie

PREPARATION TIME: 20 MINUTES
COOKING TIME: 1 HOUR 20 MINUTES
SERVES 4

For the filling:

2 large eggs
350g (12oz) coley, whiting or
    haddock fillets
400ml (14fl oz) skimmed milk
1 bay leaf
5 black peppercorns
1 blade of mace
25g (1oz) butter
1 small leek, finely sliced
2 tablespoons plain flour
1 tablespoon capers, chopped
4 small gherkins, chopped
2 tablespoons chopped parsley
1 tablespoon lemon juice

For the topping:

900g (2lb) floury potatoes, peeled
    and chopped
85g (3oz) low-fat curd cheese
4 tablespoons skimmed milk
Salt and black pepper
55g (2oz) Cheddar or Lancashire
    cheese, grated

This creamy fish pie tastes luxurious but is relatively low in fat. Pungent capers and gherkins have long been favourite flavourings in Britain and bring piquant contrast to the mild, comforting tastes and textures of fish, eggs and potato.

1 Cook the eggs in simmering water for 10 minutes, then drain and leave in fresh, cold water until cool enough to handle.

2 Meanwhile, put the fish in a large saucepan. Add the milk, bay leaf, peppercorns and mace and bring to the boil. Cover and simmer gently for 10 minutes.

3 Strain the milk into a measuring jug, discarding the bay leaf, peppercorns and mace. Set the fish aside to cool briefly.

4 Cook the potatoes in boiling, salted water for 20-25 minutes or until tender. While the potatoes are cooking, shell the hard-boiled eggs, then rinse well and pat dry. Chop and set aside. Flake the fish into chunks, discarding any remaining bone and skin, and place in a large mixing bowl.

5 In the same saucepan in which you cooked the fish, heat the butter until melted, then add the leek. Cook gently for 5 minutes, stirring often, until tender. Stir in the flour and continue cooking for 2-3 minutes over a medium heat.

6 Gradually add the reserved milk, stirring to give a smooth sauce. Bring to the boil, reduce the heat and simmer, stirring often, for 10-12 minutes. Remove from the heat and set aside.

7 To make the topping, drain the cooked potatoes, return them to the pan and mash thoroughly. Using a wooden spoon, beat in the soft cheese and milk. Add salt and pepper and continue beating until light and fluffy.

8 Heat the oven to 200°C (400°F, gas mark 6). Gently stir the eggs, fish, capers, gherkins, parsley and lemon juice into the sauce. Add salt and pepper to taste, then transfer to an ovenproof dish, about 30cm (12in) long. Top with the mashed potato and sprinkle with the grated cheese. Bake for 25 minutes until golden. Serve with roast tomatoes and a watercress salad.

Nutrients per serving

- Calories 480
- Carbohydrate 49g (of which sugars 10g)
- Protein 41g
- Fat 17g (of which saturated fat 10g)
- Fibre 3g
- Vitamins A, B_1, B_6, B_{12}

Fish, chips and mushy peas

PREPARATION TIME: 25 MINUTES
COOKING TIME: I HOUR
SERVES 4

3 tablespoons fine fresh breadcrumbs
3 tablespoons medium or fine oatmeal
4 haddock, cod or plaice fillets, about
    115g (4oz) each, skinned
Olive or vegetable oil for brushing

For the chips:
200g (7oz) potatoes, peeled and cut into
    batons about 1cm (½in) thick
400g (14oz) mixture of parsnips, swede,
    carrots and sweet potato, peeled and
    cut into batons about 1cm (½in) thick
½ teaspoon allspice berries
½ teaspoon black peppercorns
1 egg white
1 teaspoon salt

For the mushy peas:
200g (7oz) green split or marrowfat peas
1 small onion or large shallot, chopped
1 clove garlic, chopped
1 celery stick
1 bay leaf
15g (½oz) butter
Salt and pepper

Nutrients per serving
- Calories 390
- Carbohydrate 50g
  (of which sugars 10g)
- Protein 29g
- Fat 9g (of which saturated fat 3g)
- Fibre 8g
- Vitamins A, B₁, B₆, B₁₂, niacin

Avoiding the usual deep-frying method and making chips with a variety of root **vegetables** adds **nutrients** and makes this favourite a much **healthier** meal.

1 For the mushy peas, put the peas, onion, garlic, celery, bay leaf and 1 litre (1¾ pints) water in a large saucepan. Bring to the boil, then reduce the heat, cover and simmer for 1 hour, stirring occasionally, or until the peas are tender.

2 For the chips, simmer the potatoes and other vegetables in a saucepan of salted water for 5 minutes. Drain and set aside.

3 Place a heavy-based saucepan over a medium-high heat until hot, then reduce the heat to low. Add the allspice to the pan and toast, stirring constantly, for 3-5 minutes until fragrant. Remove from the pan. Add the peppercorns to the pan and toast, stirring constantly, until fragrant. Place the allspice and peppercorns in a mill or pestle and mortar and grind to a fine powder. Set aside.

4 Heat the oven to 200°C (400°F, gas mark 6). In a large bowl, whisk the egg white until frothy. Add the blanched vegetables, ground spices and 1 teaspoon salt. Toss carefully until the

vegetables are completely coated. Lightly brush or spray two baking sheets with oil. Lift the vegetables from their bowl, allowing any excess egg white to drip off. Arrange them on one baking sheet, so that they are not touching. Bake for 20 minutes.

5 Meanwhile, to prepare the fish, put the breadcrumbs and oatmeal on a large plate or shallow dish and mix. Rinse the fish briefly under the tap and shake gently to dry. Press the fillets into the crumb mixture, turning to coat them evenly. Place the coated fish on the second baking sheet and brush lightly with oil.

6 When the chips have been baking for 20 minutes, remove from the oven and turn them, for even browning. Return the tray to the oven with the tray of fish. Bake both for a further 10 minutes, or until the fish is cooked and the chips are nicely browned.

7 Remove the celery stalk and bay leaf from the mushy peas. Stir in the butter and mash lightly to give a textured mixture. Add salt and pepper to taste and serve with the baked fish and chips.

Seafood terrine

PREPARATION TIME: 45 MINUTES
COOKING TIME: 20 MINUTES, PLUS
6-8 HOURS SETTING
SERVES 6-8

250g (9oz) skinless salmon fillets
250g (9oz) small skinless monkfish fillets,
    halved if large
250g (9oz) skinless haddock fillets
250g (9oz) skinless whiting fillets
1 carrot, very finely diced
2 shallots, very finely chopped
2 celery sticks, very finely diced
2 small radishes, very finely diced
Bouquet garni made from a few sprigs
    each of parsley, thyme and dill,
    tied together
Salt
4 tablespoons flat-leaved parsley, torn
Black pepper
Juice of 1 lemon
½ teaspoon paprika
Pinch of powdered saffron
Pinch of grated nutmeg
2½ teaspoons powdered gelatine

To garnish:
1 tablespoon finely chopped shallot
Finely pared zest of 1 lemon
4 tablespoons finely chopped parsley

1 Put all the fish in a large saucepan or or casserole. Add 225ml (8fl oz) water, the carrot, shallots, celery, radishes, bouquet garni and salt. Slowly bring to the boil, then reduce the heat, cover and poach gently for 10 minutes. Remove from the heat and leave to cool in the cooking liquid.

2 When completely cool, discard the bouquet garni. Remove the fish from the pan and place on a tray. Slice the monkfish into medallions and break the remaining fish into generous bite-sized pieces. Place all the fish in a large mixing bowl. Strain the cooking liquid into a jug and transfer the strained vegetables to a plate. Add the parsley and some pepper. Set aside.

3 Place 125ml (4fl oz) of the reserved cooking liquid in a heatproof bowl. Add the lemon juice, paprika, saffron and nutmeg and stir to mix. Add salt to taste. Sprinkle the gelatine over the surface and leave to soak for 5 minutes.

4 Heat a large frying pan of water to just below boiling point. Set the bowl of gelatine bouillon in the pan and heat gently for 3-5 minutes until the gelatine has dissolved completely and the bouillon is clear.

5 Line a small Pyrex loaf pan, terrine mould or bowl with cling film, allowing a generous amount to hang over each side. Layer the fish pieces and vegetables in the mould, arranging them so that there is an attractive mix of colours and textures. Pour the gelatine mixture evenly over the fish.

6 Fold the excess cling film back over the surface of the terrine and place a lid or plate on top to weigh it down. Refrigerate for 6-8 hours or until completely set.

7 To serve, use the excess cling film to lift the fish terrine out of the mould and turn out on a serving plate, removing the cling film. Put the shallot, lemon zest and parsley in a small bowl and stir to mix. Sprinkle the mixture over the terrine, pressing it down lightly. Serve in slices with a leafy salad.

Nutrients per serving, when serving 8
- Calories 140
- Carbohydrate 2g (of which sugars 1.5g)
- Protein 22g
- Fat 4.5g (of which saturated fat 0.5g)
- Fibre 0.5g
- Vitamins A, B_6, B_{12}

A fish version of the popular old English meat dish brawn, this light, low-fat chilled terrine makes a fine summer main course.

Mussels in broth

Nutrients per serving
- Calories 190
- Carbohydrate 4g (of which sugars 3g)
- Protein 37g
- Fat 6g (of which saturated fat 1g)
- Fibre 0.5g
- Vitamins B$_{12}$

PREPARATION TIME: 15 MINUTES
COOKING TIME: 15 MINUTES
SERVES 4

2kg (4lb 8oz) live mussels
1 tablespoon olive oil
1 large onion, finely sliced
1 clove garlic, finely chopped
2cm (¾ in) cube fresh ginger, peeled and finely chopped
Small pinch of saffron strands
125ml (4fl oz) dry cider
125ml (4fl oz) fish stock (see page 88)
1 tablespoon chopped fresh dill
Salt and black pepper
1 tablespoon chopped fresh parsley

Cider adds a delicious fruity flavour to the tasty low-fat broth in which the mussels are cooked.

1 Wash the mussels in a few changes of cold water, scrubbing to remove any beards still attached to the shells. Discard any that are damaged, or opened ones that do not close when tapped. Drain off the water.

2 Heat the oil in a stockpot or large saucepan. Add the onion and garlic and fry for 5 minutes over a medium-low heat, stirring frequently, until translucent. Add the ginger and fry for a further 3 minutes. Do not let it brown.

3 Add the saffron, cider, stock, dill and some salt and pepper. Bring to the boil, add the mussels, then cover and cook for 4-5 minutes, shaking the pan occasionally, until the shells have opened.

4 Transfer the mussels to serving bowls and discard any that remain closed. Stir the chopped parsley into the broth, spoon it into the bowls and serve with crusty bread.

Crab and celeriac salad

Nutrients per serving, when serving 6
- Calories 80
- Carbohydrate 7.5g (of which sugars 7g)
- Protein 7.5g
- Fat 2.5g (of which saturated fat 0.5g)
- Fibre 0.5g

PREPARATION TIME: 15 MINUTES
SERVES 4-6 AS A STARTER

1 celeriac, about 450g (1lb), peeled and grated
Juice of 1 lemon
200g (7oz) fresh or frozen white crab meat, or drained canned crab meat (from two 170g cans)
2-3 tablespoons cider vinegar
2 tablespoons runny honey
4 teaspoons Dijon mustard
1 tablespoon low-fat fromage frais (optional)
3 tablespoons finely chopped fresh parsley or chervil
Salt and black pepper

1 Put the celeriac in a mixing bowl, add the lemon juice and toss briefly.

2 Pick over the crab meat to ensure there are no traces of shell or cartilage. Add to the celeriac and toss.

3 In a small bowl, whisk together the vinegar, honey, mustard, fromage frais, if using, and parsley. Add salt and pepper to taste, then add to the salad and toss. Serve at once with brown bread and green salad leaves.

This tangy, oil-free dressing has a sweet and mellow flavour to balance the raw celeriac and low-fat, high-protein white crab meat.

Grilled oysters
with bacon and lemon

PREPARATION TIME: 15 MINUTES
COOKING TIME: 10 MINUTES
SERVES 2

12 oysters, rinsed and scrubbed if dirty
1 unwaxed lemon
4 rashers lean back bacon, chopped
1 tablespoon chopped fresh parsley
Black pepper

Quick, **simple grilling** is a good way to turn these **low-calorie**, zinc-filled treats into a regular **favourite**. Use **lean** back bacon for this dish as it is **lower in fat** than streaky bacon. Sweet-flavoured **Wiltshire cure** bacon would be ideal.

1 Wrap a towel, thick cloth or glove around the hand in which you wish to hold the oysters. Working over a bowl to catch any juices, hold an oyster firmly so that the hinge area is exposed and the flattest side is uppermost. Take an oyster knife or other short, strong knife and insert the tip in the crack between the shells near the hinge.

2 Work the knife around in the shell until you feel it cut the muscle that attaches the oyster to the top shell. Turn the knife upwards to prise the shell apart. Remove the flat top shell and set the curved bottom section cupping the muscle and juices aside on a baking tray. Repeat with the remaining oysters.

3 Heat the grill. Pare the zest from the lemon and cut the flesh into wedges.

4 In a small, nonstick frying pan, slowly heat the chopped bacon to release its fat gently. Cook lightly for 5 minutes, stirring frequently, until just beginning to brown. Stir in the lemon zest, parsley and some black pepper.

5 Divide the bacon between the oysters, pour over the reserved juices and place under the hot grill for 3 minutes, until the bacon is crisp and the oysters are cooked. Squeeze a little juice from the lemon wedges over the top and serve at once with wholemeal bread.

Nutrients per serving
- Calories 90
- Carbohydrate 1g (of which sugars 0g)
- Protein 12g
- Fat 4g (of which saturated fat 1.5g)
- Fibre 0g
- Vitamins B_1, B_6, B_{12}

Curried prawns and rice

PREPARATION TIME: 15 MINUTES
COOKING TIME: 40 MINUTES
SERVES 4

200g (7oz) brown basmati rice
Salt and black pepper
2 tablespoons semi-skimmed milk
½ teaspoon saffron strands
2 tablespoons vegetable oil
1 large onion, finely chopped
1 red pepper, deseeded and finely chopped
2 teaspoons ground coriander
2 teaspoons ground cumin
1 teaspoon ground turmeric
225ml (8fl oz) fish stock (see page 88)
500g (1lb 2oz) cooked prawns, shelled but
    with the tails left on
500g (1lb 2oz) low-fat fromage frais
15g (½oz) fresh sprigs of coriander,
    roughly chopped
Squeeze of lemon juice

This lighter version of an old **favourite** retains the classic **Anglo-Indian** combination of flavours, using a fragrant variety of **high-fibre** wholegrain rice.

1 Put the rice in a large saucepan and cover with a generous quantity of water. Add a pinch of salt and bring the pan to the boil. Reduce the heat and simmer for 30-35 minutes (or according to the instructions on the packet) until cooked.

2 Meanwhile, heat the milk in a small saucepan or a microwave until just below simmering point. Put the saffron in a small heatproof dish or bowl, cover with the hot milk and set aside to infuse.

3 Heat the oil in a large saucepan. Add the onion and red pepper and cook gently, stirring often, for 5 minutes. Add the ground coriander, cumin and turmeric and continue cooking, stirring often, until the vegetables are tender, a further 5 minutes.

4 Add the stock and bring to simmering point. Add the prawns and cook gently for 2 minutes. Remove the pan from the heat and leave to cool for a few minutes.

5 Whisk the fromage frais gradually into the hot sauce, then whisk in the saffron-infused milk and most of the fresh coriander. Add salt, pepper and lemon juice to taste.

6 Drain the rice and spoon it into warm serving bowls. Spoon the sauce over the rice in the bowls, sprinkle with the remaining chopped coriander and serve, with a cucumber and onion salad.

VARIATION
Cooked shelled mussels, cockles and scallops are good additions to this mixture, as are any firm-textured chunks of white fish.

Nutrients per serving
- Calories 400
- Carbohydrate 54g (of which sugars 13g)
- Protein 40g
- Fat 4g (of which saturated fat 1g)
- Fibre 2g
- Vitamins A, B$_1$, B$_2$, B$_6$, B$_{12}$, C

Pan-fried scallops with ribbon vegetables

PREPARATION TIME: 10 MINUTES,
PLUS 20 MINUTES MARINATING
COOKING TIME: 8 MINUTES
SERVES 4

4 teaspoons olive oil, plus extra
    for cooking
4 teaspoons lemon juice
12 fresh scallops, halved crossways,
    with corals separate
2-3 carrots, about 350g (12oz) in total
4 courgettes, about 350g (12oz) in total

For the sauce:
6 tablespoons white wine
6 tablespoons fish or vegetable stock
½ teaspoon English mustard
½ teaspoon chopped fresh tarragon
15g (½oz) butter

1 Mix the oil and lemon juice in a bowl. Add the scallops and corals and set aside for 20 minutes to marinate. Using a potato peeler, cut the carrots and courgettes into ribbons.

2 To make the sauce, put the wine, stock and mustard in a small pan and heat gently. Remove from the heat and cover to keep it warm while you cook the vegetables and scallops. Steam the carrot ribbons for 1 minute, then add the courgette ribbons and steam for a further 2 minutes until tender. Heat the oven to very low.

3 Meanwhile, wipe some oil into a frying pan, using kitchen paper. Heat until very hot and then add the scallops and corals, in batches, reserving the marinade. Fry for about 20 seconds, then turn over and fry them on the other side for a further 20-30 seconds. Keep them warm in the oven while you cook the remaining scallops.

4 Add the reserved marinade to the sauce and whisk in the tarragon and butter. Pile the vegetable ribbons onto warmed serving plates. Arrange the scallops in a circle round the ribbons and spoon over the sauce.

Nutrients per serving
- Calories 260
- Carbohydrate 11g (of which sugars 8g)
- Protein 17g
- Fat 15g (of which saturated fat 4g)
- Fibre 3g
- Vitamins A, B_{12}, C

The trick when cooking **scallops** is to do so as quickly as possible over a high heat. The **courgette** and **carrot ribbons** are also cooked quickly until just tender. Together they make a pretty and delicious light lunch.

Cockles and mussels hotpot

PREPARATION TIME: 40 MINUTES,
PLUS 1 HOUR SOAKING
COOKING TIME: 20 MINUTES
SERVES 6

750g (1lb 10oz) live cockles
750g (1lb 10oz) live mussels
150ml (¼ pint) white wine
1 tablespoon vegetable oil
1 onion, finely chopped
1 celery stick, finely chopped
½ red pepper, finely chopped
3 tablespoons finely chopped carrot
2 tablespoons finely chopped sage leaves
400g (14oz) canned chopped tomatoes
Salt and black pepper
2 tablespoons roughly chopped parsley

Cockles and mussels have a high content of **selenium**, a cancer-fighting **antioxidant**, as well as iron and vitamin B$_{12}$. Sage and a mixture of finely chopped vegetables add different flavours and extra **nutrients** to the **simple** sauce of tomatoes and wine.

1 Wash the cockles and mussels in a few changes of cold water, scrubbing to remove any beards still attached to the shells. Discard any that are damaged, or opened ones that do not close when tapped. Place the remaining shellfish in a large plastic bowl, cover with cold water and set aside to soak for 1 hour.

2 Drain the shellfish thoroughly and place in a stockpot or large saucepan. Add the wine, cover and cook over a high heat for 2-3 minutes until all the shells have opened.

3 Strain off the cooking liquid and reserve. Discard any shellfish that have not opened. Pick half the shellfish from the shells and leave those remaining in their shells.

4 Heat the vegetable oil in a saucepan, add the onion, celery, red pepper, carrot and sage and cook over a gentle heat until softened. Add the canned tomatoes and bring to the boil, stirring frequently. Cook for 3 minutes, then add the reserved cooking liquid from the shellfish. Return to the boil and simmer for a further 3 minutes, stirring frequently.

5 Stir the cockles and mussels into the sauce and add salt and pepper to taste. Stir in the parsley and serve hot with herbed scones, pasta or rice.

VARIATION
Clams can be used instead of cockles.

Nutrients per serving
- Calories 125
- Carbohydrate 5g (of which sugars 5g)
- Protein 14g
- Fat 3.5g (of which saturated fat 0.5g)
- Fibre 1g
- Vitamins A, B$_{12}$

Poultry

and game

Poultry and game
the healthy way

Excellent sources of protein, B vitamins and minerals, poultry and game are a versatile, nutritious choice for any meal.

Full of nutrients, poultry and game are increasingly popular, reasonably priced and readily available. They both lend themselves to healthy cooking methods and interesting ingredient combinations.

Nutrient-packed poultry
Chicken and turkey are rich in vitamins and minerals, notably B_2, B_6, B_{12} and zinc. Both are also lower in fat than most red meats and, because much of it is in the skin, simply skinning birds before or after cooking greatly reduces the fat in the finished dish. With roast chicken, for example, this cuts out nearly half the fat.

Storing and thawing
Only buy poultry that smells fresh, and avoid any that has dry, discoloured, torn or blemished skin or meat. With frozen birds, look out for freezer burn – brown or greyish white patches on the skin. Always check, too, that the wrapping on pre-packaged birds is not torn or open.

• Put poultry in a refrigerator as soon as possible after purchase because bacteria multiply rapidly in warm conditions. If you have a long journey home, pack the bird in an insulated cool bag.
• Unless you are eating it within hours, unwrap the bird, set it on a large plate, cover with greaseproof paper or foil, and store at the bottom of the refrigerator.
• In general, fresh poultry should be cooked within two days of purchase, though it can be stored for up to six months in the freezer.
• Always defrost frozen birds thoroughly before cooking (see box right).
• Never refreeze poultry (or any other food) that has already been defrosted.

Roasting poultry

1 Stuffing poultry helps to flavour the meat and keep it moist and succulent while it is cooking. Stuff at the neck end, as stuffing the body cavity can limit the heat getting to the centre of the bird and therefore lengthen the cooking time. Pull back the skin, push the stuffing in as far as you can, tuck the skin flap back over the stuffing and secure it firmly with a meat skewer.

2 Ducks and geese are especially fatty birds, so it is best to cut off as much visible fat as possible before cooking. But a lot of the fat on these birds lies hidden in the skin. It adds flavour and helps to prevent the bird from drying out while roasting. Pricking the skin all over before cooking will let some of this fat drain off, as it melts with the heat.

Thawing times for frozen birds

Weight	Thawing time
1.35-2.25kg (3-5lb)	20 hrs
2.7-3.2kg (6-7lb)	30 hrs
3.5-4kg (8-9lb)	36 hrs
4.5-5kg (10-11lb)	45 hrs
5.5-9kg (12-20lb)	60 hrs

Cooking poultry properly

It is also very important to cook poultry correctly, so that any bacteria that can cause food poisoning are destroyed.
• The easiest way to check that poultry is cooked thoroughly is to use a meat thermometer. At the end of the cooking time, insert the thermometer probe into the thickest part of the meat.
• For chicken and turkey, the internal temperature of dark thigh meat should be 75°C (170°F) when fully cooked.
• The temperature of properly cooked white breast meat will be 70°C (160°F).
• If you do not have a thermometer,

3 Place the bird on a rack in the roasting tin, so that the fat that melts from it while cooking can drain away, and so that the bird does not sit in a pool of hot fat as it roasts. Before putting the bird in the oven, pour about 2.5cm (1in) of water into the tin. This will turn to steam in the hot oven and help to keep the flesh moist.

pierce the bird with a skewer or sharp knife where the meat is thickest. If the the meat is fully cooked, the juices that run out should be clear. If there is any trace of blood, continue cooking and test again until done.

Poultry also has a tendency to dry out. Hints for keeping whole birds succulent while roasting are given below left, but breast pieces, especially when skinned, risk becoming very dry. There are, however, several ways to ensure they stay reasonably moist:
• Cooking with the skin on will help to prevent the meat losing moisture and does not add significantly to the final fat content. You must remember, of course, to remove the skin before serving.
• Cutting slashes in the flesh and leaving it in a fat-free marinade for several hours helps to tenderise and moisten it.
• Basting with the marinade as the meat cooks also helps to keep it moist.
• For stir-fries or skewers, cutting the meat into small pieces allows it to cook quickly and not become too dry.

Game birds

Game birds are fattier than either chicken or turkey. However, the fat is largely the 'healthy' unsaturated kind and as most of it is in the skin, the fat content

of a finished dish can be cut greatly by either pricking the raw skin to help fat to drain off as it cooks. or serving the meat skinned.
• Goose is fattier than duck and a greater proportion of its fat is saturated.
• Duck is full of iron and, weight for weight, contains three times as much as chicken. It also provides plenty of zinc.
• Duck and goose, like chicken and turkey, are a good source of B vitamins.
• Guinea fowl is low in fat and is a good source of B vitamins and iron.
• Pigeon is high in iron and zinc.
• Grouse and pheasant are high in potassium and protein.

Venison

Nutrient-rich venison has the taste and texture of red meat, but has far less fat.
• Even lean beef is about three times fattier than venison.
• Venison is rich in iron – 100g provides about half the RDA for a woman.
• Like other red meats, venison is a good source of B vitamins and zinc.

Rabbit and hare

Rabbit and hare are nutritionally similar to chicken, although rabbit contains slightly more iron and zinc and hare is considerably richer in iron.

NUTRITIONAL CONTENT PER 100g (3½oz) SKINLESS ROAST MEAT				
	Kcals	Protein	Total fat*	Saturated fat
Chicken	148	24.8	5.4	1.6
Duck	189	25	9.7	2.7
Goose	319	29.3	22	**
Hare	192	29.9	8	**
Pheasant	213	32.2	9.3	3.1
Pigeon	230	27.8	13.2	**
Rabbit	179	27	7.7	3.2
Turkey	140	28.8	2.7	0.9
Venison	165	35.6	2.5	**

* Total fat content includes fatty compounds and other fatty acids in addition to saturated fat.
** Figures for saturated fat do not exist for these meats.

A good chicken stock, prepared with **fresh** ingredients, makes a tasty base for soups, casseroles, sauces or **gravies**. Instead of chicken, you can use other **lean** poultry, such as turkey, or a couple of **game birds**.

Chicken stock

PREPARATION TIME: 10 MINUTES,
PLUS 1-2 HOURS COOLING
COOKING TIME: ABOUT 2 HOURS
MAKES ABOUT 1.4 LITRES (2½ PINTS)

1 chicken carcass or the bones from 4 chicken
    pieces, cooked or raw
1 onion, quartered
1 large carrot, roughly chopped
1 celery stick, cut into chunks
1 bay leaf
1 sprig of parsley, stalk bruised
1 sprig of fresh thyme
8 black peppercorns
½ teaspoon salt

1 Break up the chicken carcass or bones. Place in a large saucepan and add the onion, carrot and celery. Pour in 2 litres (3½ pints) water and bring to the boil over a high heat, skimming off any scum from the surface.

2 Add the bay leaf, parsley, thyme, peppercorns and salt. Reduce the heat, cover and simmer gently for 2 hours.

3 Strain the stock through a sieve into a heatproof bowl, discarding the bones and vegetables. Cool and chill the stock, then skim off any fat that sets on the surface. Keep for up to 2 days in the fridge, or freeze for up to 3 months.

Coronation chicken

PREPARATION TIME: 20 MINUTES,
PLUS COOLING TIME
COOKING TIME: 1½ HOURS
SERVES 6

Created by Constance Spry for **Elizabeth II's** coronation in 1953, the now **classic** dish is made lighter by using **yoghurt** instead of cream.

1 chicken, about 1.6kg (3lb 8oz)
400ml (14fl oz) chicken stock (see left)
1 bay leaf
1 large sprig of parsley
1 large sprig of thyme
8 black peppercorns
2 teaspoons sunflower oil
2 shallots, finely chopped
1 tablespoon medium Madras curry paste
100ml (3½fl oz) red wine
1 tablespoon tomato purée
1 tablespoon apricot jam
1 tablespoon lemon juice
150g (5½oz) low-fat mayonnaise
150g (5½oz) low-fat yoghurt
Salt and black pepper

1 Put the chicken in a large saucepan and add enough stock to cover. Add the bay leaf, parsley, thyme and peppercorns. Bring to the boil, then reduce the heat, cover and simmer gently for about 1 hour 20 minutes, or until the chicken is cooked. Leave to cool in the stock for 30 minutes.

2 Meanwhile, heat the oil in a saucepan and cook the shallots for 4-5 minutes until soft. Add the curry paste and stir for 30 seconds, then add the wine, tomato purée, jam and lemon juice. Bring to the boil and simmer, uncovered, for 4-5 minutes, or reduced by half. Set aside to cool.

3 Remove the chicken to a plate and leave to cool completely. Remove the meat, discarding skin and bones, and cut it into thick slices. (Reserve the stock for another dish.)

4 Put the cooled sauce in a blender or food processor with the mayonnaise and yoghurt and mix until smooth. Add salt and pepper to taste. Stir in the chicken and serve on a bed of watercress, with wild rice.

Nutrients per serving
- Calories 350
- Carbohydrate 7g (of which sugars 5g)
- Protein 45g
- Fat 14g (of which saturated fat 2g)
- Fibre 0g
- Vitamins niacin, B$_6$

Old English stewed rosemary chicken

PREPARATION TIME: 10 MINUTES,
PLUS MARINATING
COOKING TIME: 45-50 MINUTES
SERVES 4

4 shallots, finely chopped
2 teaspoons grated fresh ginger
½ teaspoon ground mace
Pinch of cayenne pepper
200ml (7fl oz) red wine
1 tablespoon fresh rosemary leaves, plus
    extra sprigs to garnish
4 chicken quarters, or 8 thighs, skinned
2 tablespoons plain flour
1 tablespoon sunflower oil
15g (½oz) butter
Salt and black pepper

1 Put the shallots, ginger, mace, cayenne, red wine and rosemary leaves in a large bowl and add the chicken. Turn to coat evenly, then cover and leave to marinate in the fridge for several hours or overnight.

2 Drain the chicken thoroughly, reserving the marinade, and pat dry with kitchen paper. Sprinkle evenly with flour.

3 Heat the oil and butter in a wide, flameproof casserole, add the chicken and cook quickly until lightly browned all over. Add the reserved marinade with salt and pepper to taste.

4 Cover and simmer gently for 30-35 minutes, turning the chicken occasionally, until cooked through. Top with rosemary sprigs and serve with baked or boiled potatoes and lightly cooked Savoy cabbage or spring greens.

Nutrients per serving
- Calories 370
- Carbohydrate 7g (of which sugars 6g)
- Protein 43g
- Fat 18g (of which saturated fat 3g)
- Fibre 0g
- Vitamins niacin

Drumsticks with Gubbins sauce

Named after its inventor Nathaniel Gubbins, the original sauce dates back to the early 1900s. It was rich in butter and cream; this is a lighter version that retains the same sharp flavour.

PREPARATION TIME: 10 MINUTES
COOKING TIME: 12-15 MINUTES
SERVES 4

8 chicken drumsticks
Oil for brushing
Salt and black pepper
2 tablespoons English mustard
2 tablespoons tarragon vinegar
85g (3oz) low-fat fromage frais
15g (½oz) butter
4 sprigs of tarragon to garnish

1 Slash the drumsticks at intervals with a sharp knife. Brush lightly with oil, sprinkle with salt and pepper and cook under a medium-hot grill for 12-15 minutes, turning often, until golden brown and cooked through.

2 Meanwhile, whisk together the mustard, vinegar and fromage frais. Melt the butter in a small pan, remove from the heat, then whisk it into the fromage frais and mustard mixture. Add salt and pepper to taste.

3 Serve the grilled chicken, skinned if desired, topped with tarragon, with a bowl of the warm sauce for dipping. Accompany with char-grilled courgettes and mashed potato.

Nutrients per serving
- Calories 420
- Carbohydrate 3g (of which sugars 1g)
- Protein 43g
- Fat 27g (of which saturated fat 9g)
- Fibre 0g
- Vitamins niacin, B_6

Roast chicken with parsley and lemon stuffing

PREPARATION TIME: 15 MINUTES
COOKING TIME: ABOUT 2 HOURS
SERVES 4-6

25g (1oz) butter
1 onion, finely chopped
1 celery stick, trimmed and finely chopped
125g (4½ oz) fresh white breadcrumbs
4 tablespoons finely chopped parsley
Finely grated zest and juice of 1 lemon
Salt and black pepper
1 chicken, about 1.8kg (4lb)
1 tablespoon plain flour
200ml (7fl oz) dry cider

Fresh parsley and lemon make a classic British stuffing, and are perfect to balance the delicate flavour of a simple roast chicken.

1 Heat the oven to 190°C (375°F, gas mark 5). Melt the butter in a saucepan, add the onion and celery and cook over a medium heat for 2-3 minutes, until soft.

2 Remove from the heat and stir in the breadcrumbs, parsley, lemon zest, some salt and pepper and enough lemon juice to bind the mixture. Leave to cool.

3 Put the chicken in a roasting tin and spoon about half the stuffing into the neck end. Tuck the flap of skin over to enclose it. Put the remaining stuffing in an ovenproof dish.

4 Sprinkle the chicken with lemon juice, salt and pepper. Roast for 20 minutes per 450g (1lb) plus 20 minutes extra, until the chicken is golden brown and the juices run clear, basting from time to time. Cook the stuffing in the oven for 15-20 minutes.

5 Lift the chicken onto a warm serving plate and cover with foil. Skim off any excess fat from the juices in the tin. Place the tin over the heat, stir in the flour and cook for 1-2 minutes. Gradually add the cider, whisking, until thick. Add salt and pepper to taste. Serve the chicken and stuffing with the cider gravy and new potatoes, carrots and broccoli.

Nutrients per serving, when serving 6
- Calories 300
- Carbohydrate 14g (of which sugars 2g)
- Protein 32g
- Fat 12g (of which saturated fat 5g)
- Fibre 0g
- Vitamins niacin, B_6

Little hindle wakes

PREPARATION TIME: 30 MINUTES
COOKING TIME: 55-60 MINUTES
SERVES 4

1 bay leaf
1 small carrot, diced
1 celery stick, trimmed and sliced
1 large onion, finely chopped
1 unwaxed lemon
300ml (½ pint) dry white wine
85g (3oz) fresh wholemeal breadcrumbs
115g (4oz) ready-to-eat prunes,
    finely chopped
1 tablespoon chopped fresh sage, plus
    extra sprigs to garnish
Salt and black pepper
4 boneless, skinless chicken breasts
200g (7oz) low-fat fromage frais
3 tablespoons finely chopped
    fresh parsley

1 Put the bay leaf, carrot, celery and half the onion in a flameproof casserole. Cut a thick slice from the lemon and add it to the casserole. Add the wine and 300ml (½ pint) water. Bring to the boil, cover and simmer for 5 minutes.

2 Mix the breadcrumbs with the remaining onion, prunes and sage. Grate the zest from the remaining lemon and add it to the breadcrumbs, with salt and pepper to taste. Press the mixture together into a firm stuffing.

3 Make a horizontal cut into each chicken breast to form a pocket. Divide the stuffing between the pockets, pressing it into each. Tie string round each to secure.

4 Add the stuffed breasts to the casserole. Bring back to simmering point, cover and cook gently over a medium-low heat for 40 minutes, turning the breasts once. Remove from the heat and leave to cool.

5 Lift the cooled chicken from the casserole, remove the string and wrap in cling film, then chill. Boil the stock over high heat for 10-15 minutes, until reduced to about 100ml (3½ fl oz). Strain, cool and then stir in the fromage frais. Chill the sauce.

6 To serve, cut open the chicken and arrange on plates. Stir the parsley into the sauce, add salt and pepper to taste and pour it over and around the chicken. Serve with a leafy salad.

Spatchcocked poussins
with asparagus

Spatchcocking is a method for opening small game or poultry birds out flat, so that they cook quickly and evenly and stay beautifully succulent.

A centuries-old Lancashire dish of cold, stuffed chicken, made here with lean boneless breast rather than a whole chicken, and fromage frais instead of cream.

PREPARATION TIME: 15 MINUTES, PLUS 2 HOURS MARINATING
COOKING TIME: 30 MINUTES
SERVES 4

4 small poussins, about 400g (14oz) each
1 clove garlic, crushed
Finely grated zest and juice of
 1 unwaxed lemon
125ml (4fl oz) dry white wine
2 tablespoons olive oil
2 tablespoons chopped chives
2 tablespoons chopped parsley
2 tablespoons chopped mint
Salt and black pepper
500g (1lb 2oz) asparagus spears, trimmed

1 Using poultry shears or strong scissors, cut down either side of each poussin's backbone and remove it. Open the bird out on a board, skin side up, and press down firmly to flatten it. Prick the skin all over with a fork.

2 Put the birds in a large bowl. Add the garlic, lemon zest and juice, 6 tablespoons of the wine, 1 tablespoon of the oil and 1 tablespoon each of the chives, parsley and mint. Turn to coat evenly and leave to marinate in the fridge for 2 hours or overnight.

3 Thread two metal skewers across each other through each bird to hold it flat. Sprinkle with salt and pepper and cook under a moderately hot grill or on a barbecue, turning occasionally, for 25-30 minutes, until golden and cooked through. Baste with the marinade for the first 15 minutes.

4 Brush the asparagus spears very lightly with oil and add them to the grill or barbecue for the last 5-6 minutes of cooking, turning often.

5 Lift the poussins onto a large platter with the asparagus. Whisk together the remaining wine, oil and herbs, adding salt and pepper to taste. Spoon over the poussins and asparagus, and serve warm, with new potatoes.

VARIATION
You can use 2 guinea fowl instead of 4 poussins.

Nutrients per serving
- Calories 350
- Carbohydrate 3g (of which sugars 2.5g)
- Protein 49g
- Fat 19g (of which saturated fat 5g)
- Fibre 2g
- Vitamins B_1, B_6, niacin

Turkey likkey pie

PREPARATION TIME: 25 MINUTES
COOKING TIME: 35-40 MINUTES
SERVES 4

400g (14oz) turkey breast steaks,
 cut into 2cm (¾in) chunks
400g (14 oz) leeks, thinly sliced
150ml (¼ pint) semi-skimmed milk
1 large egg, beaten, plus extra to glaze
½ teaspoon freshly grated nutmeg
Salt and black pepper
150g (5½oz) self-raising flour
75g (2¾oz) low-fat vegetable suet

Nutrients per serving
- Calories 400
- Carbohydrate 35g
 (of which sugars 5g)
- Protein 30g
- Fat 16g (of which
 saturated fat 7g)
- Fibre 3g
- Vitamins B_1, B_6, B_{12}, niacin

1 Heat the oven to 200°C (400°F, gas mark 6). Put the turkey in a saucepan with the leeks and milk. Bring to the boil, cover and simmer for 8-10 minutes, until the leeks are soft.

2 Strain the milk into a jug, then gradually whisk into the beaten egg. Add the nutmeg, with salt and pepper to taste. Spoon the turkey and leeks into a 1 litre (1¾ pint) pie dish. Pour the egg mixture on top.

3 Sift the flour with ¼ teaspoon salt into a bowl and stir in the suet. Add 4-5 tablespoons cold water, or enough to mix to a soft dough.

4 Moisten the rim of the dish with water, then roll out the pastry on a lightly floured surface to just bigger than the dish. Cut a strip of pastry and press it round the rim of the dish. Cover with the pastry lid, pressing and crimping the edges together to seal. Use any leftover pastry to make pastry leaves to decorate the top, if desired.

5 Glaze with beaten egg, make a slit in the top with a knife for the steam to escape and place on a baking sheet. Bake for 25-30 minutes, until the pastry is golden. Serve warm, with a tomato and watercress salad.

'Likkey' – or leek – pie, is an old **West Country** dish, richly filled with leeks, bacon, cream and eggs. This **healthy adaptation** uses lean turkey breast and a reduced-fat suet crust.

Roast turkey breast
with Tudor stuffing

The Elizabethans made lavish use of spices and fruits in their cooking. This dish combines some **typical** flavours of the time in a **rich**, **sweet** stuffing that complements lean, **low-fat** turkey breast meat.

PREPARATION TIME: 15 MINUTES
COOKING TIME: 1 HOUR 15 MINUTES
SERVES 4

2 boneless turkey breasts, with skin, about 500g (1lb 2oz) each
60g (2¼oz) fresh wholemeal breadcrumbs
1 Cox's apple, cored and grated
3 canned anchovy fillets, drained and finely chopped
25g (1oz) seedless raisins, chopped
½ teaspoon ground cinnamon
¼ teaspoon ground ginger
¼ teaspoon ground mace
Salt and black pepper
1 small egg, beaten
Pinch of saffron strands
1 tablespoon honey

Nutrients per serving
• Calories 383
• Carbohydrate 17g (of which sugars 12g)
• Protein 63g
• Fat 7g (of which saturated fat 2g)
• Fibre 1.5g
• Vitamins B_6, B_{12}, niacin

1 Heat the oven to 190°C (375°F, gas mark 5). Place the turkey breasts, skin side down, on a board. Make a cut about halfway through each, down the middle, to open it out slightly.

2 Put the breadcrumbs, apple, anchovy, raisins, cinnamon, ginger and mace in a bowl and mix. Add salt and pepper to taste, with enough beaten egg to bind the mixture.

3 Spoon the stuffing onto one turkey breast, then place the second on top, skin side up. Secure with string and place in a roasting tin.

4 Cover loosely with foil and roast for about 1 hour, until cooked through. Put the saffron in a small bowl with 1 tablespoon boiling water. Leave to soak for a few minutes, then stir in the honey.

5 Brush the turkey with the saffron and honey glaze and roast, uncovered, for 10-15 minutes, brushing with the glaze occasionally, until golden brown. Serve, sliced, with roast potatoes, parsnips and onions.

VARIATION
This stuffing can also be used to stuff the neck-end of a whole turkey.

127

Devilled turkey and sweetcorn skewers

This hot and spicy dish is a great choice for an informal autumn or winter celebration such as Bonfire Night or Hallowe'en. It's low in fat, quick to cook and can be prepared in advance.

PREPARATION TIME: 10 MINUTES, PLUS 1-2 HOURS MARINATING
COOKING TIME: 20 MINUTES
SERVES 4

1 tablespoon English mustard powder
2 tablespoons tomato purée
1 tablespoon dark muscovado sugar
1 tablespoon grated fresh ginger
2 cloves garlic, crushed
1 tablespoon red wine vinegar
1 tablespoon Worcestershire sauce
550g (1lb 4oz) boneless turkey breast, cut into 2.5cm (1in) cubes
2 sweetcorn cobs, husks removed, cut into 2.5cm (1in) slices

1 Put the mustard powder, tomato purée, sugar, ginger, garlic, vinegar and Worcestershire sauce in a large bowl. Mix, then add the turkey and mix again to coat. Cover and leave to marinate in the fridge for 1-2 hours.

2 Thread the corn slices and turkey in alternating pieces onto four metal skewers.

3 Cook the skewers under a hot grill or on a barbecue, turning often, for 15-20 minutes or until the turkey is cooked through and the corn is tender and golden. Serve with crusty bread and a fresh spinach salad.

Nutrients per serving
- Calories 200
- Carbohydrate 7g (of which sugars 6g)
- Protein 33g
- Fat 4g (of which saturated fat 1g)
- Fibre 1g
- Vitamins B_6, B_{12}, niacin

Although duck is relatively high in fat, this recipe cooks out the excess from the skin, while the meat is kept moist and tender.

Duck with glazed turnips

PREPARATION TIME: 10 MINUTES
COOKING TIME: 30 MINUTES
SERVES 4

Nutrients per serving
- Calories 445
- Carbohydrate 18g (of which sugars 7g)
- Protein 27g
- Fat 26g (of which saturated fat 7g)
- Fibre 3g
- Vitamins B_1, B_6, B_{12}, niacin

4 duck breasts
8 shallots, peeled and quartered
12 baby turnips, halved
1 clove garlic, crushed
200ml (7fl oz) dry white wine
Thinly pared strip of lemon zest
  and juice of 1 unwaxed lemon
3 tablespoons runny honey
2 tablespoons fresh chopped sage
Salt and black pepper

1 Slash the skin of the duck in a diamond pattern, using a sharp knife. Heat a heavy frying pan until very hot, add the duck, skin side down, and cook over a high heat for 8-10 minutes, turning once, until browned and cooked but slightly pink inside.

2 Remove the duck from the pan to a warm place. Drain off the fat from the pan, leaving a thin coating. Add the shallots and turnips and stir over a moderate heat, for 2-3 minutes, until golden, then add the garlic.

3 Add the wine and lemon zest and simmer for about 1 minute, then cover and simmer, stirring occasionally, for 10-12 minutes or until the turnips and shallots are almost tender. Stir in the lemon juice, honey and sage and cook for a further 4-5 minutes, until caramelised and tender.

4 Add the duck breasts, with skin removed if desired, and cook for 1-2 minutes, spooning the juices over the duck. Add salt and pepper to taste. Remove to warmed plates, spoon the vegetables around and serve with steamed potatoes and spinach.

Nell Gwynn's spiced duck with oranges

Nutrients per serving
- Calories 540
- Carbohydrate 13g (of which sugars 10g)
- Protein 65g
- Fat 21g (of which saturated fat 6g)
- Fibre 0.5g
- Vitamins C, B₁, B₂, B₆, B₁₂, niacin

PREPARATION TIME: 20 MINUTES
COOKING TIME: 2 HOURS 5 MINUTES
SERVES 4

1 duck, about 2.25kg (5lb)
Pinch of cayenne pepper
¼ teaspoon ground cloves
Salt and black pepper
4 oranges, Seville if in season
125ml (4fl oz) medium sherry
1½ teaspoons cornflour
1 tablespoon chopped fresh mint
1 tablespoon runny honey
Orange wedges and mint sprigs to garnish

1 Heat the oven to 200°C (400°F, gas mark 6). Remove any excess fat from the openings of the duck. Rub the cayenne pepper, cloves, salt and pepper into the skin. Cut one orange into wedges and tuck the wedges inside the cavity.

2 Place the duck on a rack in a roasting tin and roast in the oven for 30 minutes. Prick the skin all over with a fork, then reduce to 180°C (350°F, gas mark 4) and roast for a further 1¼-1½ hours, or until cooked but with the juices running slightly pink when the thickest part is pierced. Pour off the excess fat once or twice during cooking.

3 Remove the zest from the remaining oranges, then squeeze the juice into a bowl. Remove the duck on its rack from the tin, cover with foil and set aside to rest. Skim the fat from the juices and add the sherry to deglaze the tin, stirring over a moderate heat.

4 Blend the cornflour to a paste with a little of the orange juice, then stir in the remaining juice. Add to the tin, stirring until boiling, thickened and clear. Stir in the orange zest, chopped mint and honey and boil for 1 minute. Add salt and pepper to taste.

5 To serve, cut the duck into quarters with a heavy knife or poultry shears, pour over the orange sauce and garnish with orange wedges and mint sprigs. Serve with fresh minted peas and boiled potatoes.

Very sharp Seville oranges are best in this classic dish, named after the mistress of Charles II. They are available only in January and February, so if you are using sweet oranges, add a squeeze of lemon juice to ensure a tangy flavour.

Pot-roasted pheasant
with celery and walnuts

PREPARATION TIME: 20 MINUTES
COOKING TIME: 1 HOUR
SERVES 4

1 head of celery

70g (2½ oz) walnuts, chopped

100g (3½ oz) fresh white breadcrumbs

2 pheasant or chicken livers, chopped

Finely grated zest and juice of
   1 unwaxed lemon

Salt and black pepper

1 egg white

2 pheasants, about 675g (1lb 8oz) each

2 tablespoons sunflower oil

15g (½ oz) butter

55g (2oz) pearl barley

1 bay leaf

2 slices of streaky bacon, halved

250ml (9fl oz) chicken stock
   (see page 120)

1 Heat the oven to 180°C (350°F, gas mark 4). Finely chop 1 large celery stick and mix with half the walnuts, the breadcrumbs, livers and lemon zest, with salt and pepper to taste. Add enough egg white to bind the mixture, then use to stuff each pheasant cavity.

2 Heat the oil and butter in a large, flameproof casserole, add the pheasants and cook over a medium heat until lightly browned. Remove the casserole from the heat and remove the pheasants to a plate.

3 Cut the remaining celery into thick slices and add to the casserole with the pearl barley, remaining walnuts and bay leaf. Place the pheasants on top and lay the bacon slices across the breasts.

4 Add the lemon juice and stock with salt and pepper to taste. Bring to the boil, cover, then transfer to the oven for 50-60 minutes, until the pearl barley is tender and the pheasant is cooked through. Serve at once.

Nutrients per serving
- Calories 580
- Carbohydrate 25g (of which sugars 2g)
- Protein 41g
- Fat 37g (of which saturated fat 9g)
- Fibre 1.5g
- Vitamins A, B_1, B_2, B_6, B_{12}, niacin

The season for pheasant is from the end of **September** to the end of **January**, but it is available frozen all year. Pheasant is high in **protein**, low in **fat and cholesterol**, and ideal for juicy pot-roasting.

Britain's moorland, heath and woodland have long provided both the

Traditional game

In the past, only wild animals or birds that were hunted for sport or food were known as game, although the term now extends to a number of species that are bred and farmed for food. Nearly all wild game is very low in fat, whereas game specially reared on farms, is consistently plump and tender.

Most of the game eaten in Britain is of the feathered variety. The choice of cooking method will depend on the bird's approximate age. The meat on older birds is tougher and will, therefore, need to be cooked slowly over a long period of time, using plenty of liquid – braising or stewing is ideal – while young birds can be roasted or, in some cases, may be grilled. If you buy your game from a good game dealer, he should be able to tell you the age of any bird on sale,

as well as how long it has been hung for. The longer a bird has been left to hang, the richer and more intensely flavoured its meat will become.

Birds in season

Most British game birds are at their best in winter, in the main shooting season, which officially begins with grouse on 'the glorious twelfth' of August. The strong, dark meat of red grouse is considered by some to be the finest of all game birds. It is highly valued partly because the bird is difficult to farm, ensuring its continued rarity and seasonality.

The popularity of grouse reached its height during the Victorian era, when Queen Victoria's annual move to Balmoral in late summer made shooting in the Highlands a fashionable sport amongst the aristocracy.

hunter and the cook with rich natural resources.

The wild mallard duck is at its peak in September, although the smaller teal and wigeon (the two other varieties of wild duck best for eating) are better later in the year. Wigeon has an especially delicate flavour.

Geese are mainly farmed, but they can be reared only as free range and need more food than other birds, making them less cost-effective. They are in season from late September to December, and are particularly popular at Christmas.

Pheasant has a relatively mild flavour, resembling a gamey tasting chicken. The hen, which is smaller than the cock, tends to be more plump and tender. Pigeon, also a mild-tasting bird, is often called squab when young. Older wild pigeon is strong in flavour and can be tough. Wood pigeon is a specific type of pigeon, meatier than other varieties, and available all year.

The two key varieties of partridge available in Britain are the grey partridge and the red-legged partridge, although the latter is native to France. The grey partridge is milder in flavour than the larger French bird, though both are delicate compared to other

game. Quail are tiny birds of the same family as partridge. These days they are generally farmed, resulting in a much milder flavour.

Furred game

Up to the 1700s, the entire population ate wild venison, especially in Scotland, but when landowners claimed the Highlands, the poor could only obtain this high-quality, lean meat by poaching. The late 20th-century development of farmed venison has helped revive its popularity, encouraging also new ways of cooking it. Similarly, all 'wild' British boar is farmed.

Hare and rabbit were both popular with the Greeks and Romans. Most rabbit is now farmed, but hare is still wild. Brown hare is the most common; the varying hare (whose coat changes colour) is native to Scotland.

Huffed pheasant with gooseberries

PREPARATION TIME: 30 MINUTES
COOKING TIME: 30-35 MINUTES
SERVES 4

1 small leek, thinly sliced
125g (4½ oz) gooseberries
25g (1oz) breadcrumbs
1 tablespoon chopped thyme
Salt and black pepper
4 pheasant breasts, about 125g
    (4½ oz) each
4 slices of lean back bacon
250g (9oz) self-raising flour
125g (4½ oz) light vegetable suet
1 egg, beaten, plus extra for brushing
2 tablespoons lemon juice

Nutrients per serving
- Calories 500
- Carbohydrate 54g (of which sugars 2g)
- Protein 35g
- Fat 37g (including saturated fat 18g)
- Fibre 3g
- Vitamins A, B$_1$, B$_6$, niacin

Here, 'huffed' or 'houghed' means wrapped, and in this 18th-century recipe iron-rich pheasant breasts are cooked in attractive pastry parcels.

1 Heat the oven to 200°C (400°F, gas mark 6). Put the leek, gooseberries, breadcrumbs, thyme and a pinch of salt and pepper in a bowl and mix.

2 Remove the skin from each pheasant breast and cut a deep pocket in the side. Spoon the stuffing mixture in, packing it firmly. Wrap a slice of bacon around each.

3 Sift the flour into a bowl and stir in the suet and some salt and pepper. Make a well in the centre and add the egg, lemon juice and enough cold water to mix to a soft, but not sticky, dough.

4 Divide into four and roll out each to about a 15cm (6 in) round, depending on the size of the pheasant breasts. Place a pheasant breast on each, brush the edges with egg and fold over to enclose. Pinch the edges to seal, place on a baking sheet and brush with egg to glaze.

5 Bake for 20 minutes, until the pastry is firm and golden brown, then reduce to 180°C (350°F, gas mark 4) and cook for a further 10-15 minutes. Serve warm or cold, with a crisp salad and pickles.

Partridge with port and red cabbage

PREPARATION TIME: 15 MINUTES
COOKING TIME: 45-50 MINUTES
SERVES 4

Nutrients per serving
- Calories 500
- Carbohydrate 16g (of which sugars 15g)
- Protein 45g
- Fat 27g (of which saturated fat 5g)
- Fibre 3g
- Vitamins B$_6$, C, niacin

1 onion
1 cooking apple, such as Bramley, peeled
    and cored
4 young partridge, about 275g (9½ oz)
    each
1 tablespoon sunflower oil
450g (1lb) red cabbage, finely shredded
1 bay leaf
3 tablespoons red wine vinegar
150ml (¼ pint) apple juice
100ml (3½ fl oz) ruby port
8 pickled walnuts, halved
Salt and black pepper

Partridge, seen by many as the king of game birds, has sweet, succulent meat that is also low in cholesterol.

Roast grouse with chestnuts and cranberries

PREPARATION TIME: 15 MINUTES
COOKING TIME: 40 MINUTES
SERVES 4

15g (½oz) butter
2 shallots, chopped
200g (7oz) peeled chestnuts
200g (7oz) cranberries
1 tablespoon runny honey
4 oven-ready young grouse
Salt and black pepper
2 slices of streaky bacon, halved
4 slices of white bread
1 tablespoon walnut or hazelnut oil

Nutrients per serving
- Calories 450
- Carbohydrate 38g (of which sugars 9g)
- Protein 41g
- Fat 21g (of which saturated fat 7g)
- Fibre 4g
- Vitamins B₁, B₆, niacin

Grouse is in season – and has the best flavour – between the 'glorious twelfth' of August and December 10. Young, plump birds are excellent roasted.

1 Heat the oven to 200°C, (400°F, gas mark 6). Melt the butter in a small pan, add the shallots and cook over a low heat for 5-6 minutes until soft. Add the chestnuts, cranberries and honey. Set aside to cool.

2 When cool, divide about half the mixture between the cavity of each bird. Place each on a piece of foil. Sprinkle with salt and pepper and drape a piece of bacon over the breast of each. Spoon the remaining chestnuts and cranberries around the birds.

3 Tuck the foil loosely over each grouse and roast them in the oven for 20 minutes, then open the foil and cook for a further 10-15 minutes, until browned and cooked through.

4 Stamp out four 7.5cm (3in) rounds from the bread and brush with oil. Toast under a hot grill until golden, turning once. Serve the grouse on the toasted croutes, with the cranberries, chestnuts and juices spooned over.

VARIATION
Use 2 guinea fowl instead of 4 grouse.

---

1 Heat the oven to 180°C (350°F, gas mark 4). Cut half the onion and apple into 4 wedges, and tuck a wedge of each into the cavity of each bird. Dice the remaining onion and apple.

2 Heat the oil in a heavy, nonstick frying pan, add the birds, breast side down, and cook quickly, until browned all over. Remove to a plate. Put the red cabbage in a flameproof casserole with the diced apple and onion, bay leaf, vinegar, apple juice, port and walnuts. Add salt and pepper to taste, bring to the boil and stir well.

3 Place the birds on top, breast sides up, sprinkle with salt and pepper and cover tightly. Cook in the oven for 30 minutes, then remove the lid and cook for a further 10 minutes to crisp the skin.

4 Serve each partridge on a bed of cabbage, with the juices spooned over, with baked or mashed potatoes.

VARIATION
Use young pheasants or poussins if partridge is not available.

Guinea fowl with Madeira and redcurrant

PREPARATION TIME: 10 MINUTES
COOKING TIME: 25-30 MINUTES
SERVES 4

4 guinea fowl breasts
1 tablespoon corn oil
Salt and black pepper
15g (½ oz) butter
2 shallots, finely chopped
1 tablespoon raspberry vinegar
4 tablespoons Madeira or medium sherry
1 teaspoon caster sugar
175g (6oz) redcurrants, stems removed
Redcurrant sprigs to garnish

1 Heat the grill to medium-hot. Brush the guinea fowl breasts with oil, sprinkle with salt and pepper and grill for 12-15 minutes, turning once, until golden brown and cooked through.

2 Meanwhile, heat the butter in a small, heavy-based frying pan, add the shallots and cook over a moderate heat for 5-6 minutes, until soft.

3 Stir in the vinegar, Madeira and sugar. Add the redcurrants. Heat gently until almost boiling, then simmer for 8-10 minutes until the redcurrants are soft and the liquid is syrupy.

4 Remove the skin from the guinea fowl, if desired, and transfer the breasts to serving plates. Spoon the sauce over, top with redcurrant sprigs and serve with red cabbage (see page 183) and baked potatoes.

Nutrients per serving
- Calories 240
- Carbohydrate 4g (of which sugars 4g)
- Protein 26g
- Fat 11g (of which saturated fat 4g)
- Fibre 2g
- Vitamins C, B$_6$, niacin

Pigeon salad with raspberries

PREPARATION TIME: 15 MINUTES, PLUS 12 HOURS MARINATING
COOKING TIME: 10 MINUTES
SERVES 4

English recipes for pigeon date back to the Middle Ages, when it was a popular meat. This modern dish uses a very English combination of nuts and berries.

8 pigeon breasts, skinned
100ml (3½ fl oz) red wine
2 tablespoons sherry vinegar
1 bay leaf, crumbled
3 tablespoons hazelnut oil
2 tablespoons raspberry vinegar
Salt and black pepper
125g (4½ oz) baby spinach leaves or rocket
55g (2oz) toasted hazelnuts, roughly chopped
125g (4½ oz) raspberries, defrosted if frozen

1 Put the pigeon breasts in a wide bowl with the wine, sherry vinegar, bay leaf and 1 tablespoon of the hazelnut oil. Cover and marinate in the refrigerator for 12 hours or overnight. Drain, reserving the marinade.

2 Put the remaining hazelnut oil in a screw-top jar with the raspberry vinegar and some salt and pepper. Shake to mix.

3 Heat a ridged griddle-pan to hot, then add the pigeon breasts and cook for 4-5 minutes on each side, basting with the marinade, until brown on the outside but still pink inside.

4 Toss together the spinach or rocket, hazelnuts and raspberries in a wide serving bowl. Slice the warm pigeon breasts and add to the salad. Drizzle with the dressing, toss lightly to coat evenly, transfer to plates or a large platter and serve, with crusty bread.

Nutrients per serving
- Calories 430
- Carbohydrate 3g (of which sugars 3g)
- Protein 31g
- Fat 30g (of which saturated fat 2g)
- Fibre 2g
- Vitamins C, B$_1$, B$_6$, niacin

Guinea fowl breast is lean and healthy – a rich source of B vitamins – and has an excellent flavour, enhanced here with a very simple, tangy sauce.

Roast goose with prunes and almonds

PREPARATION TIME: 20 MINUTES
COOKING TIME: 2½ HOURS
SERVES 6

1 small onion, finely chopped
1 small Bramley apple, cored and
   finely chopped
85g (3oz) ready-to-eat prunes,
   finely chopped
1 goose liver, finely chopped
40g (1½oz) fine fresh white breadcrumbs
Finely grated zest of 1 unwaxed lemon
1 tablespoon chopped sage
25g (1oz) blanched almonds, toasted and
   roughly chopped
Salt and black pepper
1 oven-ready goose, about 5kg (11lb)
2 tablespoons plain flour
300ml (½ pint) chicken stock
   (see page 120)
1 tablespoon Worcestershire sauce

Traditionally served to celebrate **Michaelmas**, on September 29, goose is naturally high in fat, but cooking it on a rack allows much of the fat to drain off.

1 Heat the oven to 220°C (425°F, gas mark 7). Put the onion, apple, prunes, liver and breadcrumbs in a bowl. Add the lemon zest, sage, almonds, salt and pepper and mix well.

2 Spoon the stuffing into the neck end of the goose, tuck the flap over it and secure with a skewer. Rub the skin with half the flour and sprinkle with salt and pepper. Place on a rack in a roasting tin and roast for 30 minutes.

3 Remove the goose from the oven and prick the skin all over with a fork. Reduce the oven to 180°C (350°F, gas mark 4) and roast for 1¾-2 hours

until the juices run clear, draining off the fat several times during cooking.

4 Lift the goose on its rack from the tin and keep it warm. Skim the fat from the tin and stir in the remaining flour over a low heat. Whisk in the stock and Worcestershire sauce. Serve with boiled potatoes and a green vegetable.

Nutrients per serving
- Calories 600
- Carbohydrate 19g (of which sugars 11g)
- Protein 59g
- Fat 44g (of which saturated fat 7g)
- Fibre 2.5g
- Vitamins A, B_1, B_2 B_6, B_{12}, niacin

Mustard rabbit cobbler

PREPARATION TIME: 20 MINUTES
COOKING TIME: 45-50 MINUTES
SERVES: 6

1 tablespoon sunflower oil
900g (2lb) rabbit meat, diced
125g (4½ oz) lean bacon, diced
1 large onion, sliced
1 clove garlic, crushed
2 carrots, sliced
150ml (¼ pint) dry white wine
300ml (½ pint) chicken stock
   (see page 120)
75g (2¾ oz) red split lentils
1 large sprig of thyme
1 bay leaf
2 tablespoons white wine vinegar
Salt and black pepper
2 tablespoons wholegrain mustard

For the cobbler topping:
225g (8oz) self-raising flour
¼ teaspoon celery salt
55g (2oz) butter
2 tablespoons chopped chives
150ml (¼ pint) skimmed milk

1 Heat the oven to 220°C (425°F, gas mark 7). Heat the oil in a large saucepan, then add the rabbit and bacon. Cook, stirring, until golden. Add the onion and garlic and cook for 1-2 minutes. Stir in the carrots, wine, stock, lentils, thyme, bay leaf, vinegar, salt and pepper.

2 Bring to the boil, reduce the heat, cover and simmer gently for 20 minutes. Meanwhile, sift the flour into a bowl, add the celery salt and rub in the butter. Stir in the chives and milk. Mix to a firm dough. Knead gently, then roll out on a lightly floured surface to 1cm (½ in) thick and stamp out 20 rounds.

3 Add the mustard to the rabbit and spoon the mixture into an ovenproof dish.

4 Put the rounds over the rabbit and brush with milk. Bake for 15-20 minutes, until golden brown.

Nutrients per serving
- Calories 520
- Carbohydrate 42g (of which sugars 6g)
- Protein 45g
- Fat 18g (of which saturated fat 8g)
- Fibre 3g
- Vitamins A, B_1, B_2, B_6, B_{12}, niacin

Country rabbit with caramelised apples

PREPARATION TIME: 15 MINUTES
COOKING TIME: 1 HOUR 15 MINUTES
SERVES 4

8 rabbit portions, about 1kg (2lb 4oz)
25g (1oz) plain flour
2 tablespoons sunflower oil
2 onions, sliced
250g (9oz) chestnut mushrooms,
   quartered
150g (5½ oz) black pudding, sliced
300ml (½ pint) dry cider
1 tablespoon Worcestershire sauce
Salt and black pepper
15g (½ oz) butter
1 tablespoon light muscovado sugar
2 Cox's apples, cored and cut
   into wedges
1 tablespoon cider vinegar

1 Toss the rabbit in the flour to coat evenly, shaking off any excess flour. Heat the oil in a wide, flameproof casserole and cook the rabbit over a moderate heat, turning often, until golden brown. Remove from the pan.

2 Add the onion to the pan and cook for 2 minutes, then add the mushrooms and cook for a further 2-3 minutes, stirring often. Add the browned rabbit, black pudding, cider and Worcestershire sauce.

3 Bring to the boil, cover and simmer gently for about 1 hour, stirring occasionally, until the rabbit is tender. Adjust salt and pepper to taste.

4 Melt the butter and sugar in another pan, then add the apples and cook gently for 2-3 minutes, stirring, until golden. Sprinkle with cider vinegar and bubble for a few seconds. Spoon the apples over the casserole and serve hot, with crusty bread or baked potatoes.

Nutrients per serving
- Calories 600
- Carbohydrate 29g (of which sugars 19g)
- Protein 60g
- Fat 22g (of which saturated fat 9g)
- Fibre 2.5g
- Vitamins B_1, B_2, B_6, B_{12}, niacin

Jugged hare with dumplings

PREPARATION TIME: 25 MINUTES
COOKING TIME: 3 HOURS
SERVES 6

1 tablespoon sunflower oil
1 hare, jointed, or 6 hare joints, about
    1kg (2lb 4oz) in total
4 slices of streaky bacon, chopped
2 onions, chopped
2 carrots, diced
2 celery sticks, diced
2 cloves garlic, crushed
Finely grated zest and juice of 1 orange
Finely grated zest of ½ unwaxed lemon
1 sprig each of thyme and marjoram
3 cloves
½ teaspoon freshly grated nutmeg
Salt and black pepper
350ml (12fl oz) red wine

For the dumplings:
400g (14oz) cold mashed potato
60g (2¼oz) plain flour
35g (1¼oz) semolina
4 tablespoons chopped parsley
1 small egg, beaten
2 teaspoons cornflour

Nutrients per serving
- Calories 540
- Carbohydrate 30g (of which sugars 6g)
- Protein 47g
- Fat 22g (of which saturated fat 5g)
- Fibre 2.5g
- Vitamins A, B₁, B₆

1 Heat the oven to 150°C (300°F, gas mark 2). Heat the oil in a large, flameproof casserole, add the hare and cook quickly to brown on all sides, working in batches if necessary. Remove from the pan. Add the bacon and cook for 2 minutes. Add the onions, carrots and celery and cook, stirring, for 3-4 minutes.

2 Add the browned hare, garlic, citrus zest and juice, herbs, cloves, nutmeg, salt, pepper and 300ml (½ pint) of the wine. Bring to the boil and cover. Transfer to the oven and cook for 2-2½ hours.

3 Meanwhile, mix the potato, flour, semolina, half the parsley, some salt and pepper and enough egg to make a firm dough. Shape into 18 small balls.

4 In a bowl, mix the cornflour with the remaining wine. Remove the casserole from the oven and place over a moderate heat. Stir in the cornflour and cook, stirring, for 2-3 minutes, until thickened. Add salt and pepper to taste.

5 Add the dumplings to the casserole, cover and simmer for a further 20 minutes. Sprinkle with the remaining chopped parsley and serve.

Rabbit and hare are both low-fat, high-protein meats. Both are rich in iron, B vitamins and phosphorus. Rabbit meat is pale and mild, whereas hare is dark and strong, and needs to be cooked for longer, in plenty of liquid.

Venison Wellingtons

PREPARATION TIME: 20 MINUTES
COOKING TIME: 45 MINUTES
SERVES 4

350g (12oz) plain flour
Salt and black pepper
175g (6oz) butter
4 venison steaks, about 125g (4½oz) each
2 tablespoons olive oil
1 onion, thinly sliced
150g (5½oz) wild or chestnut
   mushrooms, thinly sliced
2 teaspoons wholegrain mustard
Milk for glazing

A variation on the classic Beef Wellington, these individual parcels use lean venison instead, flavoured with mushrooms, onions and mustard.

1 Heat the oven to 200°C (400°F, gas mark 6). Sift the flour into a bowl, add a pinch of salt, then rub in the butter until the mixture resembles fine breadcrumbs. Stir in enough cold water to bind to a soft, not sticky, dough. Cover and chill for 5 minutes.

2 Sprinkle the venison steaks with salt and pepper. Heat half the oil in a heavy or nonstick pan, add the steaks and cook quickly to brown on all sides. Remove from the pan.

3 Add the remaining oil and cook the onion for 2-3 minutes, then add the mushrooms and cook for a further 1-2 minutes, until soft.

4 Roll out the chilled pastry on a lightly floured surface and cut into four 17cm (6½in) squares. Spread a little mustard in the middle of each square. Top each with a venison steak, then a spoonful of the onion and mushroom mixture.

5 Brush the edges with milk, then pull up each corner to meet in the middle, pressing the edges together to seal. Lift onto a baking sheet and brush with milk. Bake for 15 minutes, then reduce the oven to 180°C (350°F, gas mark 4) and cook for a further 10 minutes, until golden. Serve with cranberry sauce and bubble and squeak (see page 197).

Nutrients per serving
- Calories 840
- Carbohydrate 70g (of which sugars 3g)
- Protein 35g
- Fat 48g (of which saturated fat 26g)
- Fibre 3.5g
- Vitamins A, B_1, B_6, B_{12}, niacin

▶ **VENISON WELLINGTON**

Spiced venison and brandy terrine

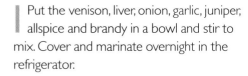

PREPARATION TIME: 15 MINUTES, PLUS OVERNIGHT MARINATING AND 2 HOURS COOLING
COOKING TIME: 2 HOURS
SERVES 8

350g (12oz) lean venison, diced
250g (9oz) lamb's liver, diced
1 large onion, chopped
2 cloves garlic, crushed
10 juniper berries, crushed
6 allspice berries, crushed
4 tablespoons brandy
10 slices of smoked streaky bacon
1 egg, beaten
Salt and black pepper

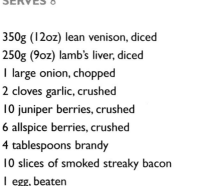

1 Put the venison, liver, onion, garlic, juniper, allspice and brandy in a bowl and stir to mix. Cover and marinate overnight in the refrigerator.

2 Heat the oven to 160°C (325°F, gas mark 3). Roughly chop 2 rashers of bacon and put in a food processor or blender with the marinated ingredients, the egg and some salt and pepper. Process until smooth.

3 Stretch the remaining bacon rashers with the back of a knife, then use them to line a 1 litre (1¾ pint) loaf tin or terrine dish, overhanging the edges. Spoon in the meat mixture and fold the bacon over to cover.

4 Cover with foil and transfer to a roasting tin. Add water to come halfway up the sides and cook in the oven for 2 hours. Remove from the roasting tin and place a heavy weight or cans of food on top. Leave to cool.

5 Remove the weight, turn the terrine out onto a plate. Slice and serve with redcurrant jelly, mixed salad and crusty bread.

VARIATION
Pheasant breast or diced rabbit can be substituted for the venison meat.

The season for venison is May to October, so this terrine is a good way to make the most of it during the summer months – perfect for picnics and lunches on lazy, outdoor days.

Nutrients per serving
- Calories 260
- Carbohydrate 1g (of which sugars 1g)
- Protein 21g
- Fat 17g (of which saturated fat 6g)
- Fibre 0g
- Vitamins A, B_2, B_6, B_{12}, niacin

Mixed game pie

PREPARATION TIME: I HOUR,
PLUS 3 HOURS MARINATING,
AND I HOUR COOLING
COOKING TIME: 2½ HOURS
SERVES 8-10

1kg (2lb 4oz) mixture of: pheasant,
   partridge, pigeon or rabbit
200g (7oz) streaky bacon, chopped
2 tablespoons dark rum
125ml (4fl oz) red wine
200g (7oz) closed cup mushrooms, sliced
2 tablespoons chopped tarragon
300ml (½ pint) chicken stock
   (see page 120)
1 onion, quartered
4 allspice berries
2 tablespoons rowan or redcurrant jelly
1 sachet of gelatine
Salt and black pepper

For the pastry:
500g (1lb 2oz) plain flour
1 tablespoon icing sugar
¼ teaspoon salt
175g (6oz) unsalted butter, plus extra
   for greasing
1 small egg, beaten

Pies, filled with
whatever game that is
in season, have been
popular since the
Middle Ages. Here,
rum and **red wine**
add a special touch.

1 Cut all the game meats into 1cm
   (½in) pieces and put in a large bowl
with the bacon, rum, wine, mushrooms
and tarragon. Cover and leave to
marinate in a cool place for at least
3 hours or overnight.

2 Put the stock in a saucepan with
   the onion and allspice. Bring to the
boil, cover and simmer for 30 minutes.
Drain the meats thoroughly and add
the marinade liquid to the pan. Boil
rapidly over a hight heat until reduced
to about 200ml (7fl oz). Strain and set
aside, reserving the stock.

3 Heat the oven to 160°C (325°F,
   gas mark 3). For the pastry, sift the
flour, sugar and salt into a bowl and
make a well in the centre. Put the
butter in a small pan, add 200ml (7fl oz)
water and bring to the boil. Remove
from the heat, stir into the flour
mixture and mix to a smooth dough.
Cover and set aside for 10 minutes.

4 Lightly grease a 23cm (9in) spring
   form cake tin and place on a
baking sheet. Cut off a third of the
dough for the lid and press the rest into
a round to line the tin, pressing it evenly
up against the sides and over the rim.

5 Spoon the meats and mushrooms
   into the tin. Roll out the remaining
pastry to make a lid, brush the edges
with beaten egg and lift over the pie.
Trim the edges and pinch together to
seal. Decorate with pastry trimmings
and pierce a hole in the centre.

6 Bake in the oven for 1½ hours,
   then remove from the oven and
carefully release the sides of the tin.
Brush the pastry with beaten egg and
bake for a further 30 minutes. Leave to
cool completely.

7 Heat the reserved stock gently
   with the rowan or redcurrant jelly,
then whisk in the gelatine until it is
dissolved. Leave until just beginning to
thicken, then pour into the pie through
the hole in the centre, using a funnel.
Cool and chill, then slice and serve with
a mixed salad or coleslaw.

**Nutrients per serving,
when serving 10**
- Calories 550
- Carbohydrate 43g (of which sugars 5g)
- Protein 30g
- Fat 28g (of which saturated fat 14g)
- Fibre 2g
- Vitamins B₁, B₆, B₁₂, niacin

Venison cottage pies

A classic family favourite, made with healthy venison rather than beef. The traditional potato topping is given extra nutrients and flavour with the addition of parsnip.

PREPARATION AND COOKING TIME: 65-70 MINUTES
SERVES 4

450g (1lb) potatoes, peeled and cut into chunks
250g (9oz) parsnips, peeled and cut into chunks
25g (1oz) butter
5-6 tablespoons semi-skimmed milk
½ teaspoon ground mace
Salt and black peppper
2 tablespoons vegetable oil
1 large onion, chopped
4 juniper berries, crushed
500g (1lb 2oz) minced venison
100g (3½ oz) small chestnut mushrooms, halved
2 tablespoons ruby port
200ml (7fl oz) beef stock (see page 148)
1 teaspoon cornflour
2 teaspoons Worcestershire sauce

1 Boil the potatoes in boiling, salted water for 15-20 minutes until soft, adding the parsnips after 10 minutes. Drain and mash, adding the butter and enough milk to make a soft mash. Add the mace with salt and pepper to taste.

2 Meanwhile, heat the oil in a large frying pan, add the onion and juniper berries and cook over a low heat, stirring often, for 10-12 minutes until the onion is soft and translucent. Remove to a bowl.

3 Add the venison to the pan and cook over a medium heat for about 10 minutes, stirring until evenly browned and in granules.

4 Heat the oven to 200°C (400°F, gas mark 6). Return the onion with the mushrooms to the frying pan. Add the port and cook over a medium heat for 2 minutes, then add the stock and bring to the boil. Cover and simmer for 15 minutes.

5 Mix the cornflour, Worcestershire sauce and 2 tablespoons cold water in a cup. Add to the venison and stir over a low heat for 1 minute. Add salt and pepper to taste.

6 Spoon the venison mixture into four small ovenproof dishes, making sure the liquid is evenly distributed. Spread the potato and parsnip mash on top and fork the top.

7 Bake for 25-30 minutes until the top is brown and the juices are beginning to bubble up around the sides. Serve with curly kale or cabbage.

Nutrients per serving
- Calories 480
- Carbohydrate 33g (of which sugars 8g)
- Protein 33g
- Fat 24g (of which saturated fat 10g)
- Fibre 5g
- Vitamins B_1, B_6, B_{12}, C, niacin

143

Beef, lamb

and pork

Beef, lamb and pork
the healthy way

Choose the right cut and cooking method to minimise fat, and benefit from meat's essential protein, vitamins and minerals.

Red meat is highly nutritious. It is a concentrated source of protein, and offers an abundance of vitamins as well as iron and zinc. Much meat is now also healthily lean, and some cuts contain no more fat than chicken or turkey.

Packed with nutrients
Meat excels as a protein food with between 29g and 35g of protein per 100g (depending on type), compared to 25.5g for Cheddar cheese, 12.5g for eggs, 25g for chicken and 8g for pulses. Meat supplies most of the B vitamins, including B_{12} – vital for cell and nerve function, and mainly found in foods of animal origin.

Beef for iron and zinc
Together with offal, red meat is one of the richest sources of iron, an essential mineral. Although you can obtain iron from beans, vegetables and wholegrain cereals, the iron in meat is in the haem form, which is more easily absorbed by the body. An average serving of roast beef will provide 21 per cent of the recommended daily intake of iron, which is essential for the manufacture of oxygen-carrying red blood cells. Low iron levels lead to tiredness, anaemia and increased susceptibility to infections.

Zinc is vital for growth and a healthy, robust immune system. Like iron, zinc is present in wholegrain cereals, but it is much more easily absorbed from red meat. An average beef serving provides 56 per cent of the daily zinc requirement.

Leaner lamb
Modern breeding techniques and new butchery methods, such as seam butchery, mean that lamb is now much leaner than in the past. In seam butchery individual muscle groups are removed by following the seams of the carcass. Any

Making a basic stock

1 A little lean meat, maybe some leftovers plus a few bones, can form the basis for a stock. For a full, rich flavour, brown the meat first in a little hot oil.

2 Vegetables, such as onions, celery, leeks and carrots, will help to enhance the flavour. These also need lightly browning in hot oil. Then, cover the meat and vegetables with cold water, and bring to the boil.

4 Strain, discard the vegetables and meat, then chill. Any fat will rest on the surface and is easy to remove.

3 Once the stock is boiling, lower the heat and skim any scum off the top. Cover and leave to simmer gently for at least 2 hours, stirring occasionally.

FAT CONTENT PER 100g (3½ oz) MEAT (all figures refer to lean, raw cuts, unless specified otherwise)					
Cut of meat	Kcals	Total fat*	Saturates	Monounsaturated	Polyunsaturated
Beef topside	116	2.7	1.1	1.2	0.2
Beef rump steak	125	4.1	1.7	1.7	0.3
Beef silverside	134	4.3	1.6	2.0	0.2
Beef mince, extra lean	174	9.6	4.0	3.6	0.6
Pork leg	107	2.2	0.9	0.9	0.4
Pork steaks	120	3.4	1.2	1.3	0.6
Lamb, average	162	8.0	3.5	2.6	0.8
Lamb breast	179	11.2	5.2	4.2	0.5
Bacon (streaky)	414	39.5	15.4	17.6	4.3
Bacon (lean back)	147	7.4	2.7	3.1	0.8
Sausage (beef)	299	24	10	11	1.4
Sausage (pork)	367	32	12.2	15	3.4
Sausage (reduced fat)	166	9.5	3.4	4.1	1.5
Gammon (boiled)	167	5.5	2.1	2.4	0.5
Liver (lamb's)	179	10.3	2.9	3	1.5
Liver (calf's)	153	7.3	2.2	1.3	1.9
Veal fillet	109	2.7	0.9	1.2	0.4
Veal escalope	106	1.7	0.6	0.7	0.3

Total fat content includes fatty compounds and other fatty acids in addition to saturated, monounsaturated and polyunsaturated fats.

visible fat between the seams is trimmed and thrown away to give lean, boneless cuts that are quick and easy to cook.

Healthy pork

Pork has become an increasingly healthy meat option. It is particularly rich in vitamin B₁, essential for energy and for preventing the build-up of toxins. One average serving provides more than the recommended daily intake.

As with lamb, selective breeding and modern butchery techniques have reduced the fat content by 30 per cent in the last 40 years. The average fat content of lean pork is now 3.5 per cent – similar to that of chicken breast. In most cuts the fat surrounds the lean flesh, rather than marbling it, making it

easy to remove or trim before cooking. Alternatively you can leave the fat on to baste the meat and keep it moist while cooking, and remove it before serving.

Cooking lean meat

Choose lean cuts as they do not need much preparation and are simple and quick to cook. However, because they do not have fat marbled through the flesh to keep the meat moist during cooking, they can become a little dry and tough.

Braising or casseroling meat allows it to cook slowly in plenty of liquid, which is ideal for very lean cuts, ensuring that it is moist and tender.

Leaving meat in a well-flavoured marinade for a few hours before cooking can also help to make it tender and

moist – especially if you include pineapple, figs or papaya in the marinade as they contain special enzymes that help to soften tough tissue.

Cuts such as steaks and escalopes can be pounded before cooking to break down tough fibres so they cook more quickly and have less time to dry out:
• Place the meat between two sheets of greaseproof paper or cling film.
• Pound it using a meat mallet or pounder, or, if you do not have a mallet, simply use a rolling pin.

The best way to ensure that you are buying good meat is to choose well-trimmed joints and cuts that look fresh. Beef and pork fillets and lamb leg steaks are generally tender, lean cuts. If in doubt, seek the advice of a reliable butcher.

At the heart of every good soup, gravy, sauce, pie and casserole lies a rich stock. It is well worth making it in large batches and freezing them, so that you always have some to hand.

Beef stock

PREPARATION TIME: 10 MINUTES, PLUS 1-2 HOURS COOLING
COOKING TIME: 2¼ HOURS
MAKES ABOUT 1.4 LITRES (2½ PINTS)

1 tablespoon sunflower oil
125g (4½ oz) lean stewing beef in one piece
1 onion, quartered
1 carrot, roughly chopped
1 celery stick, roughly chopped
2 bay leaves
1 sprig of parsley, stalk bruised
1 sprig of fresh thyme
10 black peppercorns
½ teaspoon salt

1 Heat the oil in a large, heavy-based saucepan over a high heat. Brown the beef on both sides, then remove it and set aside.

2 Reduce the heat and add the vegetables. Cook gently, stirring occasionally, until browned. Pour in 2 litres (3½ pints) water and bring to the boil.

3 Replace the beef and heat until the liquid is simmering. Skim off any scum, then add the herbs, peppercorns and salt. Reduce the heat, cover and leave to bubble for 2 hours.

4 Strain the stock through a sieve into a heatproof bowl. Discard the beef and vegetables. Cool and chill the stock, then skim off any fat from the surface. Store in the refrigerator for up to 3 days, or remove to a freezer container and freeze for up to 6 months.

VARIATIONS
For lamb or pork stock, use lean lamb or pork instead of beef. Leftovers from a joint on the bone can be used instead of fresh meat.

Roast beef with a mustard crust and Yorkshire pudding

PREPARATION TIME: 15 MINUTES
COOKING TIME: 1 HOUR 30 MINUTES
SERVES 6-8

1.5kg (3lb 5oz) rib of beef or rolled sirloin,
    any excess fat removed
Salt and black pepper
2 tablespoons English mustard powder
1 onion, sliced
1 tablespoon brown sugar
600ml (1 pint) beef stock (see left)
2-3 sprigs of thyme or rosemary
2 tablespoons cornflour, mixed with
    3 tablespoons cold water

For the Yorkshire pudding:
75g (2¾ oz) plain flour
1 egg
75ml (2½ fl oz) semi-skimmed milk
3 tablespoons light olive oil

1 Heat the oven to 220°C (425°F, gas mark 7). Rub the meat with salt and pepper. Heat a large, heavy roasting tin, add the beef and cook quickly until browned all over. Remove from the tin and set aside to cool for 5 minutes, then pat the mustard evenly over the beef.

2 To make the Yorkshire pudding batter, sift the flour into a bowl and make a well in the centre. Break the egg into the well and pour in the milk and 50ml (2fl oz) water. Beat until smooth and set aside.

3 Arrange the onion in the roasting tin and sprinkle with sugar. Place the beef on top and cook in the oven for 10 minutes per 450g (1lb) for rare, 15 minutes for medium and 20 minutes for well done, plus an extra 10, 15 or 20 minutes, reducing the oven to 180°C (350°F, gas mark 4) after 20 minutes. Remove the beef from the tin, cover with foil and place on a rack set over a plate. Leave in a warm place to rest for 30 minutes.

4 Increase the oven to 200°C (400°F, gas mark 6). For the Yorkshire pudding, pour the oil into an enamelled cast iron dish or small roasting tin and put it into the oven to heat for 5 minutes. Remove the tin and pour in the Yorkshire pudding batter. Return to the oven and cook, on an oven tray, for 20-25 minutes, until puffed and golden.

5 Meanwhile, while the beef is resting, skim off as much fat from the juices in the roasting tin as you can, using a large spoon. Pour a little of the stock into the tin and place over a medium heat. Scrape up any crusty bits from the tin and simmer for a few minutes, stirring. Add the remaining stock and the thyme or rosemary. Simmer, stirring, for 20-30 minutes. Add salt and pepper to taste.

6 Bring to the boil and thicken the gravy with cornflour, if desired, by spooning the cornflour mixture into the gravy, whisking, until it reaches your desired consistency.

7 Carve the beef and serve with the Yorkshire pudding, gravy, jacket potatoes, steamed broccoli, and horseradish and beetroot relish (see page 276).

**Nutrients
per serving,
when serving 8**
- Calories 426
- Carbohydrate 20g
  (of which sugars 4g)
- Protein 55g
- Fat 14g (of which
  saturated fat 5g)
- Fibre 1g
- Vitamins B$_{12}$, B$_{6}$,
  niacin

Few dishes can rival a magnificent traditional British roast beef with Yorkshire pudding. With a light batter, stock-based gravy and accompanying vegetables, this meal also supplies most of the nutrients we need for good health.

Devilled steaks

PREPARATION TIME: 10 MINUTES
COOKING TIME: 8 MINUTES
SERVES 4

1 tablespoon wholegrain mustard
1 tablespoon Worcestershire sauce
Pinch of cayenne pepper
4 tablespoons green tomato chutney
   (see page 272)
4 very thin steaks, cut from the topside,
   about 125g (4½ oz) each
Salt

1 Preheat the grill until hot. Mix the mustard, Worcestershire sauce, cayenne and chutney in a small bowl.

2 Sprinkle the steaks lightly with salt. Heat a nonstick frying pan until hot, add the steaks and cook quickly for 2 minutes on each side.

3 Transfer the steaks to a metal tray, then spread with the devilling ingredients. Place under the hot grill until the mixture bubbles. Remove and keep warm for about 5 minutes, to rest, then serve with potato wedges roasted in olive oil, and a salad.

Nutrients per serving
- Calories 186
- Carbohydrate 7g
  (of which sugars 7g)
- Protein 26g
- Fat 6g (of which
  saturated fat 2g)
- Fibre 0g
- Vitamins B_{12}, B_6, niacin

Colonial beef curry

Devilling food – adding **spices** and condiments to make it last – first appeared in Britain as a culinary method in the early **19th** century.

PREPARATION TIME: 20 MINUTES
COOKING TIME: 2-3 HOURS
SERVES 4

2 tablespoons sunflower oil
1 onion, finely sliced
800g (1lb 12oz) lean chuck steak, cut into
    4cm (1½ in) cubes, fat removed
2-3 tablespoons plain flour
Salt
2 tablespoons mild curry powder
½ teaspoon turmeric
1 tablespoon garam masala
600ml (1 pint) beef stock (see page 148)
2 bay leaves
1 heaped tablespoon sultanas or raisins
Juice of 1 lime

Nutrients per serving
- Calories 344
- Carbohydrate 10g (of which sugars 4g)
- Protein 42g
- Fat 15g (of which saturated fat 5g)
- Fibre 1g
- Vitamins B₂, B₆, B₁₂, niacin

1 Heat the oven to 140°C (275°F, gas mark 1). Heat half the oil in an ovenproof casserole, add the onion and cook until soft. Remove and set aside. Toss the steak in the flour to coat. Sprinkle lightly with salt, then heat the remaining oil in the casserole, add the meat and cook, stirring, until evenly browned.

2 Reduce the heat to low and return the onion to the pan. Stir in the curry powder, turmeric and garam masala and cook gently, stirring, for 2-3 minutes.

3 Add the stock, bay leaves and sultanas or raisins and bring to a simmer. Pour in some water, if needed, to cover the meat. Cover and transfer to the oven to cook for 2-3 hours until the meat is tender. Add any extra seasoning and lime juice to taste, then serve with basmati rice and mango chutney.

The oriental spices that flavour curry – popular since colonial days – may have medicinal properties too. Turmeric, for instance, is said to improve circulation and relieve digestive problems.

Boiled beef and carrots with dumplings

PREPARATION TIME: 45 MINUTES
COOKING TIME: 3 HOURS
SERVES 6-8

1 tablespoon olive oil
1.6kg (3lb 8oz) silverside beef, cut into
   4cm (1½in) chunks
1 large onion, chopped
6 large carrots, cut into chunks
1 large celery stick, cut into chunks
1 tablespoon brown sugar
1.2 litres (2 pints) beef stock
   (see page 148)
2 large sprigs of thyme
4 tablespoons chopped parsley
Black pepper

For the dumplings:
250g (9oz) plain flour, plus extra
   for dusting
1 teaspoon salt
2 teaspoons baking powder
8 tablespoons chopped chives or parsley,
   or a mixture
150ml (5fl oz) skimmed milk
2 tablespoons olive oil

**Nutrients per serving,
when serving 8**
- Calories 429
- Carbohydrate 32g (of which sugars 8g)
- Protein 45g
- Fat 14g (of which saturated fat 5g)
- Fibre 3g
- Vitamins A, B$_2$, B$_6$, B$_{12}$, niacin

1 Heat the oven to 160°C (325°F, gas mark 3). Heat the oil in a large, heavy ovenproof casserole. Add the beef and cook, turning, to brown evenly. Add the onion, carrots and celery and cook until lightly browned, then stir in the sugar. Add the stock and bring to the boil.

2 Add the thyme, then cover the meat and vegetables with parchment paper. Top with a lid, bring to a simmer, then transfer to the oven. Cook for 2 hours, until the meat is just tender.

3 Meanwhile, make the dumplings. Sift the flour, salt and baking powder into a large bowl. Add the herbs and fork through to mix.

Add the milk and oil and mix to a loose, coarse dough. Scrape the mixture from the bowl, adding a little more flour if necessary, and form into a long sausage. Cut into 12-16 pieces, then roll each into a ball. Chill on a floured tray until needed.

4 When the meat is tender, remove from the oven, season to taste and add the dumplings. Simmer gently over a low heat for 45 minutes until the dumplings are puffed and cooked. Serve with crusty bread.

Beef and vegetable pie with a filo crust

Rich pies in many forms have long graced the British table. This one is light and healthy with a filo crust and protein-rich meat and vegetable filling.

PREPARATION TIME: 1 HOUR
COOKING TIME: 1¾ HOURS
SERVES 6-8

1 kg (2lb 4oz) chuck steak, fat removed, cut into 3cm (1¼in) pieces
3-4 tablespoons plain flour
3 tablespoons olive oil
400g (14oz) shallots
450g (1lb) field mushrooms, quartered
750ml (1pint 7fl oz) brown ale
500ml (18fl oz) beef stock (see page 148)
2 tablespoons soft dark brown sugar
1 tablespoon Dijon mustard
1 bouquet garni, made from 2 celery sticks, 4 sprigs of thyme, 4 parsley stalks and 2 bay leaves, tied together
Salt and black pepper
1 egg, beaten with a little salt
140g (5oz) filo pastry, cut into 20 squares, 18cm (7in), plus 2 whole sheets

For the vegetables:
70g (2½oz) sugar snap peas
70g (2½oz) baby carrots, with green tops
70g (2½oz) broccoli florets
4 large celery sticks, cut into 2.5cm (1in) pieces

Nutrients per serving, when serving 8
• Calories 355
• Carbohydrate 28g (of which sugars 11g)
• Protein 31g
• Fat 11g (of which saturated fat 3g)
• Fibre 2g
• Vitamins C, B₂, B₆, B₁₂, niacin

Silverside is a lean cut of beef, but you can also use plain or salt brisket. The dumplings puff to twice their original size, so allow plenty of room in the casserole.

1 Toss the meat in the flour to coat. Working in batches, heat the oil in a large, deep casserole, add the meat and cook, stirring, to brown evenly. Remove to a plate. Add the shallots and cook for 5-8 minutes, until lightly browned. Add the reserved meat and the mushrooms.

2 Add the ale, stock, sugar, mustard and bouquet garni and bring slowly to a simmer, covered, then cook at a slow simmer for about 1 hour.

3 Using a slotted spoon, remove the meat and vegetables to a pie dish, about 28 x 23cm (11 x 9in). Boil the cooking liquid until reduced to 500ml (18fl oz). Taste and adjust the seasoning, adding a little more sugar if needed.

4 Meanwhile, cook the vegetables for 2-3 minutes, in batches, in boiling, salted water. Transfer them to the pie dish and mix. Strain the reduced cooking liquid, discarding the bouquet garni, then pour it over the filling. Heat the oven to 180°C (350°F, gas mark 4).

5 Brush the rim of the pie dish with some of the beaten egg. Cut the whole filo sheets to cover the top of the pie dish, and press them onto the rim. Lightly brush the remaining filo with oil and scrunch lightly to give a crumpled effect. Place them over the pie to cover completely. Cook for 20 minutes until the top is golden, and the contents hot.

Cornish pasties

PREPARATION TIME: 30 MINUTES,
PLUS 30 MINUTES RESTING
COOKING TIME: 1 HOUR
MAKES 4 SMALL PASTIES

300g (10½ oz) strong white flour, sifted
Salt and black pepper
100g (3½ oz) chilled butter, diced
3 tablespoons olive oil
1 large onion, finely chopped
150g (5½ oz) swede, peeled and cubed
225g (8oz) rump steak, trimmed of fat
    and cut into small dice
115g (4oz) potatoes, peeled and
    cut into small dice
Milk for brushing

1 For the pastry, put the flour and a pinch of salt in a large bowl with the butter. Rub in the butter until it resembles fine breadcrumbs. Gradually add the oil and enough cold water, stirring with a knife, until the mixture comes together in a ball. Wrap in cling film and chill for 30 minutes.

2 Heat the oven to 220°C (425°F, gas mark 7). Divide the pastry dough in four and roll out each piece to a circle. Using a side plate as a guide, cut each into a circle about 18cm (7in) diameter.

3 Put the chopped onion down the middle of each pastry round. Add the swede, then sprinkle with salt and pepper. Add the meat and some salt and pepper. Top with the potato.

4 Moisten one half of each circle edge with water and fold over the other half. Press the sides of the pastry together firmly but gently, to seal. Crimp the edges, tucking them in at the end.

5 Place the pasties on an oiled baking sheet, brush with milk and bake for 10 minutes, then reduce to 180°C (350°F, gas mark 4) and continue cooking for a further 35-40 minutes until golden brown. Leave for at least 15 minutes before eating, warm or at room temperature.

Nutrients per serving
- Calories 630
- Carbohydrate 70g (of which sugars 3g)
- Protein 20g
- Fat 32g (of which saturated fat 16g)
- Fibre 4g
- Vitamins B_6, B_{12}

Savoury mince

PREPARATION TIME: 25 MINUTES
COOKING TIME: 1 HOUR 30 MINUTES
SERVES 6

1 tablespoon sunflower oil
1 large onion, chopped
3 small carrots, finely chopped
700g (1lb 9oz) lean minced beef
8 slices of lean unsmoked back bacon,
    finely chopped
1 teaspoon thyme leaves
1 teaspoon tomato purée
400g (14oz) canned tomatoes
1 tablespoon tomato ketchup
2 tablespoons mushroom ketchup
    (see page 276)
1 tablespoon Worcestershire sauce
150ml (¼ pint) red wine (optional)
Black pepper

A good mince is easy to make and very versatile. Tomatoes and carrots add useful vitamins.

1 Heat the oil in a large, heavy-based saucepan, add the onion and fry gently until browned. Add the carrots and continue cooking over a low heat for about 5-8 minutes.

2 Add the beef and bacon, increase the heat and cook, stirring until evenly browned. Add the thyme and tomato purée and cook over a high heat for 5-8 minutes.

3 Add the canned tomatoes, tomato and mushroom ketchups, Worcestershire sauce, red wine, if using, and pepper to taste. Simmer over a very low heat for about 1 hour, stirring from time to time, until thick. Serve with potatoes or rice, or use instead of venison mince to make cottage pie (see page 143).

Nutrients per serving
- Calories 326
- Carbohydrate 9g (of which sugars 8g)
- Protein 33g
- Fat 16g (of which saturated fat 6g)
- Fibre 2g
- Vitamins A, B_1, B_6, B_{12}

True **Cornish** pasties are made of lard pastry filled with a fatty cut of meat. Here, the half olive oil pastry and **lean** meat make this **hearty** working man's pie much **lighter**.

Roast saddle of lamb with apricots

**Nutrients
per serving,
when serving 8**

- Calories 386
- Carbohydrate 18g
  (of which sugars 9g)
- Protein 38g
- Fat 17g (of which
  saturated fat 5g)
- Fibre 1g
- Vitamins B$_2$, B$_6$,
  B$_{12}$, niacin

PREPARATION TIME: 10 MINUTES,
PLUS 1 HOUR SOAKING
COOKING TIME: 1¼-2 HOURS
SERVES 6-8

1 saddle of lamb, boned, about 1.6kg
   (3lb 8oz), trimmed of excess fat
100g (3½oz) long-grain or basmati rice
1 clove
100g (3½oz) ready-to-eat dried apricots
3 tablespoons seedless raisins, soaked in
   water for 1 hour, then drained
2 tablespoons flaked almonds
1 teaspoon ground cinnamon
1 teaspoon ground ginger
Salt and black pepper

Valentine steaks are
loin chops with
the bone removed,
making them
heart-shaped.
A very tender
cut of lamb, it
simply needs quick
pan-grilling.

Lean lamb is high in protein and is a good
source of B vitamins, zinc and iron. Here,
a sweet-spiced stuffing adds extra nutrients.

1 Using a small knife, score the fat on the lamb
in a criss-cross pattern.

2 To make the stuffing, cook the rice in plenty
of boiling, salted water, with the clove
added, until tender. Drain and spread on a tray
to cool. Sprinkle over the apricots, raisins,
almonds, spices, salt and pepper and mix.

3 Heat the oven to 190°C (375°F, gas
mark 5). Put a roasting tin with a roasting
rack in the oven to heat. Sprinkle the lamb with
salt and pepper, then spread the rice stuffing
mixture evenly over the top.

4 Roll up the lamb and tie with string to
secure. Heat a nonstick pan over a high
heat, add the lamb and cook, turning, until
browned all over. Transfer to the roasting rack in
the oven, and pour a little water into the base of
the tray to prevent the escaping fat burning.

5 Roast in the oven for 1 hour for rare,
1 hour 15 minutes for medium rare and
1 hour 40 minutes for well-done. Leave to rest
in a warm place, covered in foil, for 20 minutes.
Carve into thick slices and serve with minted
new potatoes and spinach.

Grilled lamb valentine steaks
served with a pea and mint sauce

PREPARATION TIME: 20 MINUTES, PLUS 1 HOUR MARINATING
COOKING TIME: 35 MINUTES
SERVES 4

8 lamb valentine steaks, trimmed
3 tablespoons balsamic vinegar
Salt and black pepper
1 tablespoon sunflower or olive oil

For the sauce:
1 teaspoon butter
4 lettuce leaves, cut into fine strips
300g (10½oz) peas, frozen or fresh
Pinch of sugar
3 sprigs of mint

1 Skewer each steak diagonally with a wooden cocktail stick, snipping off the points.

2 Place the steaks in a shallow glass dish. Add the vinegar and turn the steaks to coat. Leave to marinate for about 1 hour.

3 Heat the oven to 190°C (375°F, gas mark 5). Heat an ovenproof nonstick frying pan until very hot. Sprinkle the lamb with salt and pepper, brush the pan lightly with oil and add the lamb steaks, in batches. Cook for about 5 minutes on each side until browned, then pour off the fat.

4 For medium to well-done lamb, transfer the pan to the oven for about 6 minutes. For rare, remove it to a plate, cover in foil and keep it warm.

5 To make the sauce, melt the butter in a small saucepan. Add the lettuce, peas and sugar, with salt to taste. Cover and cook for 2-3 minutes. Add 300ml (½ pint) water and the leaves from the mint sprigs, then simmer for 10-15 minutes, until the peas are very tender. Purée in a blender until smooth.

6 Remove the cocktail sticks from the lamb and serve at once with the pea sauce and new potatoes.

Nutrients per serving
- Calories 316
- Carbohydrate 9g (of which sugars 2g)
- Protein 36g
- Fat 15g (of which saturated fat 7g)
- Fibre 3g
- Vitamins A, B_1, B_6, B_{12}

The popular English combination of liver and bacon is given a new freshness with the addition of sage. Liver is very high in iron and zinc, as well as being a rich source of vitamin A, essential for healthy skin and resistance to infection.

Lamb's liver
with sage and bacon

Nutrients per serving
- Calories 250
- Carbohydrate 2g (of which sugars 1g)
- Protein 31g
- Fat 13g (of which saturated fat 4g)
- Fibre 0.5g
- Vitamins A, B₁, B₂, B₆, B₁₂, niacin

PREPARATION TIME: 30 MINUTES
COOKING TIME: 8 MINUTES
SERVES 4

300g (10½oz) sliced lamb's liver, cut into 3cm (1¼in) pieces
12 slices of lean back bacon, halved
24 cherry tomatoes
24 large sage leaves
1 tablespoon sunflower or olive oil

1 Wrap each piece of liver in half a bacon rasher. Thread a tomato onto a presoaked bamboo skewer. Thread 2 pieces of liver and bacon interspersed with 2 sage leaves onto the skewer. Add another tomato to the end and repeat with the remaining ingredients to make 12 skewers.

2 Heat a large griddle pan until hot. Brush lightly with oil and cook the skewers for 6-8 minutes, pressing them down well as they cook and turning them once. Serve at once with brown rice and a salad.

Note: Liver should be avoided by pregnant women, as its very high vitamin A content is dangerous for the unborn child.

PREPARATION TIME: 45 MINUTES
COOKING TIME: 1½ HOURS
SERVES 6

1.3kg (3lb) leg of lamb
4 tablespoons olive oil
Salt and black pepper
6 cloves garlic, peeled and cut into thin strips, plus 4 whole, unpeeled cloves
20 rosemary sprigs, tips only, plus 4 large sprigs
1.5 kg (3lb 5oz) potatoes, peeled and cubed

Traditionally, the sweet lamb of the south was served with mint which grew in the lush pastures, while Welsh and mountain lamb was served with the hardier herbs wild rosemary or thyme.

Roast leg of lamb
with garlic and rosemary

1 Heat the oven to 200°C (400°F, gas mark 6). Heat a heavy roasting tin over a high heat. Brush the lamb with 1 tablespoon of the oil, sprinkle with salt and pepper and place it in the tin. Cook over a medium heat, turning, until browned all over.

2 Remove the lamb to a board to cool for 2-3 minutes. With the tip of a small knife, pierce the lamb all over, then insert a strip of garlic and sprig of rosemary into each slit. Put the whole rosemary sprigs in the roasting tin and the lamb on top. Transfer to the oven.

3 Meanwhile, heat the remaining oil in a frying pan, add the potatoes and cook for 10 minutes until pale golden, turning constantly.

4 When the lamb has been cooking for 25 minutes, arrange the whole garlic cloves and the potatoes round the lamb and sprinkle with salt and pepper. Roast for a further 20 minutes for rare lamb, longer for medium.

5 Remove the lamb to a board, cover in foil and leave to rest in a warm place for at least 20 minutes.

Keep the potatoes warm, then transfer to a serving dish. Top with the lamb, then carve and serve with any juices from the pan, after skimming off the fat.

Nutrients per serving
- Calories 443
- Carbohydrate 43g (of which sugars 1.5g)
- Protein 29g
- Fat 18g (of which saturated fat 6g)
- Fibre 3g
- Vitamins C, B_1, B_6, B_{12}, niacin

It was once quite common to keep a pig in the yard – to be fed on scraps

Ham, bacon and sausages

Like many countries, Britain has always made the most of its pigs, using every part to produce a wide range of often highly distinctive meat products, some of which are justly famous throughout the world for their quality and taste. In earlier times, most households kept a pig in the back yard, fattening it on scraps and waste during spring and summer. In autumn, it would be killed and the meat preserved to provide a ready supply for the long winter.

A variety of hams

Ham refers specifically to the detached, cured hind leg of the pig. Gammon is also leg meat, but is cured while the leg is still attached to the side of the pig and consequently has a milder flavour. In both cases the fresh meat is salted first. For dry-salting, used only in ham production, salt is rubbed several times over the surface of the joint so that it eventually penetrates the meat. Ham or gammon can also be brined, either by soaking in a brine bath or injecting the meat with the salty liquid. The meat is then dried, smoked, or both.

Different varieties of ham are produced by varying the curing and smoking times, and also the ingredients of the salt rub or brine, which contain spices and sweeteners. Traditional British ham should be quite dry; moist flesh indicates an excess of water, for which the shopper is being unfairly charged.

The best of British

Hams still have strong associations with the places that produce them. One of the best regional hams is the sweet, delicately flavoured Bradenham, which has been made in Wiltshire since 1781. It is unsmoked,

all spring and summer, then killed in autumn.

and has an impressive black rind due to the use of molasses in the cure, which is also flavoured with juniper, coriander and other spices.

York ham is internationally famous and the style is so popular that it is now produced in other countries. Although dry-salted, it is mild in flavour and of varying degrees of smokiness. Wiltshire ham is uniquely cured like gammon, with the leg attached to the carcass. Suffolk ham, which is cured in a mixture that includes beer or stout, has a sweet flavour, while Alderton ham, a relatively new variety from Nottinghamshire, is dry-roasted to give an intense flavour, then coated with marmalade.

Bacon and sausages

Britain's favourite bacon is the mild, deep rose-pink Wiltshire cure. Ayrshire bacon is similar, but the meat is cut from the bone and the rind removed before the curing process is begun.

Unlike many Continental sausages, such as salami, the British sausage, or banger, is fresh, rather than cured, and needs to be cooked before serving. Another feature that distinguishes it from sausages produced in other countries is its high cereal content, which was once included as bulk for economic reasons, but is now a confirmed national preference.

Distinctive British sausages include the popular pepper and mace-flavoured Cumberland, a coarse-cut sausage traditionally sold in a large coil, but often also available in links. Lincolnshire sausage is flavoured with sage and thyme, Cambridge with sage, cayenne and nutmeg, and Wiltshire with ginger. Oxford sausages are traditionally made with a mixture of pork and veal.

In Scotland beef sausages, notably the square Lorne variety, are traditionally preferred. Elsewhere producers now use a range of meat, such as lamb, venison, boar and chicken.

Mr. Bones the Butcher.

Mr. Bones the Butcher.

Irish stew

Nutrients per serving
- Calories 750
- Carbohydrate 50g (of which sugars 12g)
- Protein 47g
- Fat 42g (of which saturated fat 20g)
- Fibre 5g
- Vitamins A, B₁, B₆, B₁₂, C, niacin

PREPARATION TIME: 30 MINUTES
COOKING TIME: 1 HOUR 50 MINUTES
SERVES 4

450g (1lb) lamb loin chops, about 2.5cm (1in) thick, fat removed
450g (1lb) neck fillet of lamb
Salt and white pepper
12 baby carrots, with green tops, scrubbed
12 baby onions, peeled
800g (1lb 12oz) potatoes, peeled and thickly sliced
900ml (1 pint 12fl oz) beef stock (see page 148)
4 sprigs of thyme
2 tablespoons pearl barley
1 small bunch of parsley, chopped

1 Heat the oven to 160°C (325°F, gas mark 3). Heat a nonstick frying pan until hot. Sprinkle the lamb with salt and pepper, then add it to the pan and brown lightly all over.

2 Place the lamb, carrots and onions in separate layers in a casserole dish, sprinkling each layer lightly with salt and pepper. Put the potatoes on top, then pour over the stock and add the thyme and barley. Bring to the boil, then cover and transfer to the oven for about 1 hour. Uncover and cook for 30 minutes until the meat is tender.

3 Take out of the oven and let cool a little. Remove the potato layer and reserve. Remove and reserve the onions and carrots, separately. Take the lamb off the bone and cut into even-sized pieces, discarding the bones. Skim the fat from the liquid, using a large spoon. Transfer to a saucepan and boil, skimming off further fat from the surface. Add salt and pepper to taste.

4 Clean the casserole and put the lamb, onions and carrots back into it. Pour over the gravy, to just cover the meat. Arrange the potato over the top. When ready to serve, reheat over a medium heat until piping hot. Top with the parsley and serve.

Part of a long **culinary tradition,** Irish stew was originally made with male kid or mutton and **cooked slowly** for hours over an open **peat fire.**

162

Boiled leg of lamb
in caper sauce

PREPARATION TIME: 25 MINUTES
COOKING TIME: 2¼ HOURS
SERVES 6-8

1.75 kg (3lb 13oz) leg of lamb, chump
   bone removed
1 large onion, quartered
3 carrots, quartered lengthways
3 large cloves garlic
2 small leeks, sliced
1 bouquet garni, made from 5 parsley stalks,
   6 bay leaves and 6 sprigs each of rosemary
   and thyme, tied together
Salt and white pepper

For the caper sauce:
60g (2¼oz) butter
3 tablespoons flour
4-5 tablespoons capers, rinsed and drained
1 heaped tablespoon chopped parsley

Boiling was once the best way to cook a large leg of mutton, as the gentle simmering tenderises tough meat and releases the fat. It still works deliciously well for today's healthily lean lamb.

1 Put the lamb in a large saucepan with the onion, carrots, garlic, leeks, bouquet garni and some salt and pepper. Cover completely with warm water and bring to the boil. Skim well, then reduce the heat to a low simmer. Cook for 2 hours, until tender, topping up with hot water from the kettle as necessary, but making sure it does not boil.

2 After 1½ hours simmering, remove 900ml (1 pint 12fl oz) cooking liquid and reserve for the sauce. Replace the liquid with the same volume of water from the kettle.

3 To make the caper sauce, melt the butter in a saucepan. Stir in the flour and cook for 1 minute. Add a little of the hot reserved stock. Stir well, then add the rest of the stock, whisking, until thick and creamy. Remove from the heat and whisk from time to time, to prevent a skin forming. Add the capers, with pepper to taste.

4 Remove the lamb from the poaching stock and drain on a cloth. Thin the sauce with a little more stock if necessary, then add the parsley. Serve the lamb with the caper sauce, new potatoes and mangetout peas.

Nutrients per serving, when serving 8
- Calories 361
- Carbohydrate 9g (of which sugars 4g)
- Protein 35g
- Fat 21g (of which saturated fat 11g)
- Fibre 2g
- Vitamins A, B_1, B_2, B_6, B_{12}, niacin

LANCASHIRE HOTPOT

Lancashire hotpot

PREPARATION TIME: 15 MINUTES
COOKING TIME: 2½ HOURS
SERVES 4

8 lamb cutlets, best of neck end
    if possible, trimmed of fat
450g (1lb) onions, sliced
450g (1lb) carrots, peeled and sliced
Salt and black pepper
4 tablespoons chopped fresh parsley
1 tablespoon fresh thyme leaves
900g (2lb) potatoes, peeled and
    thinly sliced
425ml (¾ pint) chicken stock
    (see page 120)
2 tablespoons olive oil

1 Heat the oven to 180°C (350°F, gas mark 4). Layer the lamb cutlets, onions and carrots in a large casserole, sprinkling each layer with salt, pepper, parsley and thyme. Arrange the potatoes in an overlapping layer on top.

2 Pour over the chicken stock. Cover and cook in the oven for 2 hours, then increase the oven temperature to 230°C (450°F, gas mark 8).

3 Remove the lid, drizzle the olive oil over the potatoes and continue cooking, uncovered, for a further 30 minutes or until the potatoes are golden.

4 Serve at once with spring cabbage or curly kale.

Nutrients per serving
- Calories 586
- Carbohydrate 56g (of which sugars 16g)
- Protein 43g
- Fat 22g (of which saturated fat 8g)
- Fibre 7g
- Vitamins A, B_1, B_2, B_6, B_{12}, C, niacin

In mining areas of Britain, cheap coal made hotpots popular, as affordable cuts often required long cooking in the fire oven. With lean meat and vegetables, the modern hotpot is a very nutritious family dish.

Pork hotpot with ale and juniper

PREPARATION TIME: 20 MINUTES
COOKING TIME: 1¾ HOURS
SERVES 4

1 tablespoon olive oil
15g (½oz) butter
900g (2lb) lean pork leg or shoulder, cut
    into 4cm (1½in) cubes, fat removed
300g (10½oz) shallots, peeled and halved
250g (9oz) parsnips, diced
1 tablespoon juniper berries, crushed
Salt and black pepper
250ml (9fl oz) brown ale
85ml (3fl oz) chicken stock
    (see page 120)
1 tablespoon tomato purée
1 tablespoon grated fresh horseradish
1 tablespoon redcurrant jelly
900g (2lb) potatoes, peeled and
    thinly sliced

1 Heat the oven to 180°C (350°F, gas mark 4). Heat half the oil and butter in a wide pan and cook the pork quickly to brown it all over. Remove from the pan. Add the shallots and parsnips with the remaining oil and butter and cook for 2-3 minutes to brown lightly.

2 Layer the pork, shallots, parsnips and juniper berries in a large casserole, sprinkling salt and pepper between the layers. Mix together the brown ale, stock, tomato purée, horseradish and redcurrant jelly, then pour into the casserole.

3 Arrange the potatoes in an overlapping layer over the casserole. Sprinkle with salt and pepper,

cover and cook in the oven for about 1 hour, then remove the lid and cook for a further 30 minutes to brown the top. Serve at once with red cabbage (see page 183).

Nutrients per serving
- Calories 652
- Carbohydrate 57g (of which sugars 13g)
- Protein 54g
- Fat 23g (of which saturated fat 8g)
- Fibre 7g
- Vitamins B_1, B_6, B_{12}, C, niacin, B_2

165

Braised gammon olives

PREPARATION TIME: 40 MINUTES
COOKING TIME: 1 HOUR
10 MINUTES
SERVES 4

8 small carrots, about 500g (1lb 2oz)
    total weight
2 Cox's apples, peeled, cored and finely
    chopped
60g (2¼oz) fresh wholemeal
    breadcrumbs
Grated zest of 1 unwaxed lemon
1 teaspoon wholegrain mustard
2 tablespoons snipped fresh chives
Salt and black pepper
2 gammon steaks, about 325g (11½oz)
    each, rind removed
1 tablespoon sunflower oil
350g (12oz) small, whole onions, peeled
2 bay leaves
300ml (½ pint) red wine
Coarsely grated zest and juice of
    1 orange
4 tablespoons redcurrant jelly

Nutrients per serving
- Calories 475
- Carbohydrate 37g
  (of which sugars 28g)
- Protein 36g
- Fat 16g (of which saturated fat 5g)
- Fibre 6g
- Vitamins A, B₁, B₆, niacin

Olives, or little meat rolls, *usually beef or veal, with a* savoury stuffing, *appeared in British cooking in the Middle Ages. This gammon version uses* lean meat *and* wholemeal *breadcrumbs.*

1 Put the carrots in a large saucepan and pour in just enough boiling water to cover. Bring to the boil, reduce the heat and cover. Cook for 15 minutes. Drain, reserving 600ml (1 pint) of the cooking liquid.

2 Meanwhile, put the apples, breadcrumbs, lemon zest, mustard and chives in a bowl. Add salt and pepper to taste and mix. Divide into four, press each portion into a sausage shape and set aside.

3 Lay the gammon steaks between large pieces of cling film and beat with a rolling pin until thin. Peel back the cling film and cut each steak in half. Place a portion of stuffing on each half. Roll the meat around the stuffing to make four packages, tucking the stuffing in at either end. Tie string around the middle to secure.

4 Heat the oil in a large, nonstick frying pan, add the gammon and cook, turning, until brown all over. Transfer to a plate. Add the onions and bay leaves to the pan and cook until golden, then transfer them to a flameproof casserole.

5 Add the reserved cooking liquid to the frying pan and bring to the boil, stirring. Pour into the casserole.

Add the carrots to the casserole and arrange the gammon olives on top. Sprinkle with salt and pepper, then add the wine, orange zest and juice.

6 Bring to the boil, then reduce the heat, cover and simmer for 40 minutes, turning the gammon olives once during cooking.

7 Transfer the meat and vegetables to a warmed dish, cover and keep warm. Boil the cooking liquid rapidly for about 10 minutes, until well reduced. Whisk in the redcurrant jelly and continue boiling, whisking, until the jelly has melted. Adjust the seasoning, then strain into a warmed serving jug.

8 To serve, remove the string from the olives and transfer them to plates, then slice them and separate the slices slightly. Add the vegetables and pour over the sauce. Serve with mashed potatoes.

Toad-in-the-hole with onion gravy

PREPARATION TIME: 10 MINUTES
COOKING TIME: 40-45 MINUTES
SERVES 4

200g (7oz) plain flour
2 eggs
500ml (18fl oz) mixture of milk and water
1 tablespoon Worcestershire sauce
Salt and black pepper
Sunflower oil for brushing
12 homemade sausages (see page 174),
   or venison sausages

For the onion gravy:
25g (1oz) butter
1 onion, thinly sliced
1 tablespoon plain flour
250ml (9fl oz) beef stock (see page 148)
1 teaspoon grainy mustard

1 Heat the oven to 220°C (425°F, gas mark 7). Put the flour, eggs, milk and water, Worcestershire sauce and some salt and pepper in a bowl and whisk to a smooth batter.

2 Brush a roasting tin lightly with oil, then arrange the sausages in it. Bake for 10 minutes until beginning to brown. Pour the batter into the roasting tin and bake for a further 30-35 minutes, until risen and golden.

3 Meanwhile, to make the onion gravy, heat the butter, add the onion and cook gently for 10-15 minutes until soft and golden. Stir in the flour and cook for about 2 minutes, stirring.

4 Add the stock and stir until boiling. Simmer for 5 minutes, then add the mustard with salt and pepper to taste. Serve with the toad in the hole and seasonal vegetables.

In this family favourite, light batter and low-fat sausages boost the protein and reduce the fat.

Nutrients per serving
- Calories 700
- Carbohydrate 60g (of which sugars 9g)
- Protein 43g
- Fat 33g (of which saturated fat 15g)
- Fibre 2g
- Vitamins A, B_1, B_2, B_6, B_{12}, niacin

Faggots in rich wine gravy

Nutrients per serving

- Calories 444
- Carbohydrate 27g (of which sugars 9g)
- Protein 37g
- Fat 17g (of which saturated fat 5g)
- Fibre 3.5g
- Vitamins A, B$_1$, B$_2$, B$_6$, B$_{12}$, niacin

PREPARATION TIME: 40 MINUTES
COOKING TIME: ABOUT 1 HOUR
SERVES 4

1 tablespoon sunflower oil
115g (4oz) pig's kidney, trimmed and cut into chunks
150g (5½oz) pig's liver, trimmed and cut into chunks
2 large onions, chopped
350g (12oz) lean minced pork
1 tablespoon ground coriander
1 teaspoon ground mace
1 teaspoon ground ginger
¼ teaspoon ground nutmeg
1 teaspoon dried sage
½ teaspoon dried thyme
100g (3½oz) rolled oats
Salt and black pepper
1 egg
2 carrots, diced
2 bay leaves
250ml (9fl oz) red wine
400ml (14fl oz) chicken stock (see page 120)

1 Heat half the oil in a large, nonstick frying pan. Add the kidney, liver and a third of the chopped onion. Cook over a high heat, stirring, for 2-3 minutes until browned. Remove from the heat and let cool briefly, then finely chop or reduce to a coarse purée in a food processor. Transfer to a large bowl.

2 Mix in the minced pork, spices and herbs. Add the oats with salt and pepper to taste and mix. Add the egg and mix again.

3 Scoop up egg-sized portions of mixture and shape into 16-18 balls. Heat the remaining oil in the pan. Add the faggots, in batches, and cook for about 5 minutes over a high heat, turning, until browned all over. Transfer to a large flameproof casserole.

4 Add the remaining onion, carrots and bay leaves to the pan and cook, stirring, for 2 minutes. Pour in the wine and bring to the boil. Pour the onion and wine mixture over the faggots. Add the stock, salt and pepper and bring to a simmer. Cover and cook for 45 minutes.

5 Transfer the faggots to a warmed dish, cover and keep warm. Boil the cooking liquid rapidly for about 5 minutes, until reduced slightly. Taste, discard the bay leaves and adjust salt and pepper. Serve the faggots and sauce with mushy peas (see page 108) and mashed potatoes.

This modern version of the humble faggot, known as savoury duck in Yorkshire and Lancashire, is full of protein and iron, while being low in fat. The rolled oats add extra fibre.

Stuffed pork tenderloin with apple sauce

PREPARATION TIME: 30 MINUTES
COOKING TIME: 45 MINUTES
SERVES 6

2 fillets of pork, about 350g (12oz) each
150g (5½oz) spinach leaves, washed
Salt and black pepper
85g (3oz) curd cheese
1 teaspoon freshly grated nutmeg
Sunflower or olive oil for brushing

For the apple sauce:
2 large Bramley apples, peeled, cored
    and roughly diced
20g (¾oz) butter
1 tablespoon sugar
1 tablespoon water

The low-fat stuffing, with iron-rich spinach, keeps the pork tender and moist as it cooks.

1 Put all the ingredients for the apple sauce in a small saucepan and cook, covered, over a gentle heat, for about 15 minutes until soft. Mash gently and set aside.

2 Meanwhile heat the oven to 190°C (375°F, gas mark 5). Trim the ends off the pork fillet and remove all visible fat. Put the spinach in a colander and run a kettle of boiling water slowly through the leaves. When cool enough to handle, squeeze dry in a tea towel.

3 Cut the fillets almost in half lengthways and open them out. Sprinkle lightly with salt and pepper. Spread the curd cheese down one side of each, and place the spinach down the other. Sprinkle with nutmeg, then fold the fillets back together and tie with string to secure. Sprinkle lightly with salt and pepper.

4 Heat an ovenproof frying pan and brush lightly with oil. Brown the fillets lightly all over, then transfer to the hot oven and cook for 15 minutes. Remove and leave to stand for at least 5 minutes in a warm place. Remove the string and slice. Serve with the apple sauce, reheated, and baked potatoes.

Nutrients per serving
- Calories 300
- Carbohydrate 7g (of which sugars 7g)
- Protein 25g
- Fat 18g (of which saturated fat 9g)
- Fibre 1g
- Vitamins A, B₁, B₆, B₁₂, niacin

Gammon in cider

PREPARATION TIME: 30 MINUTES
COOKING TIME: 1 HOUR 40 MINUTES
SERVES 6-8

Large joint of gammon, about
　　1.5kg (3lb 5oz)
4-6 cloves
2 bay leaves
1 litre (1¾ pints) medium-sweet cider
2 teaspoons Dijon mustard
4 tablespoons demerara sugar

**Nutrients per serving,
when serving 8**
- Calories 274
- Carbohydrate 10g (of which sugars 10g)
- Protein 30g
- Fat 11g (of which saturated fat 4g)
- Fibre 0g
- Vitamins B_1, B_6

1 Heat the oven to 180°C (350°F, gas mark 4). Put the gammon in a large saucepan and cover with cold water. Bring slowly to the boil, then drain and rinse.

2 Line a roasting tin with a double piece of foil, large enough to fit round the gammon. Add the gammon, skin side up, and stud the skin with cloves. Top with the bay leaves and pour in the cider. Bring the edges of the foil together to make a parcel.

3 Bring to a simmer over a medium heat, then transfer to the oven. Cook for 30 minutes per 500g (1lb 2oz). About 20 minutes before the end of the cooking time, remove from the oven and increase the temperature to 200°C (400°F, gas mark 6).

4 Open the foil carefully – the steam will be very hot. Remove the joint to a board, discarding the bay leaves, cloves and foil. Pour the cooking juices into a saucepan and set aside.

5 When the gammon has cooled a little, remove the rind and cut away all but a thin covering of the fat. Score the surface in a criss-cross fashion with a sharp knife. Mix the mustard and sugar with a little of the cooking liquid. Put the gammon back into the roasting tin and brush the mustard glaze over the top.

6 Return the gammon to the oven to brown. Meanwhile, skim the fat from the cooking juices. When the gammon is browned, carve into thin slices and spoon some cooking liquid over each serving. Serve with carrots, peas and new potatoes.

In many cider orchards, pigs are fed on windfalls, which gives their meat a sweet flavour. The salt in cured ham, once an important way for preserving meat, is here reduced by boiling the gammon in liquid.

Baked pork chops with herbs

Nutrients per serving

- Calories 200
- Carbohydrate 0g
- Protein 26g
- Fat 11g (of which saturated fat 3g)
- Fibre 0g
- Vitamins B_1, B_6, B_{12}, niacin

PREPARATION TIME: 10 MINUTES, PLUS 2-3 HOURS MARINATING
COOKING TIME: 55 MINUTES
SERVES 4

1 small bunch of thyme
1 small bunch of rosemary
1 small bunch of oregano
4 fresh or 2 dried bay leaves
4 thick pork chops, from the rib, fat removed
2 cloves garlic, peeled and halved
Salt and black pepper
Olive oil

Once a staple dish of the poor, this recipe was taken to the New World and created the forerunner of Boston Baked Beans. Iron-rich Guinness and high-fibre beans are ideal for slow cooking with succulent pork.

Pork is one of the leanest meats, and removing the fat from a chop leaves a healthy, low-fat cut, high in both vitamins B and zinc. A herb rub adds flavour to this simple dish.

1 Arrange the herbs in a shallow ovenproof dish. Using a small, sharp knife, score the chops lightly on each side. Rub them with the garlic, then sprinkle salt, pepper and oil on both sides. Place on top of the herbs and chill for 2-3 hours.

2 Heat the oven to 110°C (225°F, gas mark ¼). Place the chops, in their dish, under a hot grill, turning until lightly browned on both sides. Transfer the dish to the oven and cook for 45 minutes or until cooked through. Serve at once, with a tomato and onion salad or boiled leeks.

VARIATION
Use spare rib chops in place of the chops.

Pork and white beans in Guinness

PREPARATION TIME: 10 MINUTES,
PLUS OVERNIGHT SOAKING
COOKING TIME: 4½-5 HOURS
SERVES 6-8

300g (10½ oz) dried white haricot beans
2 tablespoons olive oil
400g (14oz) lean pork chops, fat removed,
    cut into 3cm (1¼ in) cubes
175g (6oz) smoked back bacon, cut into
    small cubes
3 sprigs of rosemary
450ml (16fl oz) Guinness
330ml (10½ fl oz) chicken stock (see page 120)
400g (14oz) canned chopped tomatoes
2 teaspoons soft brown sugar
Salt and black pepper

1 Soak the beans overnight in plenty of cold water, changing the water at least once. Heat half the oil in a large, deep casserole. Add the pork and cook, stirring, until lightly browned all over. Remove to a plate.

2 Heat the oven to 120°C (250°F, gas mark ½). Heat the remaining oil in the casserole, then add the bacon and rosemary. Stir well, then mix in the drained beans and browned pork, with the Guinness, stock, tomatoes and sugar. Bring to the boil, then remove from the heat.

3 Cover and cook in the oven for 4½-5 hours, or until the beans are tender. Add salt and pepper to taste, just before serving with green beans and crusty bread.

Nutrients per serving, when serving 8
- Calories 245
- Carbohydrate 22g
  (of which sugars 9g)
- Protein 23g
- Fat 6g (of which
  saturated fat 2g)
- Fibre 7g
- Vitamins B$_6$, B$_{12}$, niacin

Oxford sausages

Different regions of Britain produce distinct types of sausage, using varying **herbs** and **spices**, but making your own is a good way to keep the fat content low.

Cold pork with pickles

PREPARATION TIME: 15 MINUTES, PLUS 5 HOURS MARINATING, COOLING AND CHILLING
COOKING TIME: 2¼ HOURS
SERVES 6

Nutrients per serving
- Calories 327
- Carbohydrate 1g (of which sugars 1g)
- Protein 42g
- Fat 14g (of which saturated fat 5g)
- Fibre 1g
- Vitamins B₆, B₁₂, niacin

1.75kg (3lb 13oz) rib or loin of pork, 20cm (8in) long, boned and rolled
14 juniper berries
2 tablespoons coarse sea salt
1 tablespoon whole black peppercorns
5 white peppercorns
3 cloves garlic, cut into slivers
2 fennel bulbs, roughly chopped
1 pig's trotter, split lengthways (optional)
12 bay leaves
4 slices of lemon
175ml (6fl oz) white wine
400ml (14fl oz) chicken stock (see page 120)
2 tablespoons Madeira wine or Amontillado sherry (optional)
Piccalilli (see page 278) to serve

1 Ask the butcher to bone the pork, remove the rind and all but the smallest covering of fat, and to supply all the bones and trimmings.

2 Crush the juniper berries, salt, peppercorns and garlic with a pestle and mortar, then rub the mixture all over the lean side of the pork. Spread the fennel over the bottom of a heavy casserole, just big enough to take the pork, and place the pork, fat side down, on top. Add the bones, trotter, if using, bay leaves and lemon. Chill for 2 hours, or overnight.

PREPARATION TIME: 25 MINUTES,
PLUS CHILLING OVERNIGHT
COOKING TIME: 12-15 MINUTES
SERVES 4

250g (9oz) pork shoulder, diced
250g (9oz) lean boneless veal, diced
75g (2¾ oz) fresh white breadcrumbs
85g (3oz) light vegetable suet
Finely grated zest of ½ unwaxed lemon
1 tablespoon chopped parsley
1 teaspoon chopped sage
1 teaspoon chopped rosemary
1 teaspoon chopped thyme
½ teaspoon grated nutmeg
¼ teaspoon ground white pepper
½ teaspoon salt
1 small egg, beaten
Sausage casing or plain flour for coating

1 Finely chop the pork and veal in a food processor or by hand. Add the remaining ingredients, except the casings, and process or stir to mix.

2 If using sausage casings, soak them in cold water for a few minutes. Spoon the meat mixture into a piping bag fitted with a large, plain piping nozzle. Gently push a casing onto the end of the nozzle, gathering it up as much as possible.

3 Pipe the mixture gently to fill the casing, taking care not to split it, twisting the casing at intervals to make 12 sausages. Alternatively, shape the mixture into 12 sausages with floured hands.

4 Cover and chill for several hours or preferably overnight before using, to allow the flavour to mature,

then grill or fry for 15-20 minutes, turning occasionally, until golden brown and cooked through.

VARIATION
For turkey sausages, use 450g (1lb) diced boneless turkey breast and 100g (3½ oz) diced back bacon instead of the pork and veal. Add 1 small chopped onion and omit the lemon zest and herbs. Add pepper, salt and egg as in main recipe. Shape and cook as directed.

Nutrients per serving
- Calories 330
- Carbohydrate 11g (of which sugars 0g)
- Protein 30g
- Fat 19g (of which saturated fat 9g)
- Fibre 0g
- Vitamins B_1, B_{12}, B_6, niacin

3 Heat the oven to 140°C (275°F, gas mark 1). Pour the white wine and stock into the casserole, to come halfway up the meat. Cover with a disc of parchment or greaseproof paper, then the lid. Bring to a simmer, then transfer to the lowest shelf of the oven.

4 Cook for about 2 hours, until the meat is tender but still juicy. Remove to a dish and leave to cool.

5 Strain the stock into a bowl, discarding the rind and trotter. Add the Madeira or sherry, if using, and chill

to set. When set, remove the fat from the surface and cut the jelly into cubes. Slice the pork thinly and arrange on a long serving plate, with the jelly round it. Serve with pickles and warm new potatoes in vinaigrette.

This grand picnic speciality is based on the traditional dish of galantine, cold meat – often poultry or game – served with its jelly. Homemade pickles add an excellent flavour.

Collops of pork fillet with Stilton sauce

PREPARATION TIME: 30 MINUTES
COOKING TIME: 30 MINUTES
SERVES 4-6

2 pork fillets, about 350g (12oz) each, trimmed
    of fat and the silver skin
Salt and white pepper
3 tablespoons olive or sunflower oil
2 cloves garlic, halved
2 sprigs of rosemary
1 large carrot, peeled and cut into strips
4 celery sticks, cut into strips
200g (7oz) green beans, cut into strips

For the Stilton sauce:
20g (¾oz) butter
1 small shallot, finely chopped
50ml (2fl oz) dry white wine
50ml (2fl oz) dry cider
150ml (¼ pint) chicken stock (see page 120)
75ml (2½fl oz) double cream
2 teaspoons cornflour, mixed with
    4 tablespoons cold water
60g (2¼oz) Stilton cheese, rind removed,
    crumbled

In the past, collops were very fine slices of bacon or pork, but now can be slices of any meat. In the North of England, they would be served on 'Collop Monday', two days before Ash Wednesday and the start of Lent.

1 Cut each pork fillet into 5 or 6 slices, about 70g (2½oz) each. Place the slices on a board, then press firmly on each with the heel of your hand, to flatten. Sprinkle with salt and pepper.

2 Heat the oil, garlic and rosemary in a frying pan over a medium heat. Add the pork, in batches, and cook for 4 minutes on each side, until lightly browned. Remove from the pan and keep warm. Discard the oil.

3 Meanwhile, cook the carrot, celery and beans in boiling, salted water for 1-2 minutes. Drain and set aside.

4 To make the sauce, heat the butter in a small saucepan and add the shallot. Cook for 5 minutes until soft. Add the wine and cider and simmer until reduced by about half. Add the stock and simmer until reduced by half again. Strain through a fine sieve, return to the cleaned saucepan, then add the cream.

5 Bring to the boil, then add the cornflour mixture, a little at a time, until thick. Reduce the heat to very low, then add the Stilton, with pepper to taste.

6 Arrange the sauce on a serving plate, with the vegetables and collops of pork on top. Serve at once.

Nutrients per serving, when serving 6
- Calories 300
- Carbohydrate 7g (of which sugars 4g)
- Protein 16g
- Fat 22g (of which saturated fat 10g)
- Fibre 2g
- Vitamins A, B_1, B_6, B_{12}

Vegetable dishes

Vegetables
the healthy way

Delicious, nutritious and highly versatile, vegetables are an important part of any healthy diet, the fresher the better.

One of the best and simplest routes to good health is to eat plenty of fruit and vegetables. Nutrition experts generally recommend eating five portions (at least 400g/14oz) of fruit or vegetables daily. Eating a wide range of produce is important, too, and in Britain we are particularly fortunate as fresh vegetables are available throughout the year.

Promoting good health

Vegetables offer a variety of nutrients:
• Fibre, which helps the digestive system to work effectively.
• Vitamin C, which boosts immunity and promotes healing, and other antioxidant vitamins and minerals, which help protect against cancer and cardiovascular disease.
• B vitamins, especially folate, which helps prevent birth defects in unborn babies.
• Phytochemicals – compounds that occur naturally in plants and protect them against bacteria, viruses and fungi. It is increasingly believed that these help to protect our bodies against different types of cancer, heart disease and certain chronic degenerative disorders, such as cataracts and arthritis.

• Vitamins C, E and beta-carotene, which help to prevent free radicals from initiating or accelerating cancer, heart disease, cataracts, arthritis, general ageing, sun damage and sperm damage.

Packaged produce

Many people assume that fresh is best, but frozen and canned vegetables have much to offer. Frozen vegetables are processed within hours of harvesting, which preserves their vitamin content. In fact, they often contain more vitamins than 'fresh' vegetables, which can be a few days old at the point of purchase.

Losing goodness

The vitamins in vegetables are easily lost during storage, preparation and cooking, so to maximise your vitamin content

Preparation tips

Vegetables cut into thin 'ribbons', using a potato peeler, cook very quickly, helping to conserve their nutrients. It takes just 3 minutes to steam carrots cut this way.

Peeling shallots can be difficult, but if they are soaked for a few minutes first in hot water, the skin should glide off easily.

Minimising vitamin loss

• Buy small amounts of fruit and vegetables frequently and store in a cool, dark place for no more than three days.
• Never leave vegetables in water before cooking.
• Do not add bicarbonate of soda to the water when cooking vegetables.
• Choose cooking methods, such as steaming, stir-frying or grilling, which require little or no water and keep the nutrients intact.
• When boiling vegetables, keep the amount of water to a minimum. Wait until the water is boiling before adding the vegetables and save the water to make gravy, sauce, soup or stock, or simply to drink.
• Eat food as soon as you can after it is prepared. Keeping food warm results in vitamins being lost.

Steaming asparagus

Steaming asparagus standing upright prevents the fine tender tips from overcooking. If you do not have a steamer, crumple foil and put it around the base of the asparagus so that it stands upright in the pan. Then cover the tips with a 'hood' of tightly sealed foil.

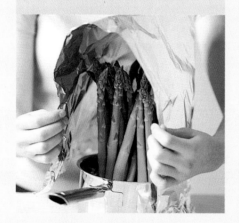

always buy the freshest produce you can, store it in the refrigerator and eat it as soon as possible. Once cut, oxidation accelerates the loss of vitamin C, so it is important to prepare vegetables as close to cooking and eating as possible.

When buying British vegetables, it is best to buy locally grown produce. It will taste better and, because it has not travelled so far, will be fresher and contain more vitamins.

Homemade stock

As well as eating vegetables as part of a meal, you can also use them in stock for soups and meat dishes. Stock is simple to make and will contain more nutrients and less salt and additives than processed stock cubes. Homemade stock will keep for up to five days in the refrigerator or up to one month in the freezer.

SEASONAL BRITISH VEGETABLES		
Vegetable	Months available (inclusive)	Nutritional information*
Asparagus	May-June	vitamins A, B$_1$, C
Beetroot	available all year	phytochemicals
Broad beans	June-Aug	vitamin C, fibre, niacin
Broccoli	Feb-Oct	vitamins A, B$_6$, C, phytochemicals
Brussels sprouts	Jan	vitamin C
Cabbage	Jan-Feb	vitamin C, phytochemicals
Carrot	Jan-Mar, July-Aug	vitamins A, B$_6$, fibre, phytochemicals
Cauliflower	Aug	vitamins B$_6$, C, phytochemicals
Celeriac	Jan-Apr	vitamin B$_6$, fibre
Celery	Aug	vitamin C
Chicory	Aug	–
Courgettes	July-Aug	vitamins A, B$_1$, B$_6$, C
Fennel	Aug-Sept	–
French beans	July-Sept	vitamin C, fibre
Jerusalem artichokes	Mar-May	vitamin B$_1$, fibre
Kale	Jan-Apr	vitamins A, C, calcium, fibre
Leeks	Jan-Feb	vitamins A, C
Lettuce	May-Sept	–
Mangetout peas	June-Sept	vitamins A, B$_1$, B$_6$, C, fibre
Marrow	Aug, Sept	–
Onions	July-Sept	phytochemicals
Parsnip	Jan-Mar	vitamin C, fibre
Peas	June-Aug	vitamins B$_1$, C, fibre,
Peppers	May-Oct	vitamin C, betacarotene, phytochemicals
Potatoes	June-Oct	vitamin B$_1$, B$_6$, C, fibre
Pumpkin	May-Sept	vitamins A, B$_1$, C
Radishes	May-Sept	vitamins B$_1$, B$_2$, C
Rocket	Feb-Mar, May-Sept	phytochemicals
Runner beans	July-Sept	vitamin C
Spinach	Jan-Feb, May-Sept	vitamins A, B$_6$, C, calcium, phytochemicals
Swede	Jan	vitamins B$_1$, C, phytochemicals
Sweetcorn	July-Sept	vitamin B$_6$, fibre
Tomatoes	June-Sept	vitamins A, B$_6$, C, phytochemicals
Turnip	Jan-Mar	vitamin C
Watercress		vitamins B$_6$, C, iron, phytochemicals

No nutrients given if one portion supplies less than 15% recommended daily allowance (RDA).

A tasty homemade vegetable stock is **useful** to have to hand, as it forms a very **healthy basis** for many vegetable and soup recipes.

Vegetable stock

PREPARATION TIME: 15 MINUTES
COOKING TIME: ABOUT 1 HOUR
MAKES ABOUT 1.7 LITRES (3 PINTS)

1 tablespoon sunflower oil
225g (8oz) leeks, chopped
1 large onion, chopped
1 large bay leaf
2-3 sprigs of fresh thyme
2-3 sprigs of parsley, stalks bruised
225g (8oz) carrots, diced
3 large celery sticks with any leaves, diced
1 teaspoon salt
5 black peppercorns

1 Heat the oil in a large, heavy-based saucepan or stockpot. Add the leeks and onion, stir well and reduce the heat to low. Cover with a tight-fitting lid and leave the vegetables to sweat for about 20 minutes, shaking the pan from time to time but without lifting the lid.

2 Add the bay leaf, thyme, parsley, carrots, celery and salt. Pour in 2 litres (3½ pints) cold water and increase the heat to medium. Bring slowly to the boil, skimming the surface of the liquid to remove any scum.

3 As soon as the water boils and all the scum has been removed, add the peppercorns and reduce the heat to low. Cover and leave to simmer for 35 minutes.

4 Strain the stock into a large, heatproof bowl and set aside to cool. Chill until needed. Alternatively, let it cool, then transfer to freezer containers, filling them three-quarters full to allow room for expansion. Cover with a lid and freeze for up to 6 months.

Glazed carrots with cider

PREPARATION TIME: 10 MINUTES
COOKING TIME: 10 MINUTES
SERVES 4

1 tablespoon olive oil
450g (1lb) carrots, trimmed, peeled or scraped, and cut into 2cm (¾in) matchsticks
1 tablespoon brown sugar
125ml (4fl oz) dry cider
1 teaspoon wholegrain mustard
Freshly chopped parsley to serve

1 Heat the oil in a frying pan, add the carrots and sauté for 3-4 minutes, stirring constantly. Sprinkle the sugar over and cook, stirring, for a further minute until the sugar has dissolved.

2 Add the cider and mustard. Bring to the boil, then half cover and simmer over a low heat for 3-5 minutes until just tender. Remove the lid, increase the heat and boil vigorously for about 1 minute to reduce the liquid. Serve sprinkled with fresh parsley.

Nutrients per serving
- Calories 92
- Carbohydrate 14g (of which sugars 13g)
- Protein 1g
- Fat 3g (of which saturated fat 0.5g)
- Fibre 3g
- Vitamins A

Carrots are an excellent source of beta carotene, a powerful antioxidant which can protect against disease. Instead of using butter for the glaze, this recipe uses healthier olive oil.

Sweet and sour red cabbage with apple

PREPARATION TIME: 15 MINUTES
COOKING TIME: 2¼ HOURS
SERVES 4

1 tablespoon sunflower oil
1 onion, sliced
1 clove garlic, crushed
1 small red cabbage, about 675g (1lb 8oz), finely sliced
2 tablespoons raspberry or red wine vinegar
4-5 tablespoons red wine
2 tablespoons soft brown sugar
1 large cooking apple, peeled, cored and sliced
Salt and black pepper

1 Heat the oven to 160°C (325°F, gas mark 3). Heat the oil in a flameproof casserole and fry the onion and garlic for 2-3 minutes.

2 Add the cabbage, stir-fry for a few minutes, then add the vinegar, wine and sugar. Bring to the boil, then remove from the heat and stir in the apple, with salt and pepper to taste.

3 Fold a large piece of aluminium foil into four. Place over the top of the casserole and secure with a lid. Put the casserole in the oven and cook for 2 hours, stirring halfway through cooking. The cabbage should be sticky and almost caramelised when ready to eat. Serve with roast or grilled meats, sausages, or with baked potatoes and cottage cheese.

Nutrients per serving
- Calories 100
- Carbohydrate 16g (of which sugars 15g)
- Protein 2g
- Fat 3g (of which saturated fat 0.5g)
- Fibre 4g
- Vitamins C

Red cabbage has been popular in Britain for many years. It was a favourite among the Victorians and is a classic accompaniment to game.

Jerusalem artichoke and herb croquettes

Jerusalem artichokes are a member of the **sunflower** family – the name comes from the Italian word for sunflower, *girasole*. They quickly became **popular** in Britain when introduced in the 17th century.

PREPARATION TIME: 20 MINUTES
COOKING TIME: 30 MINUTES
MAKES 10-12 CROQUETTES

225g (8oz) floury potatoes,
    peeled and cut into chunks
450g (1lb) Jerusalem artichokes,
    peeled and cut into chunks
Juice of ½ lemon
85g (3oz) ricotta cheese
1 tablespoon chopped chives
1 tablespoon chopped parsley
1 teaspoon chopped fresh thyme
Salt and black pepper
85g (3oz) fresh brown breadcrumbs
1 small egg, beaten with
    1 tablespoon water
1-2 tablespoons sunflower oil

1 Cook the potatoes in lightly salted, boiling water for about 15 minutes, or until tender. Drain well.

2 Put the artichokes into a saucepan of lightly salted water and add the lemon juice. Bring to the boil and simmer for about 10 minutes until tender. Drain well.

3 Put the drained artichokes and potatoes into a bowl with the ricotta and fresh herbs. Add a little salt and pepper to taste and mash well. Set aside until cool enough to handle.

4 Put the breadcrumbs in a shallow bowl and put the beaten egg into another shallow bowl. Using your hands, shape a generous tablespoon of the artichoke mixture into a small sausage about 7.5cm (3in) long. Dip briefly in the beaten egg and then roll it in the breadcrumbs. Repeat with the remaining mixture.

5 Heat a little oil in a frying pan and fry the croquettes, a few at a time, for 3-4 minutes, turning frequently, until golden. Serve with turkey, venison, pheasant or sausages.

Nutrients per serving, when serving 12
- Calories 71
- Carbohydrate 10g (of which sugars 0.5g)
- Protein 3g
- Fat 2.5g (of which saturated fat 0.5g)
- Fibre 2g

Roasting vegetables retains their **nutrients** and their colour, which is **enhanced** by the **sweet** honey glaze – a classic **British** addition to roasted foods.

Honey-roast parsnips, squash and potatoes

Nutrients per serving
- Calories 220
- Carbohydrate 44g (of which sugars 22g)
- Protein 5g
- Fat 4g (of which saturated fat 0.5g)
- Fibre 6g
- Vitamins B₁, C, B₆

PREPARATION TIME: 20 MINUTES
COOKING TIME: 50 MINUTES
SERVES 4

2 parsnips, peeled
1 small winter squash, such as acorn, pumpkin or onion squash
2 large potatoes, cut into wedges
1 tablespoon sunflower oil
2 tablespoons honey
2 teaspoons wholegrain mustard
1 tablespoon lemon juice

1 Heat the oven to 200°C (400°F, gas mark 6). Halve or quarter the parsnips and remove the woody core, then cut into chunks.

2 Halve the squash and remove the seeds. Cut into wedges and peel.

3 Cook the parsnips, squash and potatoes in boiling, salted water for 2 minutes, until slightly tender. Drain well.

4 Put the oil in a shallow ovenproof dish and heat in the oven for 2-3 minutes. Add the drained vegetables, turning them to coat well. Bake for

about 30 minutes until beginning to turn golden, turning them halfway through the cooking time.

5 Meanwhile, mix the honey with the mustard and lemon juice. When the vegetables are beginning to brown, remove them from the oven and pour the honey and mustard mixture over them. Stir to coat.

6 Return the vegetables to the oven and continue cooking for 10-15 minutes until golden. Serve hot with roast or grilled meats.

Beetroot in béchamel

Nutrients per serving
- Calories 150
- Carbohydrate 22g
  (of which sugars 10g)
- Protein 4g
- Fat 6g (of which
  saturated fat 3g)
- Fibre 3g

PREPARATION TIME: 35-40 MINUTES
COOKING TIME: ABOUT 1 HOUR
SERVES 4

4 beetroot, about 85g (3oz) each
115g (4oz) frozen chestnuts
½ tablespoon sunflower oil
6 spring onions, trimmed and cut into
    4cm (1½in) lengths
1 small clove garlic, crushed
15g (½oz) butter
15g (½oz) plain flour
175ml (6fl oz) semi-skimmed milk
Salt and black pepper

1 Put the beetroot in a large saucepan, cover with water and bring to the boil. Cover and simmer for about 45 minutes until tender. Drain and set aside to cool.

2 Put the chestnuts in a small pan, add water and simmer for 5-6 minutes until tender.

3 Heat the oil in a small frying pan and fry the spring onion and garlic for 2-3 minutes until softened. Remove from the heat and stir in the chestnuts, pressing them with the back of a spoon or spatula so that they crumble slightly.

4 Trim the top and bottom of the beetroot and peel. Slice thinly and arrange in the bottom of a shallow, ovenproof dish. Sprinkle over the spring onion and chestnut mixture.

5 Melt the butter in a small saucepan, stir in the flour and then gradually add the milk to make a fairly thin sauce. Add salt and pepper to taste.

6 Pour the sauce over the beetroot and chestnuts. Heat the grill and set the dish under the grill for about 5 minutes until the top is golden and bubbly. Serve at once, as it is or as a side dish with sausages or grilled meats.

Courgette
and pea fritters

PREPARATION TIME: 15 MINUTES
COOKING TIME: 15 MINUTES
MAKES ABOUT 20 FRITTERS

280g (10oz) frozen peas
2 large eggs, beaten
3 tablespoons plain flour
25g (1oz) Stilton cheese, crumbled
½ teaspoon chopped fresh thyme
Salt and black pepper
3 small or 2 large courgettes, about 350g (12oz) in
    total, trimmed and coarsely grated
15g (½oz) butter
½ tablespoon olive oil or sunflower oil
Lemon wedges to serve

Nutrients per fritter
- Calories 44
- Carbohydrate 4g (of which sugars 1g)
- Protein 2g
- Fat 2g (of which saturated fat 1g)
- Fibre 1g

Beetroot is **rich** in **potassium** as well as being a good source of **folate**. Cooked from raw – either boiled or roasted – it **retains** all its valuable **minerals**.

1   Cook the peas in boiling, salted water until tender. Drain thoroughly, then transfer them to a blender or food processor and purée until smooth.

2   Put the eggs in a large bowl and beat in the flour, cheese and thyme. Add salt and pepper to taste. Add the puréed peas and beat to mix, then stir in the grated courgettes.

3   Heat about half of the butter and oil in a nonstick frying pan. Add tablespoons of the courgette and pea mixture to the pan to make fritters about 6cm (2½in) in diameter. Fry for about 2 minutes until golden underneath. Turn and cook for a further 2-3 minutes. Keep them warm while you cook the rest of the mixture in the remaining butter and oil.

4   Serve hot with lemon wedges as a starter or a snack.

Fritters – small pieces of batter containing **vegetables**, fruit, meat or **fish** – can turn something ordinary into something **special**. These are made with **nutritious** peas and courgettes, plus a little **Stilton** to add a **rich**, **tangy** taste.

Brussels sprouts stir-fry

PREPARATION TIME: 10 MINUTES
COOKING TIME: 8 MINUTES
SERVES 4

175g (6oz) frozen chestnuts
1 tablespoon sunflower oil
1 leek, trimmed, finely sliced and rinsed
550g (1lb 4oz) Brussels sprouts, trimmed
   and finely sliced
225ml (8fl oz) hot chicken stock
   (see page 120)
Salt and black pepper

Nutrients per serving
- Calories 160
- Carbohydrate 22g (of which sugars 8g)
- Protein 7g
- Fat 6g (of which saturated fat 1g)
- Fibre 8g
- Vitamins C, B$_6$, B$_1$

1 Bring the chestnuts to the boil in a small saucepan of water, then cover and simmer for about 4 minutes, or until soft. Drain.

2 Heat the oil in a wok or frying pan. Add the leek and stir-fry for 30 seconds, then add the sprouts and stir-fry over a medium heat for a further 2 minutes, until the sprouts are beginning to fleck brown at the edges.

3 Add the stock, reduce the heat, cover and simmer for about 4 minutes until the sprouts are just tender but not soggy.

4 Crumble the chestnuts between your fingers and stir them into the sprouts and leeks. Cook, covered, for a further minute to heat through. Add salt and pepper to taste, then serve.

Brussels sprouts, first cultivated in Flanders, and popular for centuries here, are packed with healthy vitamins, bioflavonoids and compounds believed to ward off cancer. In this traditional dish, they are combined with chestnuts, which unlike other nuts are very low in fat.

New potatoes with fresh tomato dressing

PREPARATION TIME: 15 MINUTES
COOKING TIME: 20 MINUTES
SERVES 4

900g (2lb) new potatoes, scrubbed
1 sprig of mint

For the dressing:
450g (1lb) ripe tomatoes
2 spring onions, roughly chopped
1 large sprig of parsley
2 mint leaves
2 teaspoons white wine vinegar
2 tablespoons olive oil
Salt and black pepper

Nutrients per serving
- Calories 228
- Carbohydrate 40g (of which sugars 7g)
- Protein 5g
- Fat 6g (of which saturated fat 1g)
- Fibre 3g
- Vitamins B_6, B_1, C

The first new potatoes of the season are always a treat and are traditionally served with plentiful amounts of butter – this is a healthy alternative.

1 For the dressing, skin the tomatoes by plunging them briefly into boiling water. Peel away the skin and transfer the tomatoes immediately to a bowl of cold water. Cut into quarters and remove the core and seeds.

2 Put the spring onions and fresh herbs into a food processor and process for about 30 seconds until finely chopped. Add the tomatoes and process for about 10 seconds until coarsely chopped. Alternatively, chop very finely by hand on a board.

3 Transfer to a bowl and stir in the vinegar, olive oil, and salt and pepper to taste. Chill for 30 minutes. Cook the potatoes, with the mint, in boiling, salted water, until tender. Drain.

4 Put the potatoes in a large serving bowl and spoon the tomato dressing over the top. Serve at once. Alternatively, leave the potatoes to cool, then add the tomato dressing, stirring to coat. Chill for a further 30 minutes before serving.

Savoy cabbage and ham

PREPARATION TIME: 5 MINUTES
COOKING TIME: 8 MINUTES
SERVES 4

1 small Savoy cabbage, thinly sliced
1 small red onion, thinly sliced
4 thick slices of smoked ham or gammon, cut into strips
6 tablespoons low-fat fromage frais or crème fraîche
Salt and black pepper

This is a modern version of a favourite Victorian dish, steamed to retain the fresh flavour and colour of the cabbage, as well as its vitamins.

Put the cabbage and onion in a steamer and steam for 7-8 minutes until just tender. Transfer to a large bowl, toss with the ham and fromage frais or crème fraîche. Add salt and pepper and serve, as a light lunch or with sausages or baked potatoes.

VARIATION
Use 6 slices of Parma ham instead of the English ham or gammon.

Nutrients per serving
- Calories 110
- Carbohydrate 7g (of which sugars 6g)
- Protein 7g
- Fat 6g (of which saturated fat 2g)
- Fibre 2g
- Vitamins C

Every few months, there is something new to look forward to from the

Vegetables for all seasons

For those who enjoy eating vegetables in season, temperate Britain offers an abundance of choice all year round. There is something new to look forward to every few months, as one season closes and another timely delight comes to the fore.

Spring and summer crop

English asparagus, available in May, is hailed by many to be the finest. Enthusiasts even take portable stoves and saucepans into the fields to enjoy it at its very best – cooked immediately after picking. In the 19th century, efficient canal and rail links to Bristol and London made the Vale of Evesham the main British asparagus-growing region. There, it was often found in plum orchards, making good use of the heavy clay soil between the trees. Now, most English asparagus is grown in East Anglia and Lincolnshire.

Fresh green peas, popular in Britain since the 16th century, first appear in late spring, but are in their prime in summer. Again, they are best eaten freshly picked, as they soon start losing flavour and nutritional value. Dried peas, introduced to preserve a glut, have long been used in dishes such as pease pudding, which was traditionally eaten during Lent and was extremely popular all over the country in the 16th and 17th centuries. Its appeal gradually became restricted to the north-east of the country, where it is still relished.

Potatoes arrived in Britain in the 1590s and have become a staple part of our diet. For cooking purposes, they can be divided into floury or waxy types. Floury potatoes, good for baking, mashing and making chips, are more popular, particularly in Scotland. Farm carts selling 'mealy tatties' – boiled floury potatoes – were a familiar sight in 19th-century Scottish streets.

bounty of vegetables grown in Britain throughout the year.

The first new potatoes are highly anticipated each year. The season starts in April with small, earthy tasting Jersey Royals. Next come Cornish varieties, with harvesting moving north-west as the season progresses.

Autumn and winter pickings

Many of our summer vegetables linger into autumn, only fading with the first frosts. Runner beans and sweetcorn can last into October, while some varieties of courgette, if left unpicked, become huge, juicy marrows, ideal for stuffing.

Pumpkins are enjoying a revival in the British kitchen, but were once widely used. North American pumpkin pie is thought to derive from an old English recipe.

Young carrots and beetroot may be some of the joys of summer eating, but many root vegetables, such as parsnips, turnips and swedes, tend to be viewed as a cheap, hearty sustenance for the cold winter months. The native parsnip, a major source of carbohydrate before potatoes came to Britain, is naturally sweet, and was used in 16th and 17th-century sweet pies, as were carrots, that reached these shores in the 15th century. Carrots again served as a sweetener in the Second World War, when sugar supplies were low.

Long prized for its nutritional value, cabbage was brought to Britain by the Romans and by the Middle Ages was a national staple. Cauliflower probably came from Asia a few centuries later and Brussels sprouts arrived here only in the 18th century. Both are now also firmly part of the national diet.

A GREEN-GROCER.

Barley and mushroom cakes

Nutrients per cake
- Calories 235
- Carbohydrate 42g
  (of which sugars 1g)
- Protein 7g
- Fat 5g (of which
  saturated fat 1g)
- Fibre 0.5g

PREPARATION TIME: 25 MINUTES,
PLUS 3 HOURS COOLING AND STANDING
COOKING TIME: 1 HOUR
SERVES 4

25g (1oz) dried mushrooms
1 tablespoon olive oil, plus extra
    for greasing
1 onion, finely chopped
175g (6oz) pearl barley
475ml (17fl oz) vegetable stock
    (see page 182)
1 large egg, beaten
3 tablespoons chopped fresh tarragon
Salt and black pepper

These **nutrient-packed** vegetarian cakes
are very **low in fat** and **baked** in the oven
rather than fried. Barley, like oats, wheat
and rye, can help to **lower cholesterol**
and is **high in fibre.**

1 Put the mushrooms in a small bowl, cover with 150ml (¼ pint) hot water and leave to soak for 15 minutes, then drain, reserving the liquid, and chop. Meanwhile, heat the oil in a saucepan, add the onion and fry gently until soft and golden.

2 Add the barley and cook for 1-2 minutes, then add the chopped mushrooms, their liquid and the stock. Bring to the boil, then simmer, half-covered, for 30-40 minutes until the barley is tender and the liquid has evaporated, adding more stock if the mixture becomes too dry.

3 Remove from the heat, leave to cool for about 5 minutes then stir in the egg, tarragon and salt and pepper. Leave to stand, covered, for 2-3 hours, or overnight.

4 Heat the oven to 200°C (400°F, gas mark 6). Put a lightly greased 9cm (3½in) pastry cutter onto a lightly greased baking sheet. Spoon a quarter of the barley mixture into the cutter and press down gently with a teaspoon. Remove the cutter and repeat with the remaining mixture to make four cakes. Bake for about 20 minutes until just set.

5 Leave to stand for a couple of minutes before transferring to warmed plates. Serve with spinach and baked tomatoes, and a dollop of Greek-style yoghurt. Alternatively, serve with winter vegetable soup (see page 56).

Minted lettuce, peas and spring onions

PREPARATION TIME: 10 MINUTES
COOKING TIME: 15 MINUTES
SERVES 4

Nutrients per serving
- Calories 113
- Carbohydrate 9g (of which sugars 4g)
- Protein 6g
- Fat 6g (of which saturated fat 4g)
- Fibre 3g
- Vitamins B₁

25g (1oz) butter
225g (8oz) podded peas, about 675g
   (1lb 8oz) pod weight, or frozen
6-8 large leaves from cos, romaine or
   Webb's Wonderful lettuce, rinsed and
   cut into large pieces
4 spring onions, trimmed and finely sliced
4-6 tablespoons vegetable stock
   (see page 182)
2 tablespoons white wine (optional)
1 teaspoon sugar
1 sprig of mint
Salt and black pepper
4 tablespoons low-fat fromage frais

1 Melt the butter in a heavy-based saucepan over a gentle heat. Add the peas, lettuce and spring onions and cook, stirring, for about 1 minute.

2 Add the stock, wine, if using, sugar and mint sprig, with salt and black pepper to taste.

3 Bring to simmering point, then cover and simmer for 10 minutes, until the peas are tender.

4 Remove the mint and stir in the fromage frais. Serve immediately with crusty bread or as a side dish with roast lamb or steamed fish.

We often think of lettuce as a **salad** vegetable, but as this summery dish proves, **lettuce** can be delicious **cooked.** Fromage frais gives the **rich texture** of cream **without the fat content.**

Pease pudding castles

This updated version of the traditional accompaniment to bacon is baked in individual dishes, for a prettier and more unusual presentation.

PREPARATION TIME: 5 MINUTES
COOKING TIME: 50 MINUTES
SERVES 4

Nutrients per serving
- Calories 290
- Carbohydrate 32g (of which sugars 5g)
- Protein 18g
- Fat 10g (of which saturated fat 5g)
- Fibre 4g
- Vitamins A, B₁

175g (6oz) yellow split peas
140g (5oz) squash, such as butternut, peeled and cut into chunks
1 carrot, peeled and finely chopped
1 small onion, finely chopped
Vegetable stock (see page 182)
85g (3oz) mature Cheddar or Wensleydale cheese, grated
2 tablespoons Dijon mustard
1 large egg, beaten
Salt and black pepper

Parsnip cakes

PREPARATION TIME: 20 MINUTES
COOKING TIME: 25 MINUTES
MAKES ABOUT 16 CAKES

350g (12oz) floury potatoes, peeled and cut into evenly sized pieces
675g (1lb 8oz) parsnips, peeled and cut into evenly sized pieces
3 teaspoons sunflower oil
1 onion, finely chopped
1 clove garlic, crushed
15g (½oz) butter
4 tablespoons buttermilk
Pinch of mace or nutmeg
1 tablespoon finely chopped fresh parsley
Salt and black pepper
1 egg, beaten
115g (4oz) fresh white breadcrumbs

Nutrients per cake
- Calories 83
- Carbohydrate 13g (of which sugars 3g)
- Protein 2.5g
- Fat 2.5g (of which saturated fat 0.5g)
- Fibre 2.5g

Parsnips have been common in Britain since the Middle Ages, when the starchy vegetable was a staple food for people who could not afford the luxury of meat and game.

1 Cook the potatoes in plenty of boiling, salted water for 10 minutes until soft, adding the parsnips after 2-3 minutes. Drain.

2 Heat 2 teaspoons of the oil in a frying pan, add the onion and garlic and cook for 3-4 minutes until the onion is soft.

3 Put the drained potatoes and parsnips in a bowl with the butter and buttermilk. Mash thoroughly, then add the onion and garlic and beat together with a fork. Add the mace or nutmeg, parsley and salt and pepper. Set aside until cool enough to handle.

4 Put the egg in a shallow bowl with 1 tablespoon water. Put the breadcrumbs in a separate bowl. Shape

a tablespoon of mixture into a cake about 7.5cm (3in) in diameter. Dip briefly into the egg mixture and then in the breadcrumbs to coat. Repeat with the remaining mixture to make 14-16 cakes.

5 Brush the base of a nonstick frying pan with the remaining oil. When hot, fry the parsnip cakes, a few at a time, turning them when browned underneath. Continue cooking until evenly browned and transfer to a serving plate lined with kitchen paper. Keep them warm while you cook the remaining cakes, adding a little more oil as necessary.

6 Serve either as part of a main meat or vegetarian meal or as a snack with a tasty relish.

1 Put the split peas, squash, carrot and onion in a saucepan. Add enough stock to cover by 2.5cm (1in). Bring to the boil, then simmer, uncovered, for about 30 minutes until the peas are very tender and the liquid has evaporated. Add more stock if the mixture becomes too dry.

2 Meanwhile, heat the oven to 180°C (350°F, gas mark 4). Purée the split peas, using a hand-held blender, or in a food processor.

3 Beat the cheese, mustard, egg and some salt and pepper into the puréed peas. Transfer to four 200ml (⅓ pint) ramekin dishes set in a roasting tin. Divide the mixture between the

dishes and add boiling water to the tin, to half way up the sides of the dishes.

4 Bake on the middle shelf of the oven for about 20 minutes until just set in the centre. Remove the dishes from the tin and leave for 2-3 minutes before turning out onto warm plates. Serve with roast pork, ham or sausages.

Spring vegetable platter with fromage frais vinaigrette

PREPARATION TIME: 10 MINUTES
COOKING TIME: LESS THAN 5 MINUTES
SERVES 4

225g (8oz) baby leeks
175g (6oz) asparagus, trimmed and halved lengthways if thick
115g (4oz) baby carrots, trimmed
115g (4oz) mangetout peas, trimmed

For the vinaigrette:
4 tablespoons low-fat fromage frais
2 teaspoons white wine vinegar
½ teaspoon honey
½ teaspoon wholegrain mustard
Salt and black pepper

1 Trim the base from the leeks and cut off the upper leaves, leaving just the white flesh. Cut a slit down the length of the leek, remove the outer layer if necessary, and then rinse under cold running water, pulling the sections apart to rinse out any pieces of grit.

2 Pour about 2.5cm (1in) water into a large saucepan and bring to the boil. At the same time, fill a large bowl with cold water and ice. Add the leeks, asparagus and carrots to the boiling water, cover and cook for 1-2 minutes. Add the mangetout peas and cook for 30-60 seconds until just tender. Drain and immediately transfer to the bowl of iced water.

3 Meanwhile, put the fromage frais in a small bowl. Beat in the vinegar then add the honey and mustard, and salt and pepper to taste. Drain the vegetables thoroughly and blot them with kitchen paper to dry. Arrange them on a platter, then spoon the vinaigrette over the top and serve.

Nutrients per serving
- Calories 60
- Carbohydrate 9g (of which sugars 8g)
- Protein 4.5g
- Fat 1g (of which saturated fat 0g)
- Fibre 3g
- Vitamins C, B_6, A

Vitamin-packed spring vegetables are cooked only **briefly** to preserve their **vibrant** green as well as their **nutrients** and **sweet**, crisp flavour.

Vegetable hotpot with dumplings

PREPARATION TIME: 30 MINUTES
COOKING TIME: 1¼ HOURS
SERVES 4

1 tablespoon olive oil
15g (½ oz) butter
225g (8oz) baby or pickling onions, peeled
2 carrots, cut into wedges
1 small parsnip, peeled and cut into chunks
1 small swede, peeled and cut into chunks
350g (12oz) potatoes, peeled and halved or quartered
225g (8oz) frozen chestnuts
400ml (14fl oz) vegetable stock (see page 182)
1 sprig of fresh thyme
175g (6oz) green beans
Salt and black pepper

For the dumplings:
175g (6oz) self-raising flour
2 tablespoons chopped fresh parsley
85g (3oz) butter

1 Heat the oil and butter in a large flameproof casserole and fry the onions for 2-3 minutes until just beginning to brown.

2 Add the carrots, parsnip and swede and stir-fry gently over a low heat for 2-3 minutes. Cover and cook over a low heat for 6-8 minutes.

3 Add the potatoes, chestnuts, stock and thyme. Add salt and pepper, then cover and cook over a very gentle heat for 30-40 minutes. Meanwhile, prepare the green beans. If using runner beans, top and tail and string if necessary. Slice thinly using a sharp knife or runner bean slicer. For green beans top and tail. Add the beans to the stew and cook for a further 5 minutes.

4 To make the dumplings, put the flour and parsley into a bowl. Add a pinch of salt and rub in the butter. Stir in enough water to make a soft dough, then shape the dough into eight small dumplings.

5 Arrange the dumplings on top of the vegetables. Cover tightly and cook gently for a further 10-15 minutes until the dumplings are well risen and fluffy. Serve at once.

Nutrients per serving
- Calories 600
- Carbohydrate 86g (including sugars 18g)
- Protein 11g
- Fat 26g (including saturated fat 14g)
- Fibre 10g
- Vitamins A, B₁, B₆, C

Casseroles and hotpots have always been popular in British cuisine, especially in winter, when root vegetables provide warming, sustaining nourishment.

Cauliflower and broccoli gratin

PREPARATION TIME: 20 MINUTES
COOKING TIME: 35 MINUTES
SERVES 6

600ml (1 pint) semi-skimmed milk
55g (2oz) plain flour
½ teaspoon ground mace
2 teaspoons English mustard
Salt and pepper
115g (4oz) mature Cheddar cheese
280g (10oz) cauliflower florets
280g (10oz) broccoli florets
2 ripe tomatoes, roughly chopped
2 tablespoons Parmesan cheese, grated

1 Heat the oven to 200°C (400°F, gas mark 6). Put the milk in a pan, then whisk in the flour over a medium heat, beating until smooth. Add the mace, mustard and salt and pepper to taste. Reduce the heat to very low and cook, stirring, for 5 minutes. Remove from the heat and set aside for 2-3 minutes. Grate the cheese, then add it to the sauce and stir.

2 Cook the cauliflower and broccoli in boiling, salted water for about 6 minutes, until just tender. Drain.

3 Spoon a little of the cheese sauce into a large ovenproof dish. Arrange the cauliflower and broccoli on top and pour over the remaining sauce. Top with the tomato and sprinkle with the Parmesan. Bake for 10-15 minutes until golden, then serve.

Nutrients per serving
- Calories 216
- Carbohydrate 15g including sugars 8g)
- Protein 15g
- Fat 11g (including saturated fat 6g)
- Fibre 3g
- Vitamins C, B₁₂, niacin

Colcannon

PREPARATION TIME: 10 MINUTES
COOKING TIME: 15-20 MINUTES
SERVES 4-6

900g (2lb) floury potatoes, cut into
    chunks
1 green cabbage, such as spring or Savoy,
    about 550g (1lb 4oz), finely sliced
1 leek or 2 spring onions, finely sliced
5 tablespoons semi-skimmed milk
15g (½oz butter)
5 tablespoons vegetable stock
    (see page 182)
1 tablespoon half-fat cream (optional)
Salt and black pepper
Pinch of ground mace

Nutrients per serving
- Calories 250
- Carbohydrate 46g (including
  sugars 8g)
- Protein 8g
- Fat 4g (including saturated fat 2g)
- Fibre 7g
- Vitamins B_6, C, B_1

1 Cook the potatoes in lightly salted, boiling water until tender. Drain and return them to the pan.

2 Steam the cabbage and leek or spring onion for 2-3 minutes until tender. Alternatively, put in a large saucepan, add a little boiling water, cover tightly and cook over a high heat for 2 minutes until tender. Drain if necessary and keep warm.

3 Put the milk, butter, stock and cream, if using, into a small saucepan and heat gently until the butter has melted.

4 Mash the potatoes, adding enough warm milk mixture to give a creamy consistency.

5 Add the cabbage and onion mixture to the potatoes and mix. Add salt, pepper and mace to taste, then serve at once.

Bubble and squeak

Heat about 1 tablespoon sunflower oil in a large, nonstick frying pan and spread the colcannon in a layer, about 2.5cm (1in) thick, in the pan. Cook over a medium heat for 5 minutes, then turn by inverting onto a plate and sliding it back into the pan. Cook for a further 5 minutes, then serve.

Colcannon is a classic Irish potato dish, eaten at Hallowe'en. The English Bubble and Squeak, made from leftovers and fried before serving, is very similar. The cream and butter in Colcannon are greatly reduced here to make the dish healthy.

Roast onion tartlets

PREPARATION TIME: 20 MINUTES,
PLUS 30 MINUTES CHILLING
COOKING TIME: 40 MINUTES
MAKES 8

375g (13oz) puff pastry
2 large or 3 medium red onions,
    peeled and cut into wedges
1 teaspoon olive oil
85g (3oz) curd cheese
40g (1½oz) Cheddar cheese, grated
4 tablespoons semi-skimmed milk
2 eggs, beaten
Salt and black pepper

1 Heat the oven to 220°C (425°F, gas mark 7). Roll out the pastry and stamp out eight 11cm (4¼in) rounds. Use to line eight wells of a Yorkshire pudding tin. Refrigerate for 30 minutes.

2 Put the onion wedges in a shallow ovenproof dish, add the oil and stir to coat. Roast for 15 minutes until slightly charred, turning them from time to time. Set aside and reduce the oven to190°C (375°F, gas mark 5).

3 Prick the chilled pastry bases all over with a fork, then bake for 10 minutes until lightly golden. Reduce the oven to 180°C (350°F, gas mark 4).

4 Whisk the curd cheese, grated Cheddar and milk into the eggs. Add salt and pepper to taste. Divide the roasted onions between the pastry cases and then pour over the egg and cheese mixture. Bake in the oven for 10-15 minutes until the filling is risen and golden. Serve hot, warm or cold with green salad leaves.

Nutrients per serving
• Calories 266
• Carbohydrate 21g (of which sugars 3g)
• Protein 7g
• Fat 17g (of which saturated fat 2g)
• Fibre 0.5g

Using roasted vegetables in a tart makes them into a substantial meal rather than a side dish, and brings out their natural sweet flavour and bright colour.

Glazed roast vegetable tart

PREPARATION TIME:15 MINUTES
COOKING TIME: 45 MINUTES
SERVES 4

675g (1lb 8oz) vegetables, such as
    shallots, onions, radishes, squash,
    carrots, courgettes and garlic, peeled
    and chopped as appropriate
1 small red pepper, cut into strips
4 sprigs each of rosemary and thyme
5 tablespoons olive oil, plus extra
    for greasing
3 tomatoes, quartered

For the pastry:
85g (3oz) unsalted butter, diced
85g (3oz) plain flour
85g (3oz) semolina
Salt and pepper

1 Heat the oven to 220°C (425°F, gas mark 7). Lightly grease a deep, loose-bottomed 18cm (7in) flan tin and place it on a greased baking sheet.

2 To make the pastry, put the butter and 2 teaspoons water in a small saucepan over a low heat and melt. Mix the flour, semolina and a pinch of salt and pepper in a bowl and stir in the warm butter to make a dough. Press pieces of the dough into the flan tin to make an even flan case, bringing the edges slightly above the rim. Set aside.

3 Spread the vegetables in a single layer in a roasting tin. Scatter over the leaves from 2 rosemary sprigs and tuck the other 2 sprigs and the thyme sprigs in with the vegetables. Drizzle with oil, sprinkle with salt and pepper and stir the vegetables to coat evenly. Roast for about 45 minutes until soft and charred. After about 20 minutes, stir the vegetables and add the tomatoes to the tin.

4 Meanwhile, bake the pastry for 15 minutes until golden and set. Transfer the cooked vegetables to the baked flan case, spooning over any cooking juices. Serve with a green salad.

Nutrients per serving
• Calories 480
• Carbohydrate 44g (of which sugars 10g)
• Protein 7g
• Fat 32g (of which saturated fat 13g)
• Fibre 4g
• Vitamins A, C

Asparagus flan

PREPARATION TIME: 35 MINUTES
COOKING TIME: 35 MINUTES
SERVES 6

175g (6oz) asparagus, trimmed
3 teaspoons olive oil
6 spring onions, trimmed and cut into
   7.5cm (3in) lengths
2 eggs
100g (3½oz) fresh goat's cheese
70g (2½oz) curd cheese
4 tablespoons milk
Salt and black pepper

For the pastry:
1 egg yolk
½ teaspoon sugar
280g (10oz) plain white flour
½ teaspoon salt
115g (4oz) butter, cut into small pieces

Nutrients per serving
- Calories 430
- Carbohydrate 38g
  (of which sugars 3g)
- Protein 12g
- Fat 26g
  (of which saturated fat 15g)
- Fibre 2g
- Vitamins B_{12}, A, B_1

Asparagus adds **vitamins** and body to this creamy, **elegant** flan; roasting the vegetable enhances its **delicate flavour.**

1 Heat the oven to 190°C (375°F, gas mark 5). For the pastry, put the egg yolk, sugar and 5 tablespoons cold water in a small bowl and beat. Sift the flour and salt into a separate bowl. Rub the butter into the flour until the mixture resembles fine breadcrumbs.

2 Make a well in the centre of the flour mixture and add the egg yolk mixture. Using the back of a knife, stir until the mixture holds together, adding a little more cold water if necessary. Knead lightly, then roll out the pastry on a floured surface and use to line a 20cm (8in) flan dish. Prick the base all over with a fork and refrigerate for about 30 minutes.

3 Bake the pastry for 6-8 minutes until pale but firm. Remove from the oven and set aside.

4 If the asparagus spears are thick, cut them in half lengthways. Put in a shallow ovenproof dish and pour over 2 teaspoons oil. Roast in the oven for 10 minutes, turning once, until tender.

5 Heat the remaining teaspoon of oil in a small frying pan, add the spring onions and cook over a medium heat until slightly softened.

6 Put the eggs, goat's cheese, curd cheese and milk in a bowl and beat. Add salt and pepper to taste. Pour the egg mixture into the flan dish and arrange the asparagus and spring onions on top. Bake for 18-20 minutes until golden. Serve warm or cold with a tomato and chive salad.

Spinach and celeriac roulade

PREPARATION TIME: 30 MINUTES
COOKING TIME: 15 MINUTES
SERVES 4

350g (12oz) fresh spinach, washed and tough stalks removed
15g (½oz) butter
3 tablespoons half-fat crème fraîche
4 eggs, separated
25g (1oz) mature Cheddar cheese, grated
Salt and black pepper

For the filling:
225g (8oz) celeriac, peeled and finely grated
1 tablespoon lemon juice
4 tablespoons low-fat fromage frais
2 tablespoons reduced-fat mayonnaise

Nutrients per serving
- Calories 250
- Carbohydrate 5g (of which sugars 4g)
- Protein 14g
- Fat 16g (of which saturated fat 6g)
- Fibre 4g
- Vitamins C, B$_{12}$, A

Celeriac has a mild celery-like flavour and a delicious crunchy texture. It is not only extremely versatile, but also contains potassium, fibre and vitamin C.

1 Heat the oven to 190°C (375°F, gas mark 5). Line a 33 x 23cm (13 x 9in) swiss roll tin with baking parchment. Put the spinach into a large saucepan, cover tightly and cook over a moderate heat for a few minutes, shaking the pan occasionally, until wilted. Drain well, then chop finely.

2 Heat the butter in a small saucepan and add the chopped spinach. Cook gently until any excess liquid has evaporated. Remove from the heat and leave to cool.

3 Add the crème fraîche, egg yolks and cheese to the spinach, with salt and pepper to taste. In a clean bowl, whisk the egg whites until stiff, then fold them into the spinach and egg mixture. Spoon into the prepared tin and smooth the surface, using a palette knife.

4 Bake for 10-15 minutes until firm to the touch and golden. Turn out onto a sheet of greaseproof paper and peel away the lining paper. While still warm, carefully roll up the roulade in the greaseproof paper and place it seam side down on a cooling rack.

5 Meanwhile, to make the filling, put the celeriac into a bowl and sprinkle with lemon juice. Add the fromage frais, mayonnaise and some salt and pepper and mix well.

6 Unroll the roulade, remove the greaseproof paper and spread with the celeriac mixture. Roll up again and transfer the roulade carefully to a serving dish. Serve warm or chill. If not serving the roulade immediately, remove to room temperature about 30 minutes before serving.

Marrow stuffed
with apricots and bacon

Nutrients per serving

- Calories 434
- Carbohydrate 25g
  (of which sugars 16g)
- Protein 16g
- Fat 30g (of which
  saturated fat 7g)
- Fibre 6g
- Vitamins C, B$_6$, B$_1$

PREPARATION TIME: 20 MINUTES
COOKING TIME: ABOUT 1 HOUR
SERVES 4

1 medium to small marrow, about 1.5kg (3lb 5oz)
6-8 rashers thinly cut streaky bacon
1 tablespoon sunflower oil
1 onion, chopped
70g (2½oz) fresh brown breadcrumbs
85g (3oz) flaked almonds, lightly toasted
55g (2oz) ready-to-eat dried apricots, chopped
1 sprig of parsley, chopped
1 teaspoon chopped fresh thyme
225ml (8fl oz) vegetable stock (see page 182)
Salt and black pepper

For the sauce:
1 teaspoon English mustard
2 teaspoons chopped fresh herbs
3 tablespoons low-fat fromage frais

Breadcrumbs are ideal for stuffings, as they absorb liquids and **flavour**. The almonds and **apricots** add **fibre** and vitamins to this **classic** dish.

1 Heat the oven to 200°C (400°F, gas mark 6). Trim the marrow, cutting off about 1cm (½in) from the top to remove the stalk. Lay the marrow on its side and slice off the top 2.5cm (1in) to make a lid. Using a spoon, scoop out the seeds and pith, leaving a lining of flesh.

2 Grill the bacon for 3-4 minutes until very crisp. Cool slightly and crumble or finely chop into a bowl. Heat the oil in a small frying pan, add the onion and fry until soft. Add to the bacon.

3 Add the breadcrumbs, almonds, chopped apricots and herbs to the bacon and onion. Stir in about 85ml (3fl oz) of the stock so that the breadcrumbs are moist but not soggy. Add salt and pepper to taste.

4 Spoon the stuffing loosely into the cavity of the marrow and replace the lid. Place in a shallow baking dish and add the remaining stock to the dish. Cover tightly with foil and bake in the oven for 45-50 minutes until tender. (Pierce the flesh with a knife to check.)

5 Remove the foil and marrow lid and pour the cooking juices into a small pan. Place the marrow, uncovered, under a hot grill for 3-4 minutes until the crumbs are lightly golden.

6 Meanwhile, gently heat the stock with the mustard and herbs. When hot, remove from the heat and stir in the fromage frais.

7 To serve, cut the marrow into thick slices. Arrange on warmed plates and serve with the mustard sauce and brown rice.

Watercress and ricotta soufflé

PREPARATION TIME: 20 MINUTES
COOKING TIME: 30 MINUTES
SERVES 6 AS A STARTER

25g (1oz) butter, plus extra for greasing
25g (1oz) plain flour
300ml (½ pint) semi-skimmed milk
4 eggs, separated
115g (4oz) ricotta cheese
25g (1oz) mature Cheddar cheese, grated
½ teaspoon English mustard
Salt and black pepper
85g (3oz) watercress, trimmed and finely chopped

1 Heat the oven to 190°C (375°F, gas mark 5) and grease six 125ml (4fl oz) ramekin dishes.

2 Melt the butter in a saucepan, stir in the flour and cook for 1 minute. Gradually stir in the milk to make a smooth sauce. Remove the pan from the heat, cool slightly, then stir in the egg yolks, one at a time.

3 Add the ricotta, Cheddar, mustard and salt and pepper to taste. Add the watercress, stirring well. In a clean bowl, whisk the egg whites until stiff. Beat 1 tablespoon of egg whites into the sauce, then fold in the remainder, using a metal spoon.

4 Spoon the mixture into the prepared dish and bake for 18-20 minutes or until risen and golden. Serve at once, with crusty bread and roast tomatoes.

Nutrients per serving
- Calories 180
- Carbohydrate 6g (of which sugars 3g)
- Protein 10g
- Fat 12g (of which saturated fat 6g)
- Fibre 0g
- Vitamins B_{12}

Purple sprouting broccoli and leek bake

PREPARATION TIME: 25 MINUTES
COOKING TIME: 30 MINUTES
SERVES 2, OR 4 AS A SIDE DISH

225g (8oz) purple sprouting broccoli, trimmed and cut into evenly-sized lengths or florets
2-3 leeks, thinly sliced and rinsed
675g (1lb 8oz) potatoes, peeled and thinly sliced
25g (1oz) butter
20g (¾oz) plain flour
About 225ml (8fl oz) semi-skimmed milk
Salt and black pepper

Nutrients per serving
- Calories 500
- Carbohydrate 78g (of which sugars 13g)
- Protein 19g
- Fat 14g (of which saturated fat 8g)
- Fibre 11g
- Vitamins C, B₁, A, B₆

1 Steam the broccoli for 3-4 minutes until just tender. Cook the leeks in a little boiling water for 3-4 minutes until just tender. Drain, reserving the liquid. Cook the potato slices in lightly salted, boiling water for 5-6 minutes until tender, then drain.

2 Heat the oven to 190°C (375°F, gas mark 5). Melt 20g (¾oz) of the butter in a saucepan, stir in the flour and then gradually add the milk. Gradually add the reserved leek water, stirring, to make a thin, smooth sauce. Add salt and pepper to taste.

3 Put the broccoli in a shallow ovenproof dish and scatter the leeks over the top. Pour over the white sauce and then add the potato slices in a layer. Dot with the remaining butter and bake for 15 minutes until very hot. For a golden top, brown briefly under a hot grill. Serve with a green salad and crusty bread, or as a side dish with meat or fish.

Note: When purple sprouting broccoli is not available, use ordinary broccoli instead, cut into small florets.

Watercress has been popular in Britain since the early 19th century. Grown beside streams, it has a robust and peppery taste which goes well with the mild, low-fat ricotta.

Purple sprouting broccoli is available from late winter to early summer and, like normal broccoli, is a rich source of vitamins, potassium and antioxidants. Steaming it preserves its colour, flavour and nutrients.

Puddings

Puddings
the healthy way

You can indulge in puddings within a balanced diet if you can keep the fat and sugar content healthily low. Here's how.

It is widely believed that irresistible puddings cannot possibly be part of a healthy diet. In fact, almost anything can be eaten in moderation – balance and variety are the key to good nutrition.

Prepared according to healthy guidelines, puddings can even enhance your diet. Adding fruit boosts the vitamin content of a dessert. Using lower-fat alternatives to cream cuts the calories, while wholemeal pastry adds fibre.

Boosting vitamin content
British growers offer a wide variety of delicious fruits all year round. Rich in vitamins, especially vitamin C, we should all eat more of them.

Many traditional British puddings, such as Summer pudding and Eve's pudding (see pages 214 and 224), are already fruit-based, but you can easily use more fruit by serving puddings with a fruit coulis or sauce rather than custard or cream. For a pudding with maximum fruit and minimal preparation, pile fruit high on a meringue base (see right).

Dried fruits, nuts and seeds, such as apricots, prunes, walnuts and pumpkin seeds, can also be added to dishes such as Blackberry and apple crumble or Bread and butter pudding (see pages 226 and 229) to increase their vitamin and nutrient content. Using brown bread instead of white will also increase fibre.

Use British fruit in season (see chart), especially local produce, as it will have been picked ripe and in peak condition. Fresh produce contains more vitamins and generally has a better taste than imported fruit, which will have travelled farther and have been picked unripe to prevent damage in transit. Always wash thoroughly to remove any surface pesticides, waxes and other treatments.

Selecting fruit
Once fruit has been picked, it begins to lose its nutrient value.
• Choose ripe, but not overripe, fruit.
• Pick citrus fruits carefully; the best will feel heavy for their size and have an unblemished skin

SEASONS FOR BRITISH FRUIT AND NUTRITIONAL VALUES		
Fruit	Months available (inclusive)	Nutritional information
Apples	Jan-Feb, Sept-Dec	vitamin C, potassium, flavonoids, soluble fibre
Blackberries	June-Sept	vitamin C
Blackcurrants	June-Oct	vitamins C, E, phytochemicals
Cherries	June-Aug	vitamin C, flavonoids
Damsons	Sept	vitamin C
Elderberries	Aug-Sept	vitamin C
Gooseberries	June-Aug	vitamin C, fibre, phytochemicals
Grapes	Aug	vitamin B_6, phytochemicals
Loganberries	July-Aug	vitamin C, fibre, phytochemicals
Mulberries	Aug	vitamin C, phytochemicals
Peaches	Aug	vitamin C, fibre, phytochemicals
Pears	Sept-Mar	vitamin C, fibre
Plums	July-Oct	vitamin C, potassium, iron, carotenoids, flavonoids
Quince	Oct-Nov	vitamin C
Raspberries	May-Oct	vitamins C, E
Redcurrants	July-Aug	vitamin C
Rhubarb	Mar-May	vitamin C
Strawberries	April-Oct	vitamin C, calcium, potassium
Tayberries	June-Aug	vitamin C, fibre, phytochemicals
White currants	July-Sept	vitamin C

Making a basic meringue

1 Beat air into egg whites until it forms floppy, soft peaks when you lift it. Continue beating until it is thick enough to form stiff, upright peaks.

2 Gradually add sugar to create meringue. Caster sugar dissolves quicker for a more stable mixture. Beat in a third of the sugar until stiff peaks form again and the mixture is glossy.

3 Gently fold in the rest of the sugar, a spoonful at a time. Stop frequently and lift the whites from the bottom of the bowl to ensure thorough and even beating. Stop at stiff peak stage and be careful not to overmix, or the meringue will collapse.

Preparation tips

To avoid cutting off the stalk when preparing pears for cooking, use a potato peeler and work down from top to base.

Nuts can be roasted without added fat in a heavy-based pan over a medium heat, shaking occasionally, until just golden.

• Avoid wilted, wrinkled or bruised fruit.
• Make sure berries are firm and glossy.
 When fresh fruit is not available, use canned and dried fruits as they also provide good levels of vitamins, minerals, phytochemicals and fibre.

Lower-fat alternatives
You can make custard more healthy by using minimal sugar and semi-skimmed milk. Better still, serve yoghurt, half-fat crème fraîche or combine the two.

 Fruit fools can also be made with fromage frais, quark or Greek yoghurt rather than double cream.

Puddings with pastry
Most pastries are high in fat but this can be reduced:
• Shortcrust pastry is the most versatile pastry and is usually made with a hard fat such as butter. However, oil can be substituted as a healthier option.
• If you are making a fruit pie, reduce the fat content and boost vitamins by using more fruit and omitting the pastry base.

• Filo pastry is a very low-fat pastry with only 4.1g of fat per 100g (3½oz) of uncooked dough. Most people buy commercially made filo. Using it requires a little skill as the sheets are very thin – for some useful hints, see page 237.
• Hot-water crust is made with just a small amount of fat melted in boiling water and mixed with flour. This has a fat content of 16.5g per 100g (3½oz) and is a good lower-fat topping for raised and savoury meat pies.
• Wholemeal flour is richer in nutrients than white flour (see page 236).
• The fats generally used in pastry are butter, lard, hard margarines or suet but, in moderation, these should not affect the balance of your healthy diet (see pages 236-7). Alternatively, you can substitute whole or half quantities of oil.

Chocolate delights
If you are a chocolate lover and find it hard to cut from your diet, eat dark chocolate in moderation, as it is rich in potassium, iron and magnesium.

Berry jellies

PREPARATION TIME: 10 MINUTES,
PLUS 3 HOURS CHILLING AND SETTING
COOKING TIME: 15 MINUTES
SERVES 4

450g (1lb) raspberries, defrosted
   if frozen, plus extra for layering
Grated zest and juice of 1 unwaxed
   lemon
55g (2oz) caster sugar
2 sachets of gelatine, 11.7g each

Nutrients per serving
- Calories 82
- Carbohydrate 20g
  (of which sugars 20g)
- Protein 1.5g
- Fat 0g
- Fibre 0.5g
- Vitamins C

Traditional **homemade** jellies are not just for children. They taste quite different from the synthetic packet version and are **full of fresh fruit** vitamins and flavour.

1 Put the raspberries, lemon zest, sugar and 800ml (1 pint 9fl oz) cold water in a large saucepan. Bring to the boil, then simmer for about 10 minutes, until the raspberries are soft but not mushy.

2 Line a nonmetallic sieve with a double layer of muslin and strain the raspberry liquid into a large bowl, allowing it to drip through slowly.

3 Put the gelatine with 3 tablespoons cold water in a small bowl. Leave for 10 minutes to swell, then set the bowl over a saucepan of boiling water and heat until the gelatine dissolves.

4 Add 2 tablespoons of the raspberry liquid to the gelatine and stir to mix, then tip the gelatine mixture into the remaining raspberry liquid and stir. Leave to cool slightly.

5 Divide half the mixture between four glasses, then chill until slightly set. Add a layer of fresh raspberries, then top with the remaining raspberry mixture. Chill again to set.

6 Decorate each jelly with extra raspberries or strawberries and serve with long spoons.

VARIATIONS

For blackcurrant jelly, use blackcurrants instead of raspberries, following the recipe as directed.

For a sparkling wine jelly, halve the quantity of water and add 400ml (14fl oz) sparkling white wine in step 5, before pouring the jelly into the glasses.

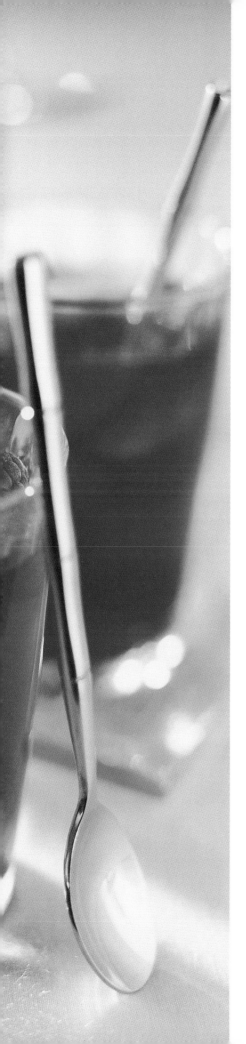

Poached pears
and quince

Quinces were once very common in Britain and in autumn the native fruit can still be bought from good fruit suppliers, while foreign varieties can be found in Middle Eastern or Cypriot shops for most of the year.

PREPARATION TIME: 15 MINUTES
COOKING TIME: 45 MINUTES, PLUS COOLING
SERVES 4-6

Juice of 1 lemon
2 quinces
1 vanilla pod, slit lengthways
5 cardamom pods, cracked
3 firm dessert pears, such as Conference or Williams, peeled and cored
1 litre (1¾ pints) perry (pear cider)
150g (5½ oz) sugar

1 Put the lemon juice into a deep bowl of cold water. Peel, quarter and core the quinces, saving the debris. Cut each quince quarter lengthways into 2 segments and add to the lemon water. Roughly chop the skin and core pieces and put them on a piece of muslin with the vanilla and cardamom pods, then tie the corners together.

2 Peel, core and slice the pears lengthways into eight, then add to the lemon water. Put the perry and sugar in a large saucepan over a low temperature and heat gently until the sugar dissolves. Add the muslin bag and bring to the boil.

3 Transfer the quince quarters to the saucepan and return to a simmer. Add the pear slices to the pan after 10 minutes and return to a simmer. Cook, partially covered, for 18-20 minutes until the fruit is tender.

4 Using a slotted spoon, transfer the fruit to a serving dish, reserving the contents of the pan.

5 Leave the muslin bag in the pan and boil the liquid until syrupy and reduced to about 400ml (14fl oz). Strain through a sieve into a jug and leave to cool. Press the muslin bag repeatedly with the back of a large spoon to extract as much of the flavoured juice as you can.

6 Discard the muslin bag and pour the juice over the fruit. Serve at room temperature or lightly chilled, with low-fat crème fraîche or yoghurt.

Note: If you cannot find quinces, use 2 large whole pears, such as black Worcesters, instead.

Nutrients per serving, when serving 6
- Calories 190
- Carbohydrate 38g (of which sugars 38g)
- Protein 0g
- Fat 0g
- Fibre 1.7g

Blackcurrant fool
with almond shorties

PREPARATION TIME: 45 MINUTES,
PLUS 4 HOURS COOLING
AND CHILLING
COOKING TIME: 15 MINUTES
SERVES 4

Nutrients per serving of fool
- Calories 235
- Carbohydrate 29g
  (of which sugars 12g)
- Protein 9g
- Fat 10g (of which saturated fat 5g)
- Fibre 3g
- Vitamins C

1 tablespoon plain flour
1 egg yolk
4 tablespoons sugar
200ml (7fl oz) semi-skimmed milk
350g (12oz) blackcurrants,
   stems removed
450g (1lb) Greek-style yoghurt

For the almond shorties:
85g (3oz) butter, softened, plus extra
   for greasing
40g (1½oz) light muscovado sugar
¼ teaspoon almond extract
115g (4oz) plain wholemeal flour
16 blanched almonds, cut into slivers

1 Put the flour and egg yolk into a
small bowl with 3 tablespoons of
the sugar. Stir in a little milk to make a
smooth paste.

2 Heat the remaining milk in a
saucepan until almost boiling, then
stir it into the paste. Return the mixture
to the pan and bring to the boil, stirring
continuously. Simmer for 3 minutes,
stirring, until thickened and smooth.
Pour into a large bowl and cover the
surface with cling film.

3 Put the blackcurrants, remaining
sugar and 1 tablespoon water into
a small saucepan and bring to the boil.

Remove from the heat, cool slightly, then purée in a blender or food processor. Pass the mixture through a fine sieve, then stir it into the custard. Cover with cling film and leave to cool.

4 When the blackcurrant mixture is cool, fold in the yoghurt, then divide between four serving glasses. Chill for at least 3 hours.

5 Meanwhile, to make the almond shorties, heat the oven to 160°C (325°F, gas mark 3) and lightly grease a large baking sheet. Cream the butter with the sugar and almond extract until very soft, then mix in the flour.

6 Divide the dough into 16 balls, about the size of prunes. Flatten each into a 4cm (1½in) round on the greased baking sheet, placing them slightly apart to allow room to spread. Lightly press a few slivered almonds into the top of each.

7 Bake for 8-10 minutes until browned and firm. Leave on the baking sheet for 2-3 minutes, until firm enough to lift without crumbling. Transfer to a wire rack to cool. Serve the fools with the almond shorties.

VARIATIONS
Gooseberries or rhubarb can be used instead of blackcurrants. Follow the main recipe, but in step 3 cook the fruit until soft before puréeing.

For a strawberry fool, purée uncooked fruit with the sugar and the juice of ½ lemon until smooth, then fold into the custard in step 4.

Nutrients per almond shortie
- Calories 100
- Carbohydrate 7g (of which sugars 3g)
- Protein 2g
- Fat 7g (of which saturated fat 3g)
- Fibre 1g

Popular in Britain since the 17th century, fools are best made with sharp fruits. Victorian cooks favoured gooseberries, but blackcurrants, a very good source of vitamin C, are delicious.

Syllabub is an English dessert dating from Tudor times. In this lighter version, yoghurt replaces some of the rich double cream in the original recipe.

Ginger syllabub with ginger wafers

PREPARATION TIME: 15 MINUTES, PLUS AT LEAST 30 MINUTES CHILLING
COOKING TIME: 30 MINUTES
SERVES 6, MAKES 18 WAFERS

Grated zest and juice of ½ orange
Grated zest and juice of ½ unwaxed lemon
2 tablespoons caster sugar
150ml (¼ pint) double cream, chilled
150ml (¼ pint) ginger wine
300g (10½oz) set natural yoghurt, chilled

For the ginger wafers:
40g (1½oz) plain flour
1 teaspoon ground ginger
40g (1½oz) butter
40g (1½oz) caster sugar
2 tablespoons golden syrup
3 pieces of stem ginger in syrup, drained and chopped

1 To make the wafers, heat the oven to 190°C (375°F, gas mark 5) and cover a baking sheet with parchment.

2 Sift the flour and ginger into a small bowl. Heat the butter, sugar, syrup and stem ginger in a saucepan, stirring until the butter has melted.

3 Remove the pan from the heat and stir in the sifted flour and ginger. Place 4 small teaspoons of the mixture, spaced well apart, on the baking sheet. Bake for about 8 minutes until bubbling and browned.

4 Leave to cool for about 1 minute or until sufficiently set to slide a large palette knife under the wafers. Transfer to a wire rack to cool. Repeat with the remaining mixture.

5 To make the syllabub, put the zests and juices in a bowl with the sugar and cream. Pour in half the ginger wine and whisk until the mixture forms soft peaks. Be careful not to overwhip, or it will separate.

6 In another bowl, stir the remaining ginger wine into the yoghurt. Pour this into the whisked mixture, then use a flexible spatula to fold until mixed. Do not stir or overmix as this will knock the air out of the whipped cream.

7 Pour the mixture into six glasses or cups and refrigerate for at least 30 minutes or for up to 2 hours, before serving with the ginger wafers.

Nutrients per serving, including 1 wafer
- Calories 190
- Carbohydrate 11g (of which sugars 9g)
- Protein 3g
- Fat 12g (of which saturated fat 9g)
- Fibre 0g
- Vitamins A

Elderflower sorbet

PREPARATION TIME: 10 MINUTES, PLUS 8 HOURS FREEZING
COOKING TIME: 7 MINUTES
SERVES 4

4 heads of elderflower
700ml (1¼ pints) water
175g (6oz) caster sugar
Grated zest of 1 unwaxed lemon and juice of 2 lemons

1 Set the freezer to the fast-freeze setting about 1 hour before starting. Pick over the elderflower heads, then rinse in cold water. Drain, then snip off the flowers into a large saucepan.

2 Add the water, sugar, lemon zest and juice. Bring to the boil, stirring until the sugar dissolves, then boil for about 7 minutes. Strain the syrup into a freezer container and leave to cool.

3 Freeze the cold syrup for about 3 hours or until sludgy. Purée until smooth in a blender or food processor, or using a hand-held blender. Freeze again, then purée the mixture twice more at intervals of about 1 hour, in order to break up the ice crystals. Leave to freeze for several hours or overnight. (Remember to turn the freezer back to the normal setting.)

Elderflowers come into blossom in our **hedgerows** in late May and June. The **aromatic** white flowers have a potent **flavour**, which is delicious in drinks and desserts.

4 Scoop out portions of sorbet into bowls. Press the broken-up mixture in the container into a layer with the back of the scoop, then freeze the leftovers, for future use.

Note: When fresh elderflower heads are not available, reduce the quantity of water to 600ml (1 pint) and boil it with the lemon and sugar as in the main recipe. There is no need to strain the syrup. Add 4 tablespoons elderflower cordial to the cooled syrup before freezing as directed.

Nutrients per serving
- Calories 115
- Carbohydrate 31g
  (of which sugars 31g)
- Protein 0g
- Fat 0g
- Fibre 0g

Rose-strawberry yoghurt ice

PREPARATION TIME: 15 MINUTES, PLUS 8 HOURS FREEZING
SERVES 6

400g (14oz) strawberries, hulled and chilled, plus extra to decorate
100g (3½oz) icing sugar
3 tablespoons rosewater
450g (1lb) Greek-style yoghurt

In Britain, there is a long tradition of making ice cream, often involving **rich** mixtures of cream and eggs. This **healthy** ice, made with **yoghurt**, is light but still **creamy**.

1 Turn the freezer to the fast-freeze setting about 1 hour before starting. Coarsely purée the strawberries in a blender or food processor, then transfer the mixture to a bowl.

2 Stir in the icing sugar, rosewater and yoghurt. Pour the mixture into a large freezer container and freeze for 3 hours, or until part frozen.

3 Transfer the mixture to a blender or food processor and purée until smooth, then return it to the freezer. Purée the mixture again once or twice more over the next 2-3 hours. Leave to freeze until firm. (Remember to turn the freezer back to the normal setting.)

4 Remove the yoghurt-ice from the freezer 30 minutes before serving. Scoop into glasses or bowls and serve decorated with strawberries.

Note: Rosewater is available in most supermarkets, as well as in Middle Eastern and Asian stores.

VARIATION
Raspberries can be used instead of the strawberries.

Nutrients per serving
- Calories 170
- Carbohydrate 23g (of which sugars 17g)
- Protein 5g
- Fat 7g (of which saturated fat 4g)
- Fibre 0.5g
- Vitamins C

213

Summer pudding

PREPARATION TIME: 20 MINUTES,
PLUS OVERNIGHT CHILLING
COOKING TIME: 3-5 MINUTES
SERVES 6

675g (1lb 8oz) mixture of blackcurrants,
    redcurrants, raspberries and
    strawberries, stemmed or hulled
200ml (7fl oz) unsweetened apple juice
2 tablespoons sugar
10 slices day-old wholemeal bread,
    about 1cm (½in) thick, crusts removed

1 Put the blackcurrants and
redcurrants in a saucepan. Add the
apple juice and sugar and bring to the
boil. Remove from the heat and set
aside to cool slightly.

2 Cut a large circle from one bread
slice, with a saucer as a guide, and
use it to line the bottom of a 1.2 litre
(2 pint) pudding basin. Line the sides by
pressing slices of bread around them,
overlapping slightly to avoid gaps. Save
a few slices for step 4.

3 Add the remaining fruit to the
currants and apple juice and mix.
Spoon the fruit into the basin on top of
the bread, pressing it down lightly.

4 Top with the remaining bread,
trimming pieces to cover the fruit
completely. Spoon the juice from the
fruit over the top and around the edge.

5 Stand the pudding in a shallow
dish to catch any juices, cover with
cling film and top with a small plate that
fits just inside the rim of the basin.
Weigh the plate down with a heavy jar
or can and refrigerate overnight.

During the 19th century, this celebration of summer fruit
was often served at **health** spas. It is a nutritious dessert,
being **very low in fat** and high in **vitamin C**.

6 To serve, remove the weight, plate
and cling film. Slide a flexible
spatula around the pudding to loosen it,
pressing it firmly against the basin.
Cover with a shallow dish and invert
both basin and dish. Lift off the basin,
and serve the pudding in slices with
fromage frais or low-fat crème fraîche.

Note: Frozen summer fruit can also be
used. It does not have to be cooked
lightly first, just used from frozen.

Nutrients per serving
- Calories 180
- Carbohydrate 38g (of which sugars 15g)
- Protein 6g
- Fat 1g (of which saturated fat 0g)
- Fibre 3g
- Vitamins C

Fresh fruit trifle

PREPARATION TIME: 40 MINUTES,
PLUS 2 HOURS COOLING AND CHILLING
COOKING TIME: 5 MINUTES
SERVES 8

1 Classic Victoria sponge (see page 253)
6 tablespoons medium sherry
15 ratafia biscuits
500g (1lb 2oz) mixture of fruit, such as
    raspberries, strawberries, blueberries,
    sliced peaches or nectarines
Extra fruit and rose petals (optional) to decorate

For the custard:
2 tablespoons cornflour
1 tablespoon caster sugar
3 egg yolks
1 teaspoon vanilla extract
600ml (1 pint) semi-skimmed milk

For the topping:
150ml (¼ pint) double cream
300g (10½ oz) thick natural yoghurt

One of the most **celebrated British** desserts, this is a luscious, **classic** trifle, lightened with extra **fresh fruit** and yoghurt.

1 Cut the sponge into large chunks. Lay the pieces on a board and spoon about half the sherry over them, then transfer them to a large trifle bowl. Add the ratafia biscuits, placing them between the pieces of sponge. Add the fruit, filling any gaps. Sprinkle over the remaining sherry.

2 For the custard, mix the cornflour with the sugar in a bowl. Add the egg yolks and vanilla with a little of the milk. Using a balloon whisk, mix to a smooth paste, adding a little extra milk if necessary.

3 Heat the remaining milk to just below boiling point, then pour it into the yolk mixture, stirring continuously with the whisk. Return the mixture to the pan and bring slowly to the boil, still stirring with the whisk. Simmer, whisking, for 2-3 minutes, until smooth and thick. Cool slightly, then pour over the fruit. Chill for about 2 hours.

4 Whip the cream to soft peaks, then fold in the yoghurt. Add to the top of the trifle. Decorate with fruit and rose petals, if using, then serve.

Nutrients per serving
- Calories 641
- Carbohydrate 64g (of which sugars 38g)
- Protein 13g
- Fat 37g (of which saturated fat 21g)
- Fibre 2.5g
- Vitamins B_{12}, C, A, B_2

Curd tart with glazed gooseberries and grapes

A traditional recipe, curd tart is creamy and rich, but made with low-fat curd cheese.

Nutrients per serving
- Calories 290
- Carbohydrate 45g (of which sugars 24g)
- Protein 6g
- Fat 11g (of which saturated fat 6g)
- Fibre 0g
- Vitamins B$_{12}$

PREPARATION TIME: 25 MINUTES, PLUS 30 MINUTES CHILLING
COOKING TIME: 1¼ HOURS
SERVES 8

150g (5½oz) plain flour
75g (2¾oz) butter
400g (14oz) curd cheese
Grated zest and juice of 1 unwaxed lemon
75g (2¾oz) caster sugar
2 tablespoons self-raising flour
55g (2oz) currants
2 eggs
4 tablespoons semi-skimmed milk

For the glazed gooseberries and grapes:

450g (1lb) dessert gooseberries
300ml (½ pint) unsweetened apple juice
350g (12oz) seedless green grapes

1 Put the plain flour in a bowl and rub in the butter until the mixture resembles fine breadcrumbs. Stir in 3 tablespoons cold water until the mixture clumps together, then bring the pastry together by hand.

2 Roll out the pastry on a lightly floured surface and use to line a 23cm (9in) round dish, 3cm (1¼in) deep. Chill for 30 minutes. Heat the oven to 200°C (400°F, gas mark 6).

3 Line the chilled pastry case with greaseproof paper and baking beans and bake for 10 minutes.

Remove from the oven and set aside. Reduce the oven temperature to 160°C (325°F, gas mark 3).

4 Beat the curd cheese with the lemon zest and juice and the sugar. Sift the flour over the mixture, then beat it in. Add the currants, eggs and milk, and beat until combined. Pour the mixture into the pastry case, then bake for 40-45 minutes until set and lightly browned. Set aside until warm.

5 To glaze the fruit, put the gooseberries in a saucepan and add the apple juice. Bring slowly to a simmer and poach the fruit for about 1 minute to soften it very slightly. Transfer the gooseberries to a bowl.

6 Boil the apple juice until reduced to about 50ml (2fl oz) of dark golden syrup. Add the grapes to the gooseberries and pour over the apple syrup. Mix well. Serve the curd tart in slices with spoonfuls of the glazed fruit arranged on top.

Nutrients per serving
- Calories 367
- Carbohydrate 47g (of which sugars 32g)
- Protein 7g
- Fat 18g (of which saturated fat 10g)
- Fibre 2.5g
- Vitamins A, C

This healthier version of a classic, with a thinner pastry crust and less sugar, still retains its wonderfully fresh lemon flavour.

Lemon meringue pie

PREPARATION TIME: 30 MINUTES,
PLUS 30 MINUTES CHILLING
COOKING TIME: 35-45 MINUTES
SERVES 6

115g (4oz) plain flour
55g (2oz) butter, diced

For the lemon filling:
Grated zest and juice of 2 unwaxed
    lemons
3 egg yolks
40g (1½oz) cornflour
50g (1¾oz) caster sugar

For the meringue topping:
3 egg whites
85g (3oz) caster sugar

1 Put the flour in a bowl and rub in the butter until the mixture resembles fine breadcrumbs. Gradually add enough cold water to make a dough, about 2-3 tablespoons. Roll out on a lightly floured surface and use to line a 23cm (9in) round dish, 3cm (1¼in) deep. Prick the pastry base all over and chill for 30 minutes. Heat the oven to 200°C (400°F, gas mark 6).

2 Line the pastry case with greaseproof paper. Fill with baking beans and bake for about 20 minutes, until browned and cooked. Reduce the oven to 180°C (350°F, gas mark 4). Remove the paper and beans and set the pastry case aside to cool slightly while you prepare the filling.

3 Pour the lemon juice into a measuring jug and make it up to 400ml (14fl oz) with cold water. Put the lemon zest, egg yolks, cornflour and sugar in a bowl. Add a little of the diluted lemon juice and stir to form a smooth thin paste, adding a little extra juice if necessary.

4 Heat the remaining diluted juice to just below boiling point. Pour onto the yolk mixture, stirring continuously, then return the mixture to the pan. Bring to the boil, stirring, then remove the pan from the heat. Pour into the pastry case.

5 For the meringue topping, whisk the egg whites until stiff. Gradually add the sugar, whisking, until stiff and glossy. Spoon this evenly over the lemon filling to cover it completely, spreading the meringue to the edge.

6 Bake for 7-10 minutes, until pale golden. Leave to cool, then chill before serving, in slices.

HOWGATE WONDER
COOKER OR EATER
QUITE SWEET, KEEPS
SHAPE WHEN COOKED
GOOD FOR BAKING

1915 BLENHEIM ORANGE X
NEWTON WONDER AT
HOWGATE LANE BEMBRIDGE
OF W

Orchards, with their glorious spring blossom and colourful autumn fruit,

Apples and pears

The Romans brought cultivated apples to Britain. They regarded them as truly gourmet produce, superior even to the luxurious fig. Today apples remain our most important fruit, perfectly suited to the cool, temperate climate. They can also be stored throughout winter, providing vitamins, nourishment and sweetness at a time when home-grown fruit is scarce.

Lost and found

Britain's Brogdale Horticultural Trust, home of the National Fruit Collection, houses over 2300 varieties of the nearly 8000 types of apple that have been given names at some point during history. About 1200 apple varieties are indigenous to Britain, but farming policy and the spread of supermarkets have resulted in most shops selling only a few locally grown examples every

year. It is difficult now to find the myriad regional varieties – Gloucester Cross, Flower of Kent, Beauty of Bath – in the regions after which they are named. However, farmers' markets and increasing consumer dissatisfaction with bland imports are encouraging a more diverse range to be enjoyed, as well as a much-needed resurgence of interest in protecting Britain's traditional orchards.

Not just Granny Smith

Apples are usually considered to be either dessert or cooking apples. For instance, the Bramley (properly called Bramley's Seedling) has such sharp, acidic flesh that it needs to be cooked to be appreciated at its best. However, several varieties, such as Britain's top seller, the Cox's Orange Pippin, can be enjoyed both ways.

are an integral part of our landscape, culture and heritage.

Two of the more unusual varieties of apple, that are not too difficult to locate, are the James Grieve, a dessert apple that can be used for cooking if it is picked early enough, and the Discovery, which has hints of raspberry and is best eaten soon after it is picked.

The Pearmain is said to be the oldest-named apple in England. It was first recorded in 1204 and the Worcester Pearmain is now the most well-known type. All the members of the Russet family, which includes the Egremont Russet, Royal Russet and Golden Russet, are delicious raw or cooked, being particularly prized for their wonderful nutty flavour.

In the 19th century, the Blenheim Orange, which comes from Oxfordshire, was considered to be the finest apple available over the Christmas period. Like the now hugely popular Cox's Orange Pippin, it is a member of the Pippin family.

Pear varieties

Many traditional orchards contain pear trees, which can produce fruit for up to 300 years. There are around 1000 varieties of pear, of which about 700 have been developed in Britain. The most common of these are the Williams, Conference and Comice pears. John Stair, a Berkshire schoolmaster, produced the Williams in 1770, and the Conference was created by Thomas Rives in 1874. It went on to win a first-class certificate at the 1885 International Pear Conference.

In Worcestershire, where perry (pear cider) was first made, the pear has been incorporated into various city and council coats of arms, and the large cooking pear, Black Worcester, is still grown in the area.

Apple batter pudding

PREPARATION TIME: 15 MINUTES
COOKING TIME: 1-1¼ HOURS
SERVES 4

25g (1oz) caster sugar, plus extra for dusting
4 dessert apples, such as Cox's, peeled,
    quartered and cored
25g (1oz) butter, diced
115g (4oz) plain flour
Pinch of ground cloves
2 eggs
25g (1oz) chopped mixed peel
300ml (½ pint) semi-skimmed milk

1 Heat the oven to 200°C (400°F, gas mark 6). Sprinkle the sugar into a 20cm (8in) diameter round ovenproof dish, about 4cm (1½in) deep.

2 Place the apple quarters in the dish, turning to coat them lightly in the sugar. Dot the butter evenly over the apples, then bake for 20 minutes. Reduce the oven temperature to 190°C (375°F, gas mark 5).

3 Meanwhile, sift the flour into a bowl and add the ground cloves. Make a well in the middle and add the eggs and mixed peel. Pour in a little of the milk, then beat it into the eggs, incorporating a little of the flour. Continue beating until all the flour has been incorporated, adding the milk a little at a time, to make a smooth batter.

4 Pour the batter over the apples and return the dish to the oven. Bake for 40-45 minutes, until the batter is risen, browned and crisp around the edges. Dust with a little sugar and serve at once.

Nutrients per serving
- Calories 330
- Carbohydrate 53g (of which sugars 35g)
- Protein 9g
- Fat 32g (of which saturated fat 10g)
- Fibre 3g
- Vitamins B$_{12}$

A homely dessert based on a classic **Yorkshire pudding,** this can also be made using **rhubarb,** cherries or **gooseberries.**

Apple pie

This light, **thin-crust** version of a **British favourite** is packed with nutrient-rich fruit.

PREPARATION TIME: 20 MINUTES,
PLUS 1 HOUR CHILLING
COOKING TIME: 40 MINUTES
SERVES 6

115g (4oz) plain flour
55g (2oz) butter, diced
675g (1lb 8oz) cooking apples, peeled,
    quartered, cored and sliced
4 tablespoons unrefined caster sugar,
    plus extra for sprinkling
¼ teaspoon ground cloves
Milk for glazing

1 Put the flour and butter in a bowl. Rub the butter into the flour until the mixture resembles fine breadcrumbs. Gradually add cold water, about 3 tablespoons, until the mixture comes together in a dough. Wrap and chill for 30 minutes.

2 Roll out the dough on a lightly floured surface to about 6cm (2½ in) larger all round than the top of a 24 x 18cm (9½ x 7in) pie dish. Cut a strip about 2.5cm (1in) wide from around the edge of the pastry. Brush the rim of the pie dish with water and press the pastry strip onto it.

3 Mix the apples with the sugar and ground cloves and pack them into the pie dish, piling it high in the middle.

4 Dampen the pastry rim with water and cover with the rolled-out pastry round. Press the edge firmly to seal it well all round. Trim off excess pastry around the rim. Decorate the rim with a scalloped effect, if desired, and use the pastry trimmings to make decorative shapes. Make a hole in the middle for steam to escape and chill for about 30 minutes. Heat the oven to 180°C (350°F, gas mark 4).

5 Stand the pie on a baking tray to catch any juices. Brush the top with a little milk and bake for about 35 minutes until the top is pale golden and the fruit is bubbling inside.

6 Brush with a little extra milk and sprinkle with caster sugar, then bake for a further 5 minutes. Set aside for 5 minutes, then serve with custard (see page 230), low-fat crème fraîche or single cream.

Nutrients per serving
- Calories 215
- Carbohydrate 35g (of which sugars 20g)
- Protein 2g
- Fat 8g (of which saturated fat 5g)
- Fibre 2g
- Vitamins C

Crispy pear dumplings

PREPARATION TIME: 30 MINUTES,
PLUS 30 MINUTES COOLING
COOKING TIME: 1 HOUR 20 MINUTES
SERVES 4

4 large, firm pears, such as Blush, peeled
   with stalks intact
600ml (1 pint) unsweetened apple juice
1 cinnamon stick
25g (1oz) sultanas
50g (1¾oz) walnut pieces, finely chopped
25g (1oz) glacé cherries, finely chopped
½ teaspoon freshly grated nutmeg
4 sheets filo pastry, about 42 x 28cm
   (16½ x 11in) each
2 tablespoons sunflower oil
250g (9oz) Greek-style yoghurt

Using **light filo** pastry rather than suet
crust reduces the **fat** content of this
delicious pudding by more than a fifth.

1 Put the pears in a saucepan just big enough
to take them. Add the apple juice and
cinnamon stick. Heat gently until simmering,
then cover and poach for 15-20 minutes,
turning once, until just tender. Leave in the
cooking liquid until cool enough to handle.

2 In a bowl, mix the sultanas, walnuts,
cherries, nutmeg and 1-2 tablespoons of
the pear cooking liquid to bind the mixture.

3 Remove the pears and set aside. Discard
the cinnamon stick and boil the juice for
about 30 minutes or until deep golden and
reduced to about 50ml (2fl oz). Leave to cool.

4 Meanwhile, cut the cores from the pears,
from the bottom, keeping the stalks intact.
Scoop out and discard the pips. Trim the bases
so that the pears can stand upright.

5 Heat the oven to 160°C (325°F, gas
mark 3). Fill each pear centre with the fruit
and nuts. Take one sheet of filo and lightly brush
with oil (keeping the other sheets covered to
prevent them drying out). Fold the sheet in
half, then brush again with oil and stand a pear
in the centre.

6 Fold the pastry up around the pear,
brushing the outside lightly with oil before
overlapping it around the stalk. Place on the
baking sheet and repeat with the remaining
pears and filo. Bake for about 35 minutes, until
crisp and lightly browned.

7 Mix the cooled, reduced apple juice with
the yoghurt and serve with the dumplings.

**Nutrients per
serving**
- Calories 400
- Carbohydrate 50g
  (of which sugars 44g)
- Protein 7g
- Fat 20g (of which
  saturated fat 5g)
- Fibre 4g
- Vitamins C

Cherry charlotte

The original charlotte filling was apple, thought to be named after Queen Charlotte, wife of George III. This version uses cherries, with wholemeal bread for added fibre.

PREPARATION TIME: 20 MINUTES, PLUS 1 HOUR SOAKING
COOKING TIME: 35-40 MINUTES
SERVES 4

600g (1lb 5oz) cherries, stoned
4 teaspoons caster sugar
6 tablespoons kirsch, medium sherry, white wine or apple juice
40g (1½oz) butter
2 tablespoons sunflower oil
11 thick slices of wholemeal bread, crusts removed

1 Put the cherries in a small, deep bowl. Add 3 teaspoons of the sugar and the kirsch, sherry, wine or apple juice. Mix well, cover and leave to soak for at least 1 hour.

2 Heat the oven to 190°C (375°F, gas mark 5). Melt the butter and oil in a small saucepan. Brush a 1.4 litre (2½ pint) ovenproof dish, about 7.5cm (3in) deep, with some of the butter and oil. Brush six slices of the bread with oil and place them, oiled side down, in the dish, to line the base and sides.

3 Tip the cherries and their juices into the dish. Cut a large round from a slice of bread and place it on top of the fruit. Cut eight small rounds from the remaining slices and arrange around the top to cover.

4 Brush the top with the remaining butter and oil. Sprinkle with the remaining sugar and bake for 35-40 minutes, until browned and crisp. Leave to stand for 5 minutes before serving with low-fat crème fraîche, yoghurt or custard (see page 230).

Nutrients per serving
- Calories 420
- Carbohydrate 57g (of which sugars 24g)
- Protein 9g
- Fat 16g (of which saturated fat 7g)
- Fibre 6g
- Vitamins C

Eve's pudding with creamy orange sauce

PREPARATION TIME: 20 MINUTES
COOKING TIME: I HOUR
SERVES 6

200g (7oz) ready-to-eat dried apricots,
    cut into chunks
4 Cox's apples, peeled, quartered, cored
    and thickly sliced
100ml (3½fl oz) unsweetened apple juice
2 eggs
50g (1¾oz) caster sugar, plus extra
    for dusting
50g (1¾oz) plain flour
85g (3oz) almonds, coarsely ground
    or very finely chopped

For the orange sauce:
Grated zest of 1 orange and juice of
    3 oranges
2 tablespoons cornflour
2 tablespoons sugar
280g (10oz) low-fat crème fraîche

1 Heat the oven to 200°C (400°F,
gas mark 6). Put the apricots and
apples in a 1.4 litre (2½ pint) ovenproof
dish, 7.5cm (3in) deep. Add the apple
juice, cover and bake for 30 minutes.
Leave to stand, uncovered, while you
prepare the sponge topping.

2 Whisk the eggs with the sugar until
very pale, thick and creamy. Sift in
the flour and add the almonds. Using a
large metal spoon, fold the flour and
nuts into the mixture until
incorporated.

3 Pour the sponge mixture over the
fruit, spreading it evenly to the
edge of the dish. Bake for 30 minutes,
until the topping is risen and browned.
Dust with sugar.

4 Make the orange sauce about
5 minutes before the pudding is
cooked. Pour the orange juice into a
jug and add water to make it up to
300ml (½ pint).

5 In a small saucepan, mix the
cornflour and sugar to a smooth
paste with the orange zest and a little
of the diluted juice. Gradually stir in
the remaining juice. Bring to the boil,
stirring continuously, then simmer for
2 minutes, still stirring. Remove from
the heat.

6 Stir in the crème fraîche and
transfer to a warmed jug. Spoon
the pudding into bowls and serve with
the orange sauce.

Nutrients per serving
- Calories 360
- Carbohydrate 51g (of which sugars 39g)
- Protein 7g
- Fat 15g (of which saturated fat 5g)
- Fibre 4g
- Vitamins C, E

The light, **fat-free** sponge on
this **classic** pudding includes
walnuts, which are high in
vitamin E and protein.

Orange roly-poly

PREPARATION TIME: 20 MINUTES
COOKING TIME: 55 MINUTES
SERVES 4

3 oranges, preferably seedless
175g (6oz) self-raising flour
75g (2¾oz) light vegetable suet
100ml (3½fl oz) semi-skimmed milk
4 tablespoons thick-cut orange marmalade
1 teaspoon sugar

Fresh oranges add a light and juicy quality to this traditional nursery pudding. Baking it gives a crunchy, slightly sticky base to contrast with the moist middle.

1 Heat the oven to 190°C (375°F, gas mark 5). Cut a sheet of non-stick baking parchment to 46 × 30cm (18 × 12in). Cut a piece of foil the same size and place the parchment over the foil.

2 Grate the zest from one of the oranges. Remove the peel and pith from all three oranges. Slice and quarter each and place the quarters in a bowl.

3 Put the flour in a separate bowl. Stir in the suet and orange zest, then mix in the milk to make a soft, but not sticky, dough. Turn out on to a floured surface and press into a neat ball, then roll out to a rectangle measuring 25 × 23cm (10 × 9in).

4 Spread the marmalade over the pastry, leaving a 2cm (¾in) border. Lay the pieces of orange on top, leaving a slightly wider border. Dampen the border with a little water and roll up the pastry from the long side, tucking in the pieces of orange as you go. Press the long edge to seal it and pinch the ends together.

5 Place the roly-poly on the parchment paper. Fold the foil and paper loosely over the top to seal, twisting the ends and turning them up slightly to catch the juices. Place on a baking tray.

6 Bake for 40 minutes. Carefully open and fold back the foil and paper, leaving the edge high to retain the juice. Baste the pudding with juice, taking care not to puncture the wrapping, and sprinkle sugar over the top. Bake for a further 15 minutes until lightly browned on top. Serve at once in thick slices, with any cooking juices poured over.

VARIATION

For apple and sultana roly-poly, peel, core and grate 450g (1lb) cooking apples. Mix with 50g (2oz) sultanas, the grated zest of 1 unwaxed lemon, 2 tablespoons light muscovado sugar and 1 teaspoon ground cinnamon. Use to fill the roly-poly instead of the marmalade and fresh oranges, then cook as directed.

Nutrients per serving
- Calories 340
- Carbohydrate 54g (of which sugars 20g)
- Protein 6g
- Fat 13g (of which saturated fat 6g)
- Fibre 3g
- Vitamins C

Deep custard tart with caramelised plums

PREPARATION TIME: 20 MINUTES,
PLUS 30 MINUTES CHILLING
COOKING TIME: 1½ HOURS
SERVES 6

Plums add **sharp-sweet** flavour and lovely **colour** to a traditional custard tart, popular since the Middle Ages.

85g (3oz) plain flour
55g (2oz) plain wholemeal flour
60g (2¼oz) butter, diced
2 eggs, plus 2 egg yolks
4 tablespoons caster sugar
1 teaspoon vanilla extract
500ml (18fl oz) semi-skimmed milk
Grated nutmeg

For the caramelised plums:
6 large plums, stoned and quartered
2 tablespoons sugar

Nutrients per serving
- Calories 320
- Carbohydrate 42g (of which sugars 26g)
- Protein 9g
- Fat 14g (of which saturated fat 7g)
- Fibre 2g
- Vitamins B$_{12}$

1 Put both flours in a bowl and rub in the butter until the mixture resembles fine breadcrumbs. Mix in 2-3 tablespoons cold water, until the mixture comes together.

2 Roll out the pastry on a lightly floured surface, then use to line a 24 x 18cm (9½ x 7in) pie dish. Trim off excess pastry and pinch round the edge to decorate. Prick the base and chill for 30 minutes.

3 Heat the oven to 200°C (400°F, gas mark 6). Line the pastry case with greaseproof paper and baking beans and bake for 20 minutes. Remove the paper and beans and bake for a further 5 minutes until dry and part-cooked. Reduce the oven to 160°C (325°F, gas mark 3).

4 Beat the whole eggs and yolks with the sugar and vanilla until well mixed. Gradually beat in the milk. Pour into the pastry case and sprinkle with a little grated nutmeg. Bake for about 50 minutes, until the custard is lightly set but still slightly wobbly. Set aside while you cook the plums.

5 Preheat the grill on the hottest setting. Place the plums, cut side up, in a shallow flameproof dish just big enough to hold them. Sprinkle with the sugar and grill for about 5 minutes until juicy and well browned in places.

6 Serve slices of the warm custard tart with the hot plums, or serve both cold.

Blackberry and apple crumble

PREPARATION TIME: 15 MINUTES
COOKING TIME: 40-45 MINUTES
SERVES 6

Nutrients per serving
- Calories 510
- Carbohydrate 53g
  (of which sugars 23g)
- Protein 8g
- Fat 31g (of which saturated fat 10g)
- Fibre 6g
- Vitamins C

450g (1lb) cooking apples, such as Bramleys
250g (9oz) blackberries
40g (1½oz) light brown sugar

For the topping:
100g (3½oz) butter
125g (4½oz) plain flour
25g (1oz) caster sugar
150g (5½oz) mixture of: chopped hazelnuts, sunflower seeds, pumpkin seeds or pine nuts
100g (3½oz) oat flakes or rolled oats

1 Heat the oven to 180°C (350°F, gas mark 4). Cut the apples into quarters and remove the core. Peel each quarter, then cut into slices. Transfer to a large ovenproof dish, about 1.4 litre (2½ pint) capacity. Add the blackberries and sugar and mix.

2 For the topping, rub the butter into the flour, then stir in the sugar, nuts and seeds and oat flakes or rolled oats. Sprinkle the topping evenly over the fruit to cover it in a thick layer.

Fruity queen of puddings

PREPARATION TIME: 15 MINUTES,
PLUS 30 MINUTES SOAKING
COOKING TIME: 45 MINUTES
SERVES 6

Tangy redcurrants, high in vitamin C and potassium, replace sweet jam in this delectable pudding, said to have been named after Queen Victoria.

125g (4½ oz) fresh white breadcrumbs
3 eggs, separated, plus 1 whole egg
100g (3½ oz) caster sugar
1 teaspoon vanilla extract
400ml (14fl oz) semi-skimmed milk
150g (5½ oz) redcurrants, stemmed
175g (6oz) raspberries

Nutrients per serving
- Calories 220
- Carbohydrate 34g
  (of which sugars 24g)
- Protein 10g
- Fat 6g (of which saturated fat 2g)
- Fibre 2g
- Vitamins C, B$_{12}$

1 Put the breadcrumbs into a 1.4 litre (2½ pint) ovenproof dish, about 7.5cm (3in) deep.

2 Beat the egg yolks with the whole egg, 25g (1oz) of the sugar and the vanilla extract. Stir in the milk. Strain the mixture through a fine sieve over the breadcrumbs. Cover and set aside to soak for 30 minutes. Meanwhile, heat the oven to 180°C (350°F, gas mark 4).

3 Bake the bread and custard base for 30-35 minutes, until set and slightly risen. Set aside to cool while you prepare the meringue.

4 Using an electric beater, whisk the egg whites until stiff. Gradually add the remaining sugar, whisking, then continue whisking until stiff and glossy.

5 Mix the redcurrants and raspberries, then place them on top of the cooked base. Pile the meringue over the fruit, spreading it out to the edge of the dish with a fork. Return the pudding to the oven for about 10 minutes to brown the meringue lightly. Serve at once.

3 Bake for 40-45 minutes, until the topping is crisp and golden and the fruit is cooked and beginning to bubble up around the edges. Leave to stand for 5 minutes before serving, with custard (see page 230).

The topping in this autumnal crumble includes nuts and seeds for added protein and fibre.

Rhubarb gingerbread puddings
with port wine sauce

PREPARATION TIME: 25 MINUTES,
PLUS 20 MINUTES COOLING
COOKING TIME: 30 MINUTES
SERVES 4

450g (1lb) tender rhubarb, sliced
125g (4½ oz) plain flour
½ teaspoon bicarbonate of soda
½ teaspoon ground ginger
½ teaspoon ground cinnamon
70g (2½ oz) golden syrup
40g (1½ oz) butter
40g (1½ oz) light muscovado sugar
2 tablespoons semi-skimmed milk
1 egg, beaten
½ teaspoon icing sugar for dusting

For the sauce:
15g (½ oz) butter
1 teaspoon cornflour
150ml (¼ pint) ruby port wine
4 tablespoons redcurrant jelly

Gingerbread dates back to **medieval** times, when **extravagant** use of spices indicated **wealth**. Based on an old recipe, this pudding combines tangy rhubarb with **sweet** ginger.

1 Heat the oven to 180°C (350°F, gas mark 4). Divide half the rhubarb between four individual 200ml (7fl oz) soufflé dishes, reserving the rest.

2 Sift the flour, bicarbonate of soda, ginger and cinnamon into a bowl. Heat the syrup, butter, sugar and milk in a saucepan, stirring, until the butter has melted. Pour into the dry ingredients and mix well. Beat in the egg.

3 Divide the mixture between the dishes, spreading it evenly over the rhubarb. Stand the dishes on a baking sheet and bake for about 25 minutes, until well risen, firm and cracked across the top. Set aside to cool slightly.

4 While the puddings are cooking, make the sauce: put the remaining rhubarb, butter and 2 tablespoons water in a small saucepan. Cover and cook over a medium heat for about 10 minutes until soft. Press the rhubarb through a sieve, discarding the fibres that remain.

5 Return the purée to a clean saucepan. Mix the cornflour to a smooth paste with the port wine. Add the redcurrant jelly to the purée and stir in the port mixture. Heat, stirring, until the mixture boils and thickens. Continue cooking, still stirring, until the jelly has melted. Remove from the heat and leave to cool slightly.

6 Dust the warm puddings with a little icing sugar and serve with the warm port wine sauce, or with ginger syllabub (see page 212).

Nutrients per serving
- Calories 430
- Carbohydrate 650g (of which sugars 40g)
- Protein 6g
- Fat 13g (of which saturated fat 8g)
- Fibre 2g

Bread and butter pudding

PREPARATION TIME: 15 MINUTES,
PLUS 30 MINUTES STANDING
COOKING TIME: 45 MINUTES
SERVES 4

6 slices of white bread, 2cm (¾ in) thick,
   crusts removed
25g (1oz) butter, softened
½ teaspoon ground mixed spice
55g (2oz) mixed dried fruit
3 eggs
25g (1oz) caster sugar, plus extra
   for dusting
600ml (1 pint) semi-skimmed milk

Nutrients per serving
- Calories 350
- Carbohydrate 46g (of which sugars 20g)
- Protein 14g
- Fat 13g (of which saturated fat 6g)
- Fibre 1g
- Vitamins B_2, B_{12}

1 Spread the bread thinly with the butter, then sprinkle it with the mixed spice. Cut each slice diagonally into quarters.

2 Arrange eight bread quarters, buttered side down, in the bottom of a 1.4 litre (2½ pint) ovenproof dish, 7.5cm (3in) deep. Sprinkle with half the dried fruit, then add half the remaining bread, buttered side up. Sprinkle with the remaining fruit and top with the remaining bread, buttered side up.

3 Beat the eggs with the caster sugar, then stir in the milk. Strain the mixture over the bread. Cover and leave to stand for at least 30 minutes, preferably 1-2 hours, or overnight in the refrigerator.

4 Heat the oven to 180°C (350°F, gas mark 4). Bake for about 45 minutes, until golden, risen and set all the way through.

5 Dust lightly with sugar and serve hot or warm.

VARIATIONS
Use 4 tablespoons chopped glacé ginger instead of the mixed dried fruit and sprinkle the buttered bread with the grated zest of 1 unwaxed lemon instead of mixed spice.

Use sultanas instead of mixed dried fruit, soaked in 4 tablespoons dry sherry for 2-3 hours.

Made with **semi-skimmed milk** and just a little butter, this **healthy version** still tastes **lusciously creamy.**

Raisin spotted dick

This comforting, lemon-scented steamed pudding is 'spotted' with succulent raisins, providing natural sweetness that keeps the added sugar content low.

PREPARATION TIME: 20 MINUTES
COOKING TIME: 1¾ HOURS
SERVES 4

Oil for greasing
115g (4oz) self-raising flour
115g (4oz) fresh white breadcrumbs
55g (2oz) low-fat vegetable suet
40g (1½oz) caster sugar
Grated zest of 1 unwaxed lemon
115g (4oz) raisins
6 tablespoons semi-skimmed milk

For the custard:
1 tablespoon cornflour
2 tablespoons caster sugar
1 teaspoon vanilla extract
3 egg yolks
600ml (1 pint) semi-skimmed milk

1 Prepare a large saucepan of boiling water with a steamer on top. Cut a sheet of greaseproof paper and foil, each about 46 x 30cm (18 x 12in). Brush the paper with a little oil and place it over the foil.

2 Put the flour in a bowl. Add the breadcrumbs, suet, sugar, lemon zest and raisins, then stir to mix well. Add the milk and mix to bind to a soft, but not sticky, dough.

3 With lightly floured hands, gently roll and press the dough into a sausage shape, 18cm (7in) long. Lay the dough lengthways on the greased paper. Bring the edges of the paper and foil together over the dough and fold

them over several times to seal. Twist the ends, like a cracker, leaving plenty of space for the pudding to rise.

4 Place the pudding in the steamer and cook for 1¾ hours. Keep the water at a constant boil, topping it up from time to time. The pudding should be well risen and the raisins plump and moist when cooked.

5 Make the custard just before the pudding is cooked. Put the cornflour, sugar, vanilla and egg yolks in a bowl. Add 1 tablespoon of the milk and stir to a smooth, thick paste. Stir in a little more milk to thin the mixture.

6 Heat the remaining milk until just before boiling, pour it into the yolk mixture, stirring, then return the mixture to the pan. Cook over a medium heat, stirring continuously, until the custard thickens and boils. Cook, still stirring, for about 30 seconds, then remove from the heat.

7 Lift the pudding from the steamer by its foil wrapping. Cut into slices and serve hot with the custard.

Nutrients per serving
- Calories 500
- Carbohydrate 83g (of which sugars 44g)
- Protein 14g
- Fat 14g (of which saturated fat 6g)
- Fibre 2g
- Vitamins B₁₂, B₆

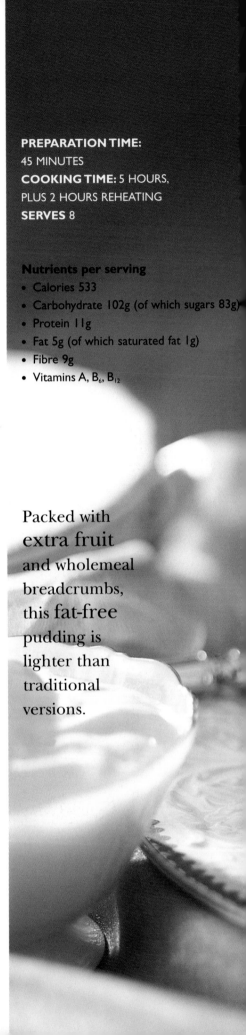

PREPARATION TIME:
45 MINUTES
COOKING TIME: 5 HOURS,
PLUS 2 HOURS REHEATING
SERVES 8

Nutrients per serving
- Calories 533
- Carbohydrate 102g (of which sugars 83g)
- Protein 11g
- Fat 5g (of which saturated fat 1g)
- Fibre 9g
- Vitamins A, B₆, B₁₂

Packed with **extra fruit** and wholemeal breadcrumbs, this **fat-free** pudding is lighter than traditional versions.

Light Christmas pudding

Oil for greasing
115g (4oz) raisins
115g (4oz) sultanas
115g (4oz) ready-to-eat prunes,
   roughly chopped
115g (4oz) ready-to-eat dried apricots,
   roughly chopped
85g (3oz) chopped mixed peel
1 carrot, finely grated
1 dessert apple, peeled, cored and grated
Grated zest and juice of 1 orange
1 teaspoon ground cinnamon
1 teaspoon grated nutmeg
2 teaspoons ground mixed spice
50g (1¾oz) plain wholemeal flour
115g (4oz) fresh wholemeal breadcrumbs
2 eggs, beaten
2 tablespoons black treacle
100ml (3½ fl oz) brandy

1 Prepare a saucepan of boiling water with a steamer on top. Lightly grease a 1.2 litre (2 pint) pudding basin. Cut a circle each of greaseproof paper and foil to cover the basin with about 10cm (4in) to spare. Grease the paper, lay it on the foil and make a pleat in the middle, to allow room to spread.

2 Mix the raisins, sultanas, prunes, apricots and mixed peel in a large bowl. Stir in the carrot, apple, orange zest and juice. Sift the cinnamon, nutmeg, mixed spice and flour into a bowl, then add to the fruit with the breadcrumbs and mix well.

3 Beat the eggs with the treacle, then add the brandy and pour it over the pudding mixture. Stir until thoroughly combined, then turn the mixture into the prepared basin and press down well. Cover with the pleated paper and foil, then tie or crumple it firmly around the basin rim.

4 Steam for 5 hours, topping up the boiling water regularly. Remove the paper and foil. Cover with a clean tea towel and leave until cold. Unwrap and cover with double-thick kitchen paper, then wrap the entire basin in foil. Store in the refrigerator for up to 1 month.

5 To reheat, steam the pudding over boiling water for 2 hours. Slide a flexible spatula down around the side of the pudding to loosen it from the basin. Cover with a serving dish, invert both basin and dish, then lift off the basin. Slice and serve with brandy orange cream.

BRANDY ORANGE CREAM
Beat together 2 tablespoons icing sugar, 4 tablespoons brandy and the grated zest of 1 orange with 225g (8oz) low-fat soft cheese, then fold in 300ml (½ pint) fromage frais.

Creamy rice pudding

PREPARATION TIME: 10 MINUTES
COOKING TIME: 1 HOUR 20 MINUTES
SERVES 4

55g (2oz) pudding rice
600ml (1 pint) semi-skimmed milk
2 fresh bay leaves
Grated zest of 1 unwaxed lemon
2 tablespoons caster sugar
Pinch of freshly grated nutmeg

Nutrients per serving
- Calories 150
- Carbohydrate 27g
  (of which sugars 15g)
- Protein 6g
- Fat 3g (of which saturated fat 1.5g)
- Fibre 0g
- Vitamins B$_{12}$

Aromatic bay leaves have a long tradition in sweet dishes, and here they add an **exotic flavour** to this traditional **nursery** pudding.

1 Heat the oven to 180°C (350°F, gas mark 4). Put the rice in a saucepan and add plenty of cold water. Bring slowly to the boil, stir well, then remove from the heat and drain in a sieve. Transfer to a large ovenproof casserole, big enough to allow room for the rice to swell as it cooks.

2 Pour in the milk. Crumple the bay leaves to release their aroma, then add them to the pudding with the lemon zest, sugar and nutmeg. Stir,

cover and bake for 1-1¼ hours, stirring after 45 minutes, then at 10-15 minute intervals (unless you prefer a skin on top), scraping the residue from the side of the casserole into the milk each time. Serve hot, warm or chilled, as it is or with stewed fruit or fresh berries.

VARIATION
Add 25g (1oz) raisins halfway through cooking.

Chocolate mousse

PREPARATION TIME: 25 MINUTES
PLUS 2-3 HOURS CHILLING
COOKING TIME: 5-7 MINUTES
SERVES 4

1 tablespoon powdered gelatine
3 tablespoons cocoa powder,
    plus extra for dusting
1 tablespoon brandy
2 eggs, separated, plus 2 egg yolks
75g (2¾oz) caster sugar
250g (9oz) low-fat fromage frais,
    plus 4 tablespoons for decorating

Nutrients per serving
- Calories 260
- Carbohydrate 28g
  (of which sugars 27g)
- Protein 16g
- Fat 9g (of which saturated fat 3g)
- Fibre 1.5g
- Vitamins B$_2$, B$_{12}$

1 Put 2 tablespoons cold water in a small, heatproof bowl that fits over a small saucepan. Sprinkle the gelatine evenly over the water, without stirring, and leave to soak until swollen.

2 Dissolve the cocoa powder in 3 tablespoons boiling water, then stir in the brandy and set aside.

3 Prepare a saucepan of hot (not boiling) water. Place the egg yolks in a large heatproof bowl that fits over the saucepan. Add the sugar and stand the bowl over the pan. Using an electric beater, whisk the mixture for 3-5 minutes until thick, pale and smooth. Remove the bowl from the saucepan.

4 Stand the gelatine over a small saucepan of hot (not boiling) water and leave until completely melted and clear. Stir the dissolved cocoa into the gelatine, then whisk the mixture into the creamed egg yolks. Use a flexible spatula to scrape the mixture down and off the side of the bowl.

5 In a clean bowl, whisk the egg whites until stiff. Stir the fromage frais into the chocolate mixture, then stir in a spoonful of the whisked whites. Fold in the remaining whites.

6 Divide the mousse between four glasses or dishes and chill until set. Serve topped with a little fromage frais and dusted with cocoa powder.

Lightened with fromage frais and lifted with a little brandy, this smooth chocolate mousse is a creamy alternative to high-fat recipes.

Baking

Baking
the healthy way

Eating cakes and biscuits may make you feel guilty but they need not be unhealthy or out of bounds if you make your own.

Showered as we are with dietary facts, it is sometimes easy to forget that eating should be a pleasure and not just a means of giving the body the vital nutrients it requires. Happily, baked goods can satisfy both these needs, especially if you make your own.

Not only can you avoid the additives and preservatives found in commercial baked products, but you can also add healthy ingredients, such as dried fruits, nuts and seeds, which will boost their nutritional value. When you are baking at home, you can, of course, also control the amount and type of fat that you use.

Butter or margarine?
Margarine used to be considered a healthier option than butter, largely because the softer varieties are much lower in saturated fats.

But, in fact, the hydrogenation process used to make hard margarines (the type usually used in baking) from vegetable, seed or fish oils converts unsaturated fats into saturated fats. Partial hydrogenation, used to manufacture softer margarines, changes some of the unsaturated fats into trans fatty acids or 'trans fats'. Both saturated and trans fats can raise blood cholesterol, leading to an increased risk of heart disease and stroke.

While butter and margarine contain vitamins A and D (margarine is fortified with the vitamins), it is now widely thought that the natural goodness of butter – in moderation – is preferable. And most people prefer the taste.

Alternatives to butter
If you wish to avoid using butter, try a margarine high in monounsaturates as these are usually made with olive oil and should contain few or no trans fats. Alternatively, try olive and vegetable oils, which can also be used for baking.

Many recipes still work well if half the butter is replaced with oil. For shortcrust pastry you can, instead of fat, use a healthier light, mild olive oil. Reduced-fat and low-fat spreads do not work well in baking recipes.

Flour power
The flour that you use in your home baking is important for the success of each loaf, cake or pie and also affects its nutritional content.

Wholemeal flour offers more nutritionally than white but produces heavier baked goods. If you have not used wholemeal flour before or wish to keep your baking light, mix one-third wholemeal flour with two-thirds white.
• Wholemeal wheat and wholegrain bread are good sources of fibre, which is important for maintaining bowel health and preventing heart disease.
• Wheat is also an important source of selenium, a vital part of the body's antioxidant defence system.
• Weight for weight, wholemeal flour contains three times as much fibre as white, as well as significantly higher levels of several of the B vitamins.

Two grades of flour are available. Strong flour is usually used for breads, whereas normal flour has a finer texture and is better when baking cakes.

Sugar and spice
Sugar enhances the taste of foods and is a major 'hidden' ingredient in many shop-bought cakes and biscuits. Although a little is not harmful, it contributes nothing to the diet except calories. When you

Griddle cakes

Cooked on a very hot surface, griddle cakes need little, if any, oil. Drop a spoonful of batter high above the griddle. They can be easily turned when a crust has formed.

NUTRITIONAL VALUES OF DIFFERENT FATS PER 100g (3½oz)				
Product	Total fat*	Saturated	Monounsaturated	Polyunsaturated
Butter	82	54	19.8	2.6
Hard margarine	82	31	37	11
Suet	87	48	32	2
Lard	99	41	44	10
Olive oil	100	14	70	11
Sunflower oil	100	12	20	63

*Total fat content includes fatty compounds and other fatty acids in addition to saturated, monounsaturated and polyunsaturated fats.

bake your own cakes and biscuits you can control the sugar content and add extra nutritious ingredients.
• Spices, such as nutmeg and cinnamon, add a lovely flavour to biscuits and cakes, so the sugar content can be reduced.
• Currants, sultanas and other dried fruits add natural sweetness to cakes and biscuits, and also contribute vitamins and minerals.

Nutritionally, white and brown sugar and honey are similar. Some recipes may suggest using unrefined brown sugar, honey, molasses or syrup for their taste.

Bread

Freshly baked crusty bread is wonderfully tempting, but in the past it has unfairly gained a reputation for being fattening, when the culprit is usually what is spread on it. Bread is a healthy source of energy and nutritionists recommend that we all eat more of it, especially the wholemeal varieties.

It is an excellent, slow-release form of carbohydrate, which makes it satisfying, and it also supplies fibre, B vitamins and iron. The average slice of bread contains only about 75 calories (roughly the same as a small banana).

But any additional butter or margarine, can easily double the calories – so it is important to spread fats thinly or omit them and, for a light lunch or snack, use your own healthy alternative toppings such as Homemade herbed curd cheese (see page 44) or Parsley-coated smoked mackerel pâté (see page 46).

Homemade breads will usually be richer in nutrients than bought loaves, especially if made with wholegrain flours, good-quality oils and extras such as nuts and seeds. They will also contain less water and air than commercial loaves.

Preparing filo pastry

1 Filo pastry can often be substituted for shortcrust or puff pastry to give a lighter result. Take care when unrolling filo sheets. Remove only what you need or they will dry out and become crumbly.

2 Keep any sheets that you are waiting to use well covered with a damp cloth, to prevent them from drying out.

3 Layer the filo sheets as instructed in the recipe. Brush each layer lightly with a little oil or melted butter.

Cornish fairings

These light, delicious ginger biscuits have long been associated with fairs in the south-west counties of England.

PREPARATION TIME: 15 MINUTES
COOKING TIME: 10 MINUTES
MAKES ABOUT 22 BISCUITS

70g (2½ oz) butter
2 rounded tablespooons golden syrup
150g (5½ oz) plain flour
1 level teaspoon bicarbonate of soda
1 teaspoon ground ginger
¼ teaspoon mixed spice
Pinch of salt
Grated zest of 1 small, unwaxed lemon
25g (1oz) golden caster sugar
Sunflower oil for greasing

1 Heat the oven to 190°C (375°F, gas mark 5). Put the butter and syrup into a small saucepan and heat gently until the butter has melted. Remove from the heat and leave to cool for a couple of minutes.

2 Sift the flour, bicarbonate of soda, spices and salt into a bowl, then stir in the lemon zest and sugar. Add the warm butter mixture and mix gently but thoroughly.

3 Using your hands, and while the mixture is still soft and warm, pull off marble-sized pieces of the dough and roll into about 22 balls. Place on a lightly oiled baking sheet, spaced well apart, and with your fingers press each one down gently into a biscuit shape.

4 Bake for 8 minutes or until golden brown and still slightly soft in the middle. (They firm up as they cool.) Remove to a wire rack to cool completely. Store in an airtight container.

Nutrients per biscuit
• Calories 56
• Carbohydrate 8g (of which sugars 3g)
• Protein 1g
• Fat 3g (of which saturated fat 2g)
• Fibre 0g

Chorley cakes

PREPARATION TIME: 30-40 MINUTES, PLUS 30 MINUTES RESTING
COOKING TIME: 30 MINUTES
MAKES 6 CAKES

For the pastry:
225g (8oz) plain flour
115g (4oz) strong white flour
1 teaspoon baking powder
25g (1oz) golden caster sugar
150g (5½ oz) butter, diced
Pinch of salt
About 125ml (4fl oz) skimmed milk
Sunflower oil for greasing
1 egg, beaten, to glaze

For the filling:
225g (8oz) currants
55g (2oz) light muscovado sugar
25g (1oz) butter, melted

1 Sift the flours and baking powder into a food processor. Add the sugar, butter and salt. Process until the mixture resembles breadcrumbs then, with the machine still running, slowly pour in enough milk to form a fairly stiff dough. Alternatively, rub the butter into the dry ingredients in a large bowl, adding milk to make a stiff dough.

2 Wrap the dough in cling film and refrigerate for 30 minutes. Heat the oven to 190°C (375°F, gas mark 5). For the filling, mix together the currants, sugar and melted butter.

3 Roll out the pastry to a thickness of about 5mm (¼in). Using a large saucer or small plate as a template, cut out six rounds of pastry, each about 20cm (8in) in diameter.

4 Divide the filling between the pastry rounds and spread it evenly. Moisten the edges of the pastry with water, then draw the edges up together to meet in the middle and form a package, pinching the edges together lightly to seal.

5 Turn the package upside down so that the edges are underneath. Using a rolling pin, gently roll out each package until the currants are just beginning to show through. They will now be about 10cm (4in) in diameter.

6 Place on a lightly greased baking sheet and brush all over with beaten egg. Make two parallel slits on top of each cake and bake for about 30 minutes or until golden brown.

7 Remove to a wire rack to cool for at least 20 minutes. Serve warm.

Similar to Eccles cakes, these Lancashire specialities are made with a light shortcrust pastry and filled with currants.

Nutrients per cake
- Calories 580
- Carbohydrate 84g (of which sugars 41g)
- Protein 8g
- Fat 26g (of which saturated fat 16g)
- Fibre 2g

Shrewsbury biscuits

PREPARATION TIME: 20 MINUTES,
PLUS 30 MINUTES RESTING
COOKING TIME: 15 MINUTES
MAKES ABOUT 30 BISCUITS

115g (4oz) butter, softened
115g (4oz) golden caster sugar, plus extra to dust
1 egg, beaten
225g (8oz) plain flour, sifted
55g (2oz) currants
Grated zest of 1 unwaxed lemon
Sunflower oil for greasing

Nutrients per biscuit
- Calories 80
- Carbohydrate 11g (of which sugars 5g)
- Protein 1g
- Fat 3g (of which saturated fat 2g)
- Fibre 0g

1 Cream the butter and sugar together in a bowl until pale and fluffy.

2 Beat in the egg, a little at a time. Stir in the flour, then the currants and lemon zest.

3 With lightly floured hands, bring the mixture together and turn it out onto a floured board. Roll out gently to a thickness of about 5mm (¼in). Using a round pastry cutter, about 5.5cm (2¼in), stamp out about 30 rounds.

4 Place the rounds on two lightly oiled baking sheets and refrigerate for about 30 minutes, until firm. Meanwhile, heat the oven to 180°C (350°F, gas mark 4).

5 Bake for about 15 minutes or until firm to the touch. Transfer to a wire rack and dust lightly with caster sugar. Leave to cool completely before serving.

Traditional to Shrewsbury for at least three centuries, these crisp biscuits, speckled with currants, can also be flavoured with nutmeg, cinnamon or caraway – add a level teaspoon to the mixture.

Oatcakes

Oatmeal is high in soluble fibre and helps to lower blood cholesterol levels, which makes these oatcakes healthy as well as delicious and versatile.

PREPARATION TIME: 15 MINUTES
COOKING TIME: 20 MINUTES
SERVES 8

225g (8oz) medium oatmeal
½ teaspoon salt
¼ teaspoon baking powder
25g (1oz) butter, melted, plus extra for greasing

Nutrients per biscuit, when making 12 biscuits
- Calories 136
- Carbohydrate 21g (of which sugars 0g)
- Protein 2g
- Fat 5g (of which saturated fat 2g)
- Fibre 2g

1 Heat the oven to 160°C (325°F, gas mark 3). Put the oatmeal, salt and baking powder in a bowl and pour in the melted butter. Mix well, adding just enough boiling water, about 5 tablespoons, to make a stiff dough.

2 Tip the mixture onto a floured board and roll out to a thickness of about 1cm (½in). Using an upturned glass or pastry cutter, stamp out 12 small, or 8 medium, rounds and transfer them to a lightly greased baking sheet.

3 Bake for about 20 minutes or until just firm. Transfer to a wire rack to cool. Serve with cheese, or, for a simple canapé, spread smaller oatcakes with a little quark and top with smoked salmon and chopped dill.

Richmond maids of honour

PREPARATION TIME: 30 MINUTES, PLUS 1 HOUR CHILLING
COOKING TIME: 30-40 MINUTES
MAKES 12 TARTLETS

Sunflower oil for greasing
225g (8oz) ready-rolled puff pastry
225g (8oz) curd cheese
1 egg
Grated zest of 1 large, unwaxed lemon
15g (½oz) butter, melted
55g (2oz) golden caster sugar

1 Heat the oven to 200°C (400°F, gas mark 6) and lightly oil a muffin or bun tin. Lay the pastry out on a board and, using a pastry cutter or glass, stamp out 12 rounds, about 7.5cm (3in) in diameter.

2 Press the pastry rounds into the prepared tin and refrigerate for about 1 hour.

3 Put the curd cheese, egg, lemon zest, butter and sugar in a bowl and beat together. Divide the mixture between the chilled pastry shells and bake for 30-40 minutes, or until the filling is puffed up and golden.

4 Remove the tarts from the tin to a wire rack to cool a little. Serve warm, freshly baked, or gently reheated in a low oven.

Nutrients per tartlet
• Calories 138
• Carbohydrate 12g (of which sugars 6g)
• Protein 3g
• Fat 9g (of which saturated fat 3g)
• Fibre 0g
• Vitamins B$_2$, B$_{12}$

These **dainty** little tarts, so named by Henry VIII, are made with **low-fat** curd cheese. Low-fat **filo pastry**, lightly brushed with melted butter, can be used instead of puff pastry.

Flapjacks with apricots

PREPARATION TIME: 15 MINUTES
COOKING TIME: 25 MINUTES
MAKES 24

100g (3½ oz) butter, plus extra for greasing
75g (2¾ oz) light muscovado sugar
3 heaped tablespoons honey
350g (12oz) porridge oats (not jumbo oats)
Pinch of salt
100g (3½ oz) dried apricots, chopped
1 banana, mashed

1 Heat the oven to 180°C (350°F, gas mark 4) and lightly butter a 23 x 33cm (9 x 13in) swiss roll tin.

2 Melt the butter, sugar and honey in a saucepan, then add the oats and salt. Stir to mix, then add the apricots and mashed banana. Mix well. Tip the mixture into the prepared tin, smoothing the surface with the back of a metal spoon to compress it.

3 Bake for 20-25 minutes, or until firm and golden brown.

4 Cut into 24 squares while still warm, then leave to cool completely in the tin. Once cooled, store in an airtight jar or tin.

Nutrients per flapjack
• Calories 125
• Carbohydrate 19g (of which sugars 8g)
• Protein 2g
• Fat 5g (of which saturated fat 2g)
• Fibre 1g

Flapjacks contain **healthy oats**, and this recipe uses **less butter**, and **honey** instead of syrup. The addition of **apricots** and **banana** ensures that they are still wonderfully moist.

Spiced oatmeal parkin

PREPARATION TIME: 20 MINUTES
COOKING TIME: ABOUT 1 HOUR
MAKES 8 SERVINGS

Sunflower oil for greasing
175g (6oz) self-raising flour
175g (6oz) medium oatmeal
Pinch of salt
85g (3oz) butter, diced
1 teaspoon ground ginger
¼ teaspoon ground nutmeg
85g (3oz) light muscovado sugar
2 rounded tablespoons black treacle
1 egg
150ml (¼ pint) buttermilk

Nutrients per serving
- Calories 300
- Carbohydrate 45g (of which sugars 12g)
- Protein 6g
- Fat 12g (of which saturated fat 6g)
- Fibre 2g

The north of England has some wonderful recipes for parkin, the **oatmeal-based** gingerbread traditionally baked for **Guy Fawkes Night** in November. Not only can it be made in advance, it also improves with keeping.

1 Heat the oven to 160°C (325°F, gas mark 3). Lightly oil a 900g (2lb) loaf tin and line it with baking parchment. Put the flour, oatmeal and salt in a bowl and stir to mix. Rub in the butter until the mixture resembles breadcrumbs, then stir in the ginger, nutmeg and sugar.

2 Warm the treacle in a small saucepan until just melted, then beat in the egg. Pour the warmed treacle and egg mixture into the dry ingredients, add the buttermilk and stir well.

3 Tip the mixture into the tin and bake for 60-70 minutes, until a skewer or cocktail stick inserted into the middle comes out clean.

4 Remove the tin to a wire rack and leave to cool in the tin. When completely cold, turn out onto a plate, cut into squares and serve.

Scotch pancakes

PREPARATION TIME: 15 MINUTES
COOKING TIME: ABOUT 20 MINUTES
MAKES ABOUT 24 PANCAKES

150g (5½ oz) white self-raising flour
75g (2¾ oz) wholemeal self-raising flour
1 teaspoon salt
2 large eggs
300ml (½ pint) skimmed milk
Sunflower oil for greasing

Also known as drop scones, these quick little pancakes include wholemeal flour, for added flavour and fibre.

1 Sift the flours and salt into a bowl. Whisk together the eggs and milk, then gradually whisk them into the dry ingredients, using a large balloon whisk.

2 Heat a griddle or large heavy-based frying pan until medium-hot. Lightly oil the griddle or pan, using kitchen paper. Drop 1 tablespoon batter onto the hot griddle or pan to form a round pancake. Repeat to make three more pancakes.

3 As soon as bubbles appear on the surface, about 1-2 minutes, turn the pancakes and cook for a further 1-1½ minutes or until just cooked. Remove to a wire rack and cover with a tea towel to keep warm, if desired, while you cook the remaining pancakes.

4 Leave to cool, top with low-fat crème fraîche and a sliver of smoked salmon, and serve with drinks. Alternatively, eat warm with a little jam.

Nutrients per pancake
- Calories 50
- Carbohydrate 7g (of which sugars 1g)
- Protein 2g
- Fat 1g (of which saturated fat 0g)
- Fibre 0.5g

Welsh cakes

Made with **moist fruit** and **warm spices**, these griddled cakes have a **reduced fat** content.

PREPARATION TIME: 15 MINUTES
COOKING TIME: 20 MINUTES
MAKES ABOUT 16 CAKES

225g (8oz) self-raising flour
½ teaspoon ground cinnamon
Pinch of ground nutmeg
Pinch of salt
100g (3½oz) butter, diced
75g (2¾oz) golden caster sugar
75g (2¾oz) mixed dried fruit
1 egg, beaten
1 tablespoon skimmed milk
Sunflower oil for greasing

1 Sift the flour, cinnamon and nutmeg into a bowl and add the salt. Add the butter and rub it in until the mixture resembles breadcrumbs. Stir in the sugar and dried fruit.

2 Add the beaten egg and milk and mix briefly to a soft but firm dough, adding a splash more milk if needed.

3 Roll out gently on a floured board to a thickness of about 5mm (¼in) and, using a scone cutter or upturned glass, stamp out about 12 rounds. Roll out the remaining scraps and stamp out a further 4 rounds.

4 Lightly wipe a griddle or frying pan with oil, using kitchen paper. Heat to medium-hot, then add the cakes, in batches. Cook for about 4-5 minutes, then turn them and continue to cook until golden brown but still soft inside, about a further 5-6 minutes.

5 Remove to a wire rack and leave to cool slightly before serving.

Nutrients per cake
- Calories 140
- Carbohydrate 19g (of which sugars 8g)
- Protein 2g
- Fat 6g (of which saturated fat 4g)
- Fibre 0.5g

Buttermilk scones

PREPARATION TIME: 10 MINUTES
COOKING TIME: 12-15 MINUTES
MAKES ABOUT 9 SCONES

225g (8oz) self-raising flour
½ teaspoon baking powder
¼ teaspoon salt
25g (1oz) golden caster sugar
25g (1oz) butter, diced
150-175ml (5-6fl oz) buttermilk
Sunflower oil for greasing

1 Heat the oven to 230°C (450°F, gas mark 8). Sift the flour into a bowl and add the baking powder, salt and sugar. Add the butter and rub it in until the mixture resembles breadcrumbs.

2 Slowly mix in enough buttermilk to make a soft but manageable dough. With floured hands, combine the mixture into a ball and very gently press it out on a floured board to a thickness of about 2.5cm (1in).

3 Using a floured 5.5cm (2¼in) scone cutter, stamp out about 9 rounds and place them on a lightly oiled baking sheet.

4 Bake for 12-15 minutes until golden brown and well risen.

5 Remove the scones to a wire rack and leave to cool slightly. Serve warm with a smear of butter, quark or low-fat crème fraîche and jam.

Nutrients per scone
- Calories 124
- Carbohydrate 25g (of which sugars 3g)
- Protein 3g
- Fat 2g (of which saturated fat 1.5g)
- Fibre 1g

Buttermilk, which is very **low in fat,** makes these scones wonderfully **light** and **soft.** They also rise well with only the **minimum** of raising agents, unlike so many commercial varieties.

Potato scones

PREPARATION TIME: 20 MINUTES
COOKING TIME: 12-15 MINUTES
MAKES 8 SCONES

1 large floury potato, about 250g (9oz),
    peeled and cut into chunks
25g (1oz) butter
50g (1¾oz) plain flour, sifted
¼ teaspoon salt
¼ teaspoon baking powder
Sunflower oil for brushing

Very popular in Scotland, these are delicious eaten just as they are, warm from the griddle, or the next day for tea – with just a smear of jam. Potatoes, which are the main carbohydrate in these pancakes, are also high in potassium.

1 Cook the potato in boiling water until tender. Drain thoroughly and return the potato to the pan.

2 Add the butter and mash until smooth. Weigh out 200g (7oz) of the mash, saving any left over for another dish or occasion.

3 Put the flour, salt and baking powder into a bowl and add the warm, weighed-out mash. Mix well to make a soft dough.

4 With floured hands, shape into two balls then roll out each, on a floured board, to form two rounds about 5mm (¼in) thick. Prick all over with a fork and cut each into quarters.

5 Heat a griddle or heavy-based frying pan to medium-hot and brush very lightly with oil. Transfer four quarters of scone to the hot griddle or frying pan and cook for 3-4 minutes on each side, turning them carefully with a large spatula, until golden brown. Repeat with the remaining quarters.

6 Transfer to a wire rack. Eat while still warm, with a bowl of vegetable soup, or serve the next day, spread with a little low-fat curd cheese.

Nutrients per scone
- Calories 80
- Carbohydrate 10g (of which sugars 0g)
- Protein 1g
- Fat 4g (of which saturated fat 2g)
- Fibre 0.5g

Barm brack

PREPARATION TIME: 20 MINUTES,
PLUS 3-3½ HOURS RISING
COOKING TIME: 40 MINUTES
SERVES 8

450g (1lb) strong white flour
¼ teaspoon grated nutmeg
½ teaspoon mixed spice
Pinch of salt
55g (2oz) golden caster sugar
7g sachet of easy-blend dried yeast
25g (1oz) butter, diced, plus extra
    for greasing
About 250ml (9fl oz) tepid skimmed milk
225g (8oz) mixed currants and sultanas
55g (2oz) chopped mixed peel
1 tablespoon golden granulated sugar

This fruit-packed Irish loaf is similar to both bara brith from Wales and Selkirk bannock from the Scottish Borders. It is traditionally served at Hallowe'en, when rings or coins are wrapped up and hidden inside the dough before it is baked.

1 Sift the flour, spices and salt into a bowl. Stir in the caster sugar and yeast, then rub in the butter. Make a well in the centre, then add enough tepid milk to the well to form a soft dough, adding more liquid if needed.

2 Turn the dough out onto a floured board and, using lightly floured hands, knead until smooth, about 10 minutes. Knead in the dried fruit and peel, a handful at a time.

3 Place in a lightly greased bowl, cover and put in a warm (not hot) place for 2 hours, or until well risen.

4 Lightly butter a deep 18cm (7in) cake tin, then knock back the dough by punching it with your fists. Shape the dough into the tin. Cover loosely and leave in a warm place for another hour or so, or until the dough has risen nearly to the top of the tin. Meanwhile, heat the oven to 220°C (425°F, gas mark 7).

5 Bake for 15 minutes, then reduce the heat to 190°C (375°F, gas mark 5) and continue to cook until the base sounds hollow when tapped, a further 20 minutes.

6 Meanwhile, bring 1 tablespoon water to the boil in a small saucepan, add the granulated sugar and dissolve over a low heat. Once the barm brack is done, remove from the oven, brush the top with the glaze and return it to the oven for 2-3 minutes.

7 Turn out onto a wire rack to cool. Serve warm, sliced, as it is or lightly spread with butter.

Nutrients per serving
- Calories 287
- Carbohydrate 61g (of which sugars 18g)
- Protein 6g
- Fat 3g (of which saturated fat 2g)
- Fibre 2g

From Scottish oatcakes to Bath buns, baked goods in Britain maintain

British breads and flours

Baking is one of the most ancient human skills and Britain, like many other countries, enjoys a national tradition that encompasses a large number of regional variations.

Well into the 19th century, only relatively wealthy households had ovens. These were wood-fired and slow to heat up, so it was more practical to have day-long, baking sessions. In poor households breads were baked on a griddle over an open fire or the dough was made at home, then taken to a public bakehouse.

While bread has remained a constant staple in everyone's diet across society, its ingredients and the way it is cooked have changed according to the flours and grains available. Prevailing fashions and regional preferences have also had a marked influence on the shape and style of baked goods.

Types of flour

Barley grows well in Britain and was used as early as 5000 years ago to make bread. However, wheat has gradually become the most popular breadmaking grain, thanks in part to its high gluten content, which helps to give a consistent rise and a light-textured loaf. Barley meal or flakes are still used, but usually only in mixed-grain loaves.

Oats are famously associated with Scotland, where they grow exceptionally well, producing fatter and juicier grains than are grown in England. Cut into

strong regional characteristics.

various grades of meal (pinhead, coarse, medium, fine) as well as ground into flour and processed into rolled oats, they are a common addition to wheat-flour breads. They are also made into oatcakes, which are an unleavened flatbread or crackerbread that keeps well.

Spelt, sold as flour and used in baked and processed goods, is an ancient type of wheat with an inedible outer husk that common wheat lacks. Its current resurgence is partly due to increasing interest in old and lost varieties of wheat, but also to its low-gluten content, which means that people who are allergic to common wheat may tolerate small amounts of spelt.

Regional loaves and cakes

The names of most British loaves today refer to their shape, from bloomer to cob. Dough mixes used to vary from region to region, some being enriched with milk, butter or lard. However, many traditional recipes have been lost and wherever you are in Britain, most bread is now made from simple white, brown or mixed-grain doughs. Many traditional tea-time breads, filled with fruit and spices, maintain strong regional differences and it is still possible to enjoy locally distinctive baked goods. Selkirk bannocks from Scotland, Welsh bara brith, Cornish saffron buns and fat rascals from Yorkshire are typical, each with their locally distinctive mix of dried fruit and spices.

Many cooks in Scotland and northern England still use the griddle for baking, despite the invention of the coal-fired range in the 19th century and the gas and electric cooker in the 20th century.

Sally Lunn

Nutrients per slice
- Calories 279
- Carbohydrate 49g (of which sugars 7g)
- Protein 12g
- Fat 5g (of which saturated fat 3g)
- Fibre 4.5g

PREPARATION TIME: 20 MINUTES, PLUS 3½ HOURS RISING
COOKING TIME: 30 MINUTES
SERVES 8

450g (1lb) strong white flour, sifted
Pinch of salt
25g (1oz) golden caster sugar
7g sachet of easy-blend dried yeast
250ml (9fl oz) tepid semi-skimmed milk
2 eggs, beaten, plus 1 egg yolk, beaten, to glaze
Sunflower oil for greasing
200g (7oz) quark

Legend has it that a beautiful young girl named Sally Lunn sold these cakes in the streets of 19th-century Bath, but the name could be a corruption of *soleil lune,* meaning 'sun' and 'moon' - referring to its golden crust and white filling.

1 Put the flour, salt, sugar and yeast in a large bowl, mix and make a well in the centre. Mix the milk and egg in another bowl, then tip into the well in the dry ingredients and mix.

2 With floured hands, turn the dough out onto a floured board and knead for about 10 minutes until smooth and no longer sticky. Place in a lightly oiled bowl and cover. Leave in a warm (not hot) place for 2-2½ hours, or until well risen.

3 Lightly oil a deep cake tin, 18cm (7in) in diameter. Tip the risen dough onto a floured board and knock back by punching it with your fists. Shape into a ball then place it in the tin. Cover loosely and leave to rise in a warm place for about 1½ hours or until almost risen to the top of the tin. Meanwhile, heat the oven to 200°C (400°F, gas mark 6).

4 Brush the risen dough with the egg yolk and bake for about 30 minutes or until golden brown.

5 Tip the cake out onto a wire rack and leave for at least 30 minutes before slicing horizontally into three. Spread the two lower layers with quark, replace the top layer and serve at once while still warm.

Dundee cake with whisky

PREPARATION TIME: 30 MINUTES, PLUS OVERNIGHT SOAKING
COOKING TIME: 1¾-2 HOURS
SERVES 12

250g (9oz) sultanas
250g (9oz) currants
250g (9oz) raisins
50g (1¾oz) glacé cherries
50g (1¾oz) mixed peel
300ml (½ pint) whisky
150g (5½oz) butter, softened
150g (5½oz) light muscovado sugar
3 large eggs
1 heaped teaspoon mixed spice
25g (1oz) ground almonds
200g (7oz) plain flour
1 teaspoon baking powder
Apricot jam, melted, and mixed nuts, to decorate

1 Put all the fruit and peel with the whisky in a bowl and leave overnight to soak.

2 When ready to cook, heat the oven to 160°C (325°F, gas mark 3) and line a deep 23cm (9in) diameter cake tin with baking parchment. Cream the butter and sugar together until light, then add the eggs, one at a time. Add the soaked fruit, then sift in the mixed spice, ground almonds, flour and baking powder. Mix well.

3 Tip the cake mixture into the prepared tin. Bake for 1¾-2 hours until cooked through, or when a skewer inserted in the middle comes out clean. (Cover loosely with foil if the top looks too brown during cooking.)

4 Leave to cool completely before turning out. Brush with melted apricot jam and decorate with mixed nuts. The cake will keep for up to 2 weeks, if well wrapped.

Nutrients per serving
- Calories 475
- Carbohydrate 74g
  (of which sugars 61g)
- Protein 5g
- Fat 13g (of which
  saturated fat 7g)
- Fibre 2g

Packed with all the iron, potassium and fibre of dried fruit, this recipe uses a high proportion of fruit to sugar and fat.

Dark muscovado chocolate cake

PREPARATION TIME: 20 MINUTES
COOKING TIME: 1½ HOURS
SERVES 10

Sunflower oil for greasing
300g (10½oz) dark chocolate (70% cocoa solids)
175g (6oz) butter
200g (7oz) dark muscovado sugar
2 large eggs
2 rounded tablespoons low-fat natural yoghurt
    (not the set variety)
150g (5½oz) plain flour
1 rounded teaspoon baking powder

1 Heat the oven to 160°C (325°F, gas mark 3).
Lightly oil a 900g (2lb) loaf tin and line it with
baking parchment.

2 Melt the chocolate and butter in a small
saucepan and over a very low heat, then
leave to cool for a few minutes. Put the sugar
and eggs in a bowl and beat. Stir in the yoghurt.

3 Transfer the melted chocolate mixture to a
large bowl and add the egg mixture. Sift in
the flour and baking powder and mix well. Tip
the mixture into the prepared tin.

4 Bake for 1-1½ hours, covering loosely with
foil for the last 20 minutes or so to prevent
scorching. Test by inserting a skewer into the
centre; it should come out almost clean, with a
few moist crumbs attached.

5 Remove the tin to a wire rack to cool
completely before turning the cake out.
Remove the lining and wrap the cake in foil.
Refrigerate for at least 1 day before slicing.
Serve as it is, or as a dessert with some
raspberries and low-fat crème fraîche.

Nutrients per serving
- Calories 440
- Carbohydrate 52g (of which sugars 38g)
- Protein 4g
- Fat 25g (of which saturated fat 15g)
- Fibre 0.5g

Classic Victoria sponge

Named after Queen Victoria, this light, moist sponge, filled with jam and sprinkled with icing sugar, is delicious – and as British as can be.

PREPARATION TIME: 20 MINUTES
COOKING TIME: 20 MINUTES
SERVES 6

175g (6oz) butter, slightly softened, plus extra
    for greasing
175g (6oz) golden caster sugar
3 large eggs, beaten
175g (6oz) self-raising flour
Strawberry jam and sifted icing sugar to finish

Nutrients per serving
- Calories 470
- Carbohydrate 53g
  (of which sugars 31g)
- Protein 7g
- Fat 27g (of which
  saturated fat 16g)
- Fibre 1g

1 Heat the oven to 180°C (350°F, gas mark 4). Lightly butter two 20cm (8in) sandwich tins and line them with baking parchment. Put the butter and sugar in a bowl and beat well until pale and creamy.

2 Add half the beaten egg with 2 teaspoons of the flour, to prevent the mixture curdling. Beat again until incorporated, then add the remaining egg. Once well mixed, sift in half the flour and fold it in gently, using a large metal spoon. Sift and fold in the remaining flour.

3 Spoon the mixture into the prepared tins and smooth the surface with the back of a spoon. Bake for about 20 minutes or until golden and slightly springy but firm to the touch. The cakes will have begun to shrink away a little from the sides of the tin.

4 Leave for 1-2 minutes, then turn out carefully onto a wire rack and remove the lining.

5 Once cold, spread one cake with jam and set the other on top. Sprinkle with icing sugar just before serving. Alternatively, serve a piece of plain sponge with some fresh or poached summer fruit or berries, as a dessert.

This has less butter than regular chocolate cake, but the yoghurt and muscovado sugar make it **wonderfully moist** and almost **treacly** in flavour.

Moist carrot cake
with nuts

PREPARATION TIME: 25 MINUTES
COOKING TIME: 50 MINUTES
SERVES 8

125ml (4fl oz) sunflower oil, plus extra for greasing
3 eggs
1 teaspoon vanilla extract
100g (3½oz) unsweetened desiccated coconut
100g (3½oz) raisins
100g (3½oz) walnuts or hazelnuts,
    roughly chopped
About 400g (14oz) carrots, peeled and
    coarsely grated
225g (8oz) self-raising wholemeal flour
150g (5½oz) light muscovado sugar
1 teaspoon ground cinnamon

This delicious, **moist** carrot cake is packed with **fruit and nuts**. Although delicious served as it is, it can also be topped with **light cream cheese** and a scattering of **nuts** for extra **health** and **flavour**.

1 Heat the oven to 180°C (350°F, gas mark 4). Lightly oil a 900g (2lb) loaf tin and line it with baking parchment. Put the oil, eggs and vanilla extract into a small bowl and beat well.

2 Put the coconut, raisins and nuts in another large bowl and add the oil and egg mixture. Stir in the grated carrot, flour, sugar and cinnamon and mix well.

3 Tip the mixture into the prepared tin and smooth down the top. Bake for about 50 minutes or until a skewer inserted into the middle comes out clean.

LIGHT CREAM CHEESE TOPPING
Beat 200g (7oz) low-fat cream cheese with 2 tablespoons runny honey. Spread on top of the cake once it has cooled completely.

Nutrients per serving
- Calories 500
- Carbohydrate 51g
  (of which sugars 34g)
- Protein 10g
- Fat 29g (of which
  saturated fat 9g)
- Fibre 6g
- Vitamins B_1, B_6, B_{12}

Somerset apple cake

Apple cakes typically come from the orchard-clad areas of **southern England**. Apples are a good source of **vitamin C** and also contain **bioflavonoids**, which help to protect against cancer and heart disease.

PREPARATION TIME: 20 MINUTES
COOKING TIME: 1¼ HOURS
SERVES 8

Nutrients per serving
- Calories 460
- Carbohydrate 62g
  (of which sugars 35g)
- Protein 8g
- Fat 12g (of which saturated fat 12g)
- Fibre 4g
- Vitamins B₁₂, B₆

Sunflower oil for greasing
175g (6oz) butter, softened
175g (6oz) light muscovado sugar
3 eggs, beaten
1 rounded tablespoon black treacle
225g (8oz) wholemeal self-raising flour
100g (3½ oz) self-raising flour
¼ teaspoon ground nutmeg
½ teaspoon ground cinnamon
¼ teaspoon ground ginger
675g (1lb 8oz) cooking apples, peeled
    and chopped
About 3 tablespoons skimmed milk

1 Heat the oven to 160°C (325°F, gas mark 3). Lightly oil a round 24cm (9½ in) cake tin and line it with baking parchment. Cream the butter and sugar together until smooth, then beat in the eggs a little at a time. Add the treacle and stir well to mix.

2 Sift in the flours and spices, stir to mix, then add the apple. Add enough milk to make a soft batter and mix lightly.

3 Tip the mixture into the prepared tin and bake for about 1¼ hours or until a skewer inserted in the middle comes out clean.

4 Leave to cool in the tin for at least 20 minutes, then turn the cake out onto a wire rack to cool. Serve warm as it is or with a little low-fat crème fraîche.

Seed cake

PREPARATION TIME: 30 MINUTES
COOKING TIME: 50 MINUTES
SERVES 8

Sunflower oil for greasing
175g (6oz) butter, softened
175g (6oz) golden caster sugar
1 tablespoon caraway seeds
2 large eggs, separated
175g (6oz) self-raising flour, sifted
Pinch of salt
55g (2oz) ground almonds

1 Heat the oven to 180°C (350°F, gas mark 4). Grease a 900g (2lb) loaf tin and line it with baking parchment.

2 Put the butter and sugar in a bowl and beat together until light and creamy. Add the caraway seeds and stir well to mix. Beat in the egg yolks, one at a time, then fold in the flour, salt and ground almonds.

3 In a clean bowl, whisk the egg whites until stiff. Fold them into the cake mixture, a little at a time.

4 Tip the mixture into the prepared tin and bake for about 50 minutes or until a skewer inserted in the middle comes out clean.

5 Transfer the tin to a wire rack and leave to cool for about 30 minutes before turning the cake out onto the rack to cool completely. Slice when cold and serve at tea time with some low-fat crème fraîche and strawberries, as a summery dessert.

Nutrients per serving
- Calories 390
- Carbohydrate 40g (of which sugars 23g)
- Protein 5g
- Fat 23g (of which saturated fat 12g)
- Fibre 1g
- Vitamins A, B₁₂

This **traditional** cake was a great **tea-time** favourite in 18th-century rural **Britain**, when it was eaten to **celebrate** the seed-planting time of year.

Saffron buns

PREPARATION TIME: 30 MINUTES, PLUS 3 HOURS RISING
COOKING TIME: 15 MINUTES
MAKES 12 BUNS

250ml (9fl oz) tepid milk
1 rounded teaspoon saffron strands
500g (1lb 2oz) strong white bread flour
Good pinch of salt
7g sachet of easy-blend dried yeast
50g (1¾oz) golden caster sugar
200g (7oz) mixed dried fruit and
    chopped mixed peel, with no more
    than 50g (1¾oz) peel
50g (1¾oz) butter, melted
1 large egg, beaten
Sunflower oil for greasing
3 teaspoons runny honey, warmed

Popular in Cornwall, saffron buns, both fruited and plain, are a glorious yellow. Throughout the Middle Ages and up until the 19th century, saffron crocuses were grown in Essex, in Cambridgeshire and possibly in Cornwall too.

1 Put half the tepid milk in a bowl, add the saffron strands and leave to infuse for about 20 minutes.

2 Sift the flour and salt into a large bowl, then stir in the yeast, sugar, fruit and peel. Add the melted butter, egg and remaining tepid milk, then pour in the saffron milk and strands. Mix well and, with floured hands, remove the mixture to a floured board. Knead for up to 10 minutes until smooth and elastic, adding frequent light dustings of flour if it is very sticky.

3 Place in a lightly oiled bowl, cover and leave in a warm (not hot) place for 1½-2 hours until well risen.

4 Turn the dough onto a floured board and punch it down. Divide into 12 pieces and shape each piece into a round bun. Place on a lightly oiled baking sheet, cover loosely and leave for 45-60 minutes until risen again. Meanwhile, heat the oven to 220°C (425°F, gas mark 7).

5 Bake the buns for 15 minutes until golden, then remove to a wire rack. Brush with the honey while still warm, then leave to cool slightly. Serve warm or cold with a cup of tea.

VARIATION
To make into a single loaf, shape the dough into a 900g (2lb) loaf tin at stage 4. To bake, proceed as for the buns, but after the first 25 minutes reduce the oven temperature to 200°C (400°F, gas mark 6) and continue to bake for a further 20-30 minutes until golden and cooked. (The base will sound hollow when tapped.)

Nutrients per bun
- Calories 260
- Carbohydrate 49g (of which sugars 19g)
- Protein 7g
- Fat 5g (of which saturated fat 3g)
- Fibre 2g

In small quantities, butter is not unhealthy, and adds a **delicious richness** to breads and cakes. Britain's **lush** pastures help produce some of the world's **best** butters, notably those from the West Country and the Channel Islands.

Kentish huffkins

Nutrients per huffkin
- Calories 160
- Carbohydrate 30g (of which sugars 1.5g)
- Protein 4g
- Fat 3g (of which saturated fat 2g)
- Fibre 1g

PREPARATION TIME: 15 MINUTES, PLUS ABOUT 2 HOURS RISING AND PROVING
COOKING TIME: 15 MINUTES
MAKES 12 HUFFKINS

7g sachet of easy-blend dried yeast
1 teaspoon sugar
450g (1lb) strong white bread flour
1 rounded teaspoon salt
40g (1½ oz) butter, diced, plus extra for greasing
About 225ml (8fl oz) tepid mixture of semi-skimmed milk and water

Soft, oval-shaped bread rolls with a characteristic dent in the middle – often filled with jam – huffkins were traditionally baked throughout Kent, especially at the end of the hop-picking season.

1 Put the yeast, sugar, flour and salt in a large bowl, then rub in the butter. Make a well in the centre and gradually add enough tepid milk and water to the well to make a stiff dough, working it in to the dry ingredients as you go. Turn the dough onto a floured surface and, with floured hands, knead for up to 10 minutes until smooth and elastic.

2 Place the dough in a lightly greased bowl. Cover and leave in a warm (not hot) place for 1-1½ hours, or until well risen.

3 Knock back the risen dough by punching it with your fists, then divide the mixture into 12 pieces. Shape each into an oval and place on a lightly greasing baking sheet. Make a small dent in the middle of each oval with your fingertip. Loosely cover and leave to prove in a warm place for 30-40 minutes. Meanwhile, heat the oven to 220°C (425°F, gas mark 7).

4 Bake for about 15 minutes or until the huffkins sound hollow when tapped on the base. Remove to a wire rack to cool. Serve warm with jam.

Stottie cake

Nutrients per serving (¼ cake)
- Calories 272
- Carbohydrate 56g (of which sugars 0.75g)
- Protein 3.5g
- Fat 2g (of which saturated fat 1g)
- Fibre 9g

PREPARATION TIME: 20 MINUTES, PLUS 1 HOUR 20 MINUTES RISING AND PROVING
COOKING TIME: 15 MINUTES
MAKES 2 STOTTIE CAKES

575g (1lb 4½ oz) strong white bread flour
1 heaped teaspoon salt
1 teaspoon caster sugar
7g sachet of easy-blend dried yeast
25g (1oz) butter, diced, plus extra for greasing
About 350-375ml (12-13fl oz) tepid water

Stottie is a white bread from Newcastle, and a delicious way to boost the carbohydrate content of a meal. It is typically filled with ham and pease pudding, but roasted vegetables and salad leaves also make a wonderful filling.

1 Put the flour, salt, sugar and yeast in a large bowl and mix well. Add the butter and rub it in until the mixture resembles breadcrumbs. Make a well in the centre, then gradually add enough tepid water to the well to make a stiff dough, mixing gently.

2 Turn the dough out onto a floured board and knead, with floured hands, for up to 10 minutes until smooth and elastic. Place in a lightly greased bowl, cover and leave in a warm (not hot) place for at least 1 hour, or until well risen.

3 Knock back the risen dough by punching it with your fists, then divide it in half. Shape each piece into a round about 20cm (8in) in diameter. Place on a lightly oiled baking sheet, loosely cover and leave in a warm place for about 20 minutes.

4 Meanwhile, heat the oven to 220°C (425°F, gas mark 7). Make a dimpled surface in the dough by gently pressing all over with your fingertips. Bake for about 15 minutes or until golden. Remove to a wire rack to cool.

5 Serve split in half with the filling of your choice, savoury or sweet.

Wholemeal bread

PREPARATION TIME: 20 MINUTES,
PLUS 2-3 HOURS RISING
MAKES 1 LARGE LOAF

750g (1lb 10oz) wholemeal flour
2 teaspoons salt
7g sachet of easy-blend dried yeast
Sunflower oil for greasing

1 Put the flour, salt and yeast in a bowl and mix. Make a well in the middle, gradually pour in 450-475ml (16-17fl oz) tepid water, and combine. (You might need a little more or a little less liquid: the dough should come together, leaving the sides of the bowl.)

2 Tip the mixture onto a floured surface and knead for at least 10 minutes, until smooth. Place in an oiled bowl, cover and leave in a warm (not hot) place for 1½-2 hours until almost doubled in size.

3 Knock back the dough by punching it with your fists, then turn it out onto the floured surface and knead very briefly. Shape it into an oval, tuck the edges underneath and place in an oiled 900g (2lb) bread tin. Loosely cover again and leave in a warm place for 30-60 minutes until risen. Meanwhile, heat the oven to 230°C (450°F, gas mark 8).

4 When risen, lightly dust the surface of the dough with a little flour and slash the top to decorate, if desired.

5 Bake for 15 minutes then reduce to 200°C (400°F, gas mark 6) and cook for a further 20 minutes or so, until done. (It should sound hollow when tapped on the base.) Remove to a wire rack and leave to cool completely before cutting.

VARIATIONS: WHITE LOAF
Use strong white bread flour (preferably unbleached) in place of wholemeal.

GRANARY AND WALNUT LOAF
Use 400g (14oz) strong white flour and 350g (12oz) granary flour in place of wholemeal, and incorporate 55g (2oz) chopped walnuts towards the end of kneading.

Nutrients per slice
- Calories 97
- Carbohydrate 19g
  (of which sugars 0.5g)
- Protein 4g
- Fat 0.05g
- Fibre 3g
- Vitamins B_1, B_6

Homemade bread is incredibly easy and rewarding. It is also much healthier than commercial bread, being free of added enzymes and preservatives.

Irish soda bread

Nutrients per wedge (⅛ loaf)
- Calories 224
- Carbohydrate 46g (of which sugars 5g)
- Protein 10g
- Fat 1.5g (of which saturated fat 0g)
- Fibre 4.5g
- Vitamins B$_6$, B$_1$

PREPARATION TIME: 10 MINUTES
COOKING TIME: 35-40 MINUTES
MAKES 1 LOAF

300g (10½ oz) plain wholemeal flour
175g (6oz) plain flour, sifted
25g (1oz) wheatgerm
1 rounded teaspoon salt
1 rounded teaspoon bicarbonate of soda
1 teaspoon sugar
About 450ml (16fl oz) buttermilk or
   semi-skimmed sour milk

1 Heat the oven to 220°C (425°F, gas mark 7). Put the flours, wheatgerm, salt, bicarbonate of soda and sugar in a large bowl, mix and make a well in the centre.

2 Gradually add enough buttermilk or sour milk to the well to make a soft dough, beating with each addition. The dough should be loose and moist, but not too sloppy.

3 Using floured hands, turn the dough out onto a floured baking tray and knead lightly into a round, about 23cm (9in) in diameter. Using a floured knife, cut a shallow cross on top.

4 Bake for 20 minutes, then reduce the heat to 200°C (400°F, gas mark 6) and bake for a further 15-20 minutes until the crust is brown and the loaf sounds hollow when tapped on the base.

5 Transfer to a wire rack to cool before cutting it into slices. Serve warm, when it needs no butter. Use for toast the following day, topped with low-fat spread.

IRISH SODA BREAD

The wholesome mixture of **flours** and addition of nutrient-rich **wheatgerm** gives this traditional soda bread a healthy boost. The wheatgerm also produces an attractive **gold** fleck through the dough.

261

Preserves

and drinks

Preserves and drinks
the healthy way

Homemade jams, pickles, chutneys and cordials taste great, often reflecting the superior quality of the ingredients used.

There are many good reasons why it is worth taking the time and making the effort to prepare your own preserves and cordials. Apart from the satisfaction, you can also be sure that your family and friends are eating the very best because you control the ingredients that go into them.

While some expensive preserves taste almost as good as homemade, many commercial products are inferior and contain a variety of additives such as acidity regulators, antioxidants, gelling agents, colourings and preservatives. These generally have little effect on health but in those people who are susceptible, artificial colourings and organic compounds called salicylates can trigger allergic reactions.

Jams and sweet preserves

Jams and sweet preserves are often perceived as being unhealthy because of their high sugar content. By making them yourself you can adjust the sugar and flavourings to taste.

• Delicious homemade sweet preserves can usually be prepared using larger quantities of healthy fruit and far less sweetener than in commercial ones.

• All sweet preserves are fairly high in readily absorbed sugar, so that eating them on their own will result in a rapid rise in blood sugar levels. But when eaten with a slow energy-releasing carbohydrate, such as wholemeal toast, the sugar is absorbed more slowly, which helps to keep blood sugar levels stable, preventing hunger and stress.

After dating and labelling, store in a cool, dark place, then, once opened, in the refrigerator. Most of the jams and chutneys in this chapter will keep for as long as commercial products.

Savoury preserves

Chutneys and pickles are used to enhance the flavour of a main dish, and so are only consumed in small quantities. Most are also fat free, which makes them a healthier option than mayonnaise in sandwiches.

Shop-bought preserves tend to contain an unhealthy proportion of 'hidden' salt or sodium. The body needs sodium to function properly. It regulates and maintains the body's fluid balance and is also essential for nerve and muscle function. But in Britain, the average adult eats 9g (about 2 level teaspoons) of salt per day, 50 per cent more than the 6g per day recommended by the World Health Organisation.

Doctors and nutritionists believe that for their health's sake, most people should cut down their salt intake as

Pectin

All jams and jellies are a mixture of fruit, sugar and water that has been boiled to setting point. The setting point will vary, depending on the amount of pectin, acid and sugar present. Pectin occurs naturally in the cells of fruit. When it combines with sugar, it thickens. Acid helps to speed up the release of pectin from the fruit. Blackcurrants, apples, damsons and redcurrants are rich in both pectin and acid and make excellent jams and jellies. Apricots, greengages, loganberries, raspberries and plums have less pectin and acid in their cells and make runnier jam, unless more pectin is added. Cherries, strawberries and rhubarb, all popular jams, contain virtually no natural pectin or acid and do not set well, unless supplemented with commercially made pectin or by adding lemon juice – 2 tablespoons per 1.8kg (4lb) of fruit.

Making cordial

1 Wash thoroughly any flowers or ripe soft fruit you are using to flavour the cordial, and remove stalks and leaves where necessary.

2 If using soft fruit, boil it in a pan with water to cover until the juice runs freely. Strain off the juice, add a similar volume of sugar and heat very gently until the sugar dissolves. For flower cordials, make a syrup first by dissolving sugar in an equal volume of boiling water. Stir in the flowers, leave overnight, then strain.

3 Once cooled, bottle the syrupy cordial. To drink, dilute to taste.

---

excessive consumption has been strongly linked to high blood pressure, which can eventually lead to a stroke, heart disease or kidney failure.

Making your own savoury preserves allows you to limit the salt level, helping to reduce your overall dietary intake.

Equipment

If you make preserves often, you may want to invest in a special preserving pan. For sweet jams and jellies, you can use a copper or brass pan, but this should not be used when preparing savoury preserves, as they contain acidic vinegar, which will react adversely with the copper.

If you plan to make sweet and savoury preserves, buy a large, heavy-based pan made of aluminium or stainless steel. This will not conduct the heat as evenly or as well as a copper pan, but it is more versatile and considerably cheaper.

The pan should be wide in relation to its depth to allow for rapid evaporation before the sugar is added, and for quick boiling afterwards.

Fruit cordials

Drinks based on homemade fruit cordials make a refreshing alternative to alcohol. They can also help to add a dose of vitamin C to your daily diet.
• Many people find commercial cordials overly sweet; if you make your own you can adjust sweetness to suit individual preference. Reducing the sugar in both elderflower cordial and lemonade (see pages 280-1) improves the taste and enhances the citrusy tang.

• Elderflowers, rich in beta carotene and vitamin C, are often an ingredient in cordials, and have long been used in folk medicine as a remedy for colds, flu and other respiratory ailments. They are a natural decongestant.
• Drinks such as lemon barley (see page 280) are wonderfully soothing for invalids and refreshing at any time.

Alcohol

Drinks containing alcohol, such as Rum and ginger charmer (page 283) and Sloe gin (page 284), can be enjoyed as part of a healthy, balanced diet.

Research has shown that one or two units of alcohol a day can help to reduce the risk of heart disease by up to 30 per cent. Moderate drinkers have the lowest death rate, lower even than teetotallers.

Preserving tips

Warming sugar

It is best to warm the sugar before adding it, to prevent a sudden drop in the temperature of the fruit as it cooks. Put it in an ovenproof bowl in a preheated, low oven for 10 minutes or in a microwave on full power for 1-2 minutes. For the best results, use preserving sugar – the large crystals dissolve more easily than those of ordinary sugar, and the finished jam will be clearer and brighter.

Testing for the setting point

Drop 1 teaspoon of the hot preserve mixture onto a chilled saucer and leave to cool for 1-2 minutes. Push the mixture gently with the side of your finger. If the surface wrinkles, the preserve is ready to pot. If it does not, continue cooking.

Sterilising and warming jars

Wash heatproof jars thoroughly in detergent and water and rinse well. Place them in a large saucepan of boiling water for 10 minutes, then carefully remove and dry upside down in a low oven for a further 10 minutes.

Potting and covering jams and chutneys

As soon as the preserve is in the jars, cover the surface of each one with a waxed paper circle and leave to cool. Then top with a metal or plastic screw-on lid, or dampen a cellophane circle and stretch it tightly over the top of the jar and secure around the rim with a couple of elastic bands.

Storing preserves and chutneys

Label and date each jar and store in a cool, dark place.

Strawberry jam

Delicious on **scones**, bread or in sponge cakes, **homemade strawberry jam** tastes best and is free of the artificial colourings found in many of the cheaper commercial brands.

PREPARATION TIME: 20 MINUTES
COOKING TIME: 20-30 MINUTES
MAKES ABOUT 4.5KG (10LB)

3.2kg (7lb) strawberries, small and
 firm if possible
Juice of 2 lemons
2.7kg (6lb) preserving or granulated sugar

1 Put two saucers in the refrigerator or freezer, to chill. Do not wash the strawberries. Remove any stems and lightly brush off any grit or dirt. Put in a large pan with the lemon juice.

2 Heat gently until the juices start to run, then use a potato masher to break up the fruit to the required texture, leaving whole berries if desired. Continue cooking and stirring until reduced to a thick slush.

3 Warm the sugar (see left) and add to the pan. Increase the heat and stir continuously until the sugar dissolves. Bring to a steady boil and cook for 8-10 minutes, stirring frequently. Test for setting point by dropping a teaspoon of jam onto a cold saucer (see left). If it is not ready, continue boiling and testing every 10 minutes until it is.

4 Remove from the heat and use a jug to pour the jam into clean, warmed jars (see left). Cover and seal immediately (see left), then label and date each jar. Store in a cool, dark place for up to a year.

VARIATION
For raspberry jam, use 2.7kg (6lb) fresh or frozen raspberries and 2.7kg (6lb) granulated sugar. Omit the lemon juice. Cook and pot as directed, but start testing for the setting point after 5 minutes.

Nutrients per 15ml tablespoon
- Calories 40
- Carbohydrate 10g (of which sugars 10g)
- Protein 0g
- Fat 0g
- Fibre 0.2g

Orange marmalade

PREPARATION TIME: 50 MINUTES,
PLUS OVERNIGHT SOAKING
COOKING TIME: 2 HOURS
MAKES 4.5KG (10LB)

1.3kg (3lb) Seville oranges
3 litres (5¼ pints) water
2.7kg (6lb) preserving or granulated sugar
Juice of 2 lemons

Nutrients per 5ml teaspoon
- Calories 12
- Carbohydrate 3g (of which sugars 3g)
- Protein 0g
- Fat 0g
- Fibre 0.07g

Bitter Seville oranges, which are available in
late January and February, are best for a tangy,
clear British breakfast marmalade.

1 Rinse the oranges in hot water to
soften the peel a little. Remove any
green stalks and slice off any blemishes.

2 Set a nylon sieve over a large
bowl. Cut each orange in half
crossways. Squeeze out the juice, then
pour it into the sieve. Scrape out any
remaining flesh and pips into the sieve.
Cut the remains of each orange half
into three, then chop to fine or chunky
pieces, as desired, in a food processor
or by hand.

3 Put the water into a large pan and
add the chopped peel. Squeeze
out as much juice as possible from the
flesh and pips in the sieve and add to
the pan. Turn the pips and bits of
orange into a square of muslin and tie
in a bundle. Drop the bundle into the
pan, stir well, cover and leave overnight.

4 The next day, bring the contents of
the pan to a boil, then reduce the
heat and simmer gently, uncovered and
stirring occasionally, until the mixture
thickens and is reduced by about half.
Put two saucers in the fridge or freezer
to chill.

5 Meanwhile, warm the sugar (see
page 266) and add to the pan with
the lemon juice. Simmer, stirring
continuously, until the sugar dissolves.

6 Increase the heat and boil for
about 10 minutes. Put a teaspoon
of mixture onto a chilled saucer to test.
If it is not ready, continue boiling and
stirring, testing every 10 minutes, until it
is. When ready, remove from the heat.
Allow to stand for 10 minutes, then
take out and discard the bag of pips.

7 Use a jug to pour the marmalade
into clean, warmed jars. Hold the
jar over the pan and fill almost to the
brim. Seal, label and date each jar. Store
in a cool, dark place for up to a year.

Wonderful in
tarts or on
bread, this
creamy curd
is quick and
easy to make
at any time of
the year.

Lemon curd

PREPARATION TIME: 30 MINUTES
COOKING TIME: 30 MINUTES
MAKES 1.3KG (3LB)

700g (1lb 9oz) granulated sugar
6 eggs
215g (7½oz) unsalted butter,
    cut into small pieces
300ml (½ pint) lemon juice,
    about 10 lemons
Thinly pared zest of 6 unwaxed lemons,
    cut into long strips, with a potato
    peeler

Quince cheese

PREPARATION TIME: 45 MINUTES
COOKING TIME: 45-60 MINUTES
MAKES ABOUT 900G (2LB)

2.7kg (6lb) quinces, washed and
   roughly chopped
Granulated sugar (see step 1, below)
Sunflower oil for greasing

1 Put the chopped quinces in a large pan
with just enough water to cover. Cook
gently until reduced to a pulp. Use a
wooden spoon to push the fruit pulp, a
little at a time, through a sieve into a clean
bowl. Weigh the pulp, then put into a large
pan with an equal weight of sugar. Mix well.

2 Cook over a low heat, stirring
continuously, until the mixture is very
thick, and starting to leave the sides of
the pan.

3 Lightly oil jars or cups, then line with
cling film. Spoon the thickened mixture
into the jars or cups and leave in a cool
place to set. Cover with foil and store in
the refrigerator for up to 3 months. Serve
with Cheshire or Wensleydale cheese.

Nutrients per 5ml teaspoon
- Calories 50
- Carbohydrate 14g (of which sugars 14g)
- Protein 0g
- Fat 0g
- Fibre 0g

Fruit cheeses were popular
in 17th-century England. You
can buy **British quinces**
only in autumn, but Cypriot
and **Middle Eastern** shops
sell imported ones all year.

---

1 Sit a large heatproof bowl over a
pan of simmering water, making
sure the bottom of the bowl does not
touch it. Put the sugar and eggs in the
bowl and whisk lightly.

2 Add the butter, lemon juice and
zest. Cook over a low heat for
about 20 minutes, stirring frequently,
until the mixture is as thick as whipped
cream. Remove from the heat and lift
the bowl from the pan. Remove and
discard the lemon zest.

3 Spoon into clean, warmed jars and
seal each jar with a circle of waxed
paper and cellophane (see page 266).
Label and date, then store in the
refrigerator for up to 4 weeks.

Nutrients per 5ml teaspoon
- Calories 19
- Carbohydrate 3g
(of which sugars 3g)
- Protein 0.2g
- Fat 0.7g
(of which saturated fat 0.5g)
- Fibre 0g

269

Blackberry and apple jelly

PREPARATION TIME: 30 MINUTES,
PLUS OVERNIGHT DRAINING
COOKING TIME: 1½ HOURS
MAKES 1.6KG (3LB 8OZ)

1.8kg (4lb) ripe blackberries,
   stalks removed
900g (2lb) Bramley apples, wiped and
   roughly chopped, with core
1.2 litres (2 pints) water
Preserving or granulated sugar
   (see step 3, below)

Brambles bring a glorious
natural bounty to
autumn hedgerows.
Wild berries taste best
and should be picked
before the first frosts
and not after the
29th of September, or
Michaelmas, according
to superstition.

1 Put the fruit into a large pan and add
   the water. Bring to a boil, then
simmer, stirring frequently, for 1 hour
until soft and pulpy. Mash lightly with a
potato masher, then let cool slightly.

2 Pour into a jelly bag with a bowl
   set underneath to catch the juice.
Leave overnight. Avoid squeezing the
bag, as this will make the jelly cloudy.

3 Put two saucers in the refrigerator
   or freezer to chill. Measure the
juice in the bowl, then pour it into a
large, clean pan. Warm the juice, but do
not boil. Remove from the heat and
add 450g (1lb) sugar for each 600ml

(1 pint) juice. Stir over a gentle
heat until all the sugar has melted.
Increase the heat and boil vigorously
for 8 minutes, stirring constantly.
Remove from the heat.

4 Test for setting by dropping a
   teaspoon of jelly mixture onto a
chilled saucer (see page 266). If it is not
ready, continue boiling and test every
8 minutes.

5 Pour the jelly into clean, warmed
   jars (see page 266). Cover and seal
immediately, then label and date each
jar. Store in a cool, dark place for up to
a year.

Nutrients 5ml teaspoon
- Calories 18
- Carbohydrate 5g
  (of which sugars 5g)
- Protein 0g
- Fat 0g
- Fibre 0g

Gooseberry and mint jelly

This jelly is a **delightful alternative** to mint sauce, for serving with a joint of lamb, adding an **extra tang** to the traditional accompaniment.

PREPARATION TIME: 45 MINUTES
COOKING TIME: ABOUT 1¾ HOURS, PLUS OVERNIGHT DRAINING
MAKES ABOUT 1.3KG (3LB)

1.8kg (4lb) small underripe gooseberries, topped and tailed
Juice of 1 lemon
Preserving or granulated sugar
  (see step 2, below)
2 large bunches of fresh mint

Nutrients 5ml teaspoon
- Calories 14
- Carbohydrate 4g (of which sugars 4g)
- Protein 0g
- Fat 0g
- Fibre 0g

1 Put the berries in a large pan with the lemon juice and just enough cold water to cover the fruit. Simmer gently for about 1 hour, stirring frequently, until it is a very soft pulp. Pour into a jelly bag with a bowl set underneath to catch the juice. Leave overnight to drain.

2 Put two saucers in the refrigerator or freezer to chill. Measure the juice in the bowl and pour it into a large, clean pan. Add 450g (1lb) sugar for every 600ml (1 pint) of juice. Bring to a gentle boil, stirring, until the sugar has melted. Lightly crush one of the bunches of mint, using a rolling pin, then drop it into the boiling liquid.

3 Test for setting by dropping a teaspoon of the jelly mixture onto a chilled saucer (see page 266). If it is not ready, continue boiling and test every 8 minutes.

4 When the setting point is reached, take the pan off the heat. Remove the bunch of mint and squeeze it in a strainer over the jelly mixture. Stir and skim off any scum on the surface.

5 Cut the hard stalk bottoms from the remaining bunch of mint, saving the leaves. Chop the mint finely, then stir it into the jelly. Leave to stand for about 10 minutes. Use a jug to pour the jelly into small clean, warmed jars and seal, label and date the pots (see page 266). Store in a cool, dark place for up to a year.

Green tomato chutney

Nutrients per 15ml tablespoon
- Calories 23
- Carbohydrate 6g (of which sugars 6g)
- Protein 0.2g
- Fat 0.1g (of which saturated fat 0g)
- Fibre 0g

PREPARATION TIME: 30 MINUTES, PLUS 2 MONTHS MATURING
COOKING TIME: 2 HOURS
MAKES 3.2KG (7LB)

25g (1oz) fresh ginger, crushed
25g (1oz) whole white mustard seeds
1.3kg (3lb) green tomatoes, roughly chopped
450g (1lb) cooking apples, peeled, cored and roughly chopped
450g (1lb) marrow, peeled, seeded and chopped
450g (1lb) onions, peeled and roughly chopped
115g (4oz) stoned dates, finely chopped
225g (8oz) seedless raisins
900g (2lb) soft brown sugar
2 teaspoons salt
½ teaspoon cayenne pepper
1 litre (1¾ pints) white malt vinegar

1 Tie up the ginger and mustard seeds in a square of muslin, then put into a very large pan with all the other ingredients. Cook over a low heat, stirring continuously, until the sugar dissolves. Increase the heat and bring to a boil, then reduce the heat and simmer gently for about 2 hours, stirring often. The mixture should be quite thick. Remove and discard the ginger and mustard seed bundle.

2 Spoon into clean, warmed jars (see page 266) and set aside to cool. Seal the jars with lids. Label and date the jars, then store them in a cool, dark place. Leave to mature for 2 months before eating and keep for up to a year.

Chutney, a word derived from *chatni*, Hindi for **spiced relish**, reflects the influence of **Indian** food on the British. Recipes using **mango** and **tamarind** were adapted to make use of local **orchard** and **garden** fruits, usually apples and tomatoes. If you would rather avoid the pungent cooking aromas, you can make this uncooked version.

Uncooked chutney

Nutrients per 15ml tablespoon
- Calories 33
- Carbohydrate 6g (of which sugars 6g)
- Protein 0.1g
- Fat 0g
- Fibre 0g

PREPARATION TIME: 20 MINUTES
MAKES 1.3KG (3LB)

225g (8oz) dessert apples, peeled, cored and roughly chopped
225g (8oz) onions, roughly chopped
225g (8oz) dates, roughly chopped
225g (8oz) sultanas
225g (8oz) soft dark brown sugar
150ml (¼ pint) spiced vinegar (see page 279)
1 teaspoon salt
1 pinch each of black pepper, dried mustard and cayenne pepper

1 Put all the ingredients in a large plastic or ceramic bowl and mix well until the sugar has dissolved.

2 Turn the mixture into cleaned, dry jars, filling almost to the top. Seal with lids (see page 266). Label and date, then store in a cool, dry place. Leave for at least 2 weeks before using. It will keep for up to 6 weeks.

Plum chutney

PREPARATION TIME: 45 MINUTES,
PLUS 3-4 WEEKS MATURING
COOKING TIME: 1¾-2¼ HOURS
MAKES 1.8KG (4LB)

450g (1lb) onions, peeled and finely chopped
25g (1oz) root ginger, lightly crushed
2 teaspoons each whole cloves, whole allspice
    and whole black peppercorns
1.2kg (2lb 10oz) plums, halved and stoned
900g (2lb) cooking apples, peeled,
    cored and chopped
600ml (1 pint) white malt vinegar
450g (1lb) soft dark brown sugar
1 tablespoon salt

1 Put the onions in a large pan with just enough cold water to cover them. Simmer until soft. Meanwhile, tie up the ginger and whole spices in a square of muslin. Add to the onions, with the plums.

2 Place over a moderate heat, then stir in the apples, vinegar, sugar and salt. Cook, stirring, until the sugar dissolves, then increase the heat and bring to a boil. Reduce the heat and simmer gently, stirring often, for 1½-2 hours, until thick. Remove and discard the bundle of spices.

3 Spoon the hot chutney into clean, warmed jars (see page 266). Leave to cool, then seal the jars with lids. Label and date, then store in a cool, dark place. Allow the chutney to mature for 3-4 weeks before using. It will keep for up to a year.

Nutrients per
15ml tablespoon
- Calories 26
- Carbohydrate 7g
    (of which sugars 0.1g)
- Protein 0g
- Fat 0g
- Fibre 0g

The sight of fruit pickers in the fields and punnets of fragrant berries on

Soft fruits and berries

The appearance in our shops and gardens of colourful and fragrant soft fruits and berries is a sweet reward for the long wait through the chillier seasons of the year. Whether they are used for making puddings or preserved in jams and jellies, these succulent fruits, with their strong seasonal resonance, have had an enormous influence on British culinary traditions.

Nature's sweetest harvest
Some berries have a very short season. Mulberries are available only in August and black, red and white currants are confined to the months of June, July and August. Even strawberries, which first appear in June, and blackberries, from July, have a season that seldom exceeds four months. Yet when they are combined with the preservative properties of sugar, vinegar or alcohol, these fruits can be kept to

be enjoyed at any time. A few, such as raspberries and blackberries, also freeze very well, so you can preserve a glut and enjoy them at any time of the year.

Wild and cultivated
Blackberries – known as brambles in some parts of the country – are indigenous to Britain, but it was not until the 20th century that they were widely cultivated. At one time, due to the plentiful supply in hedgerows, they were often viewed as fruit for the poor and their culinary qualities ignored. They are now more valued, especially when paired with apples in a pie or crumble.

Scotland's cooler, wetter climate is particularly suited to growing raspberries and, for more than a century, most of Britain's raspberries have been cultivated there. The longer midsummer days also coincide with the cropping and picking season. As well as the familiar deep scarlet, raspberries can also be white, orange or purple. They

market stalls announces each year the welcome arrival of summer.

are delicate and easily spoilt, making fresh raspberries in season a particular treat. Loganberries and tayberries are both blackberry-raspberry hybrids. Since they were crossbred from different types of blackberry and raspberry, they have quite different flavours and appearances, the tayberry being much sweeter and darker than the sharp, red loganberry.

Edward I introduced gooseberries to Britain in 1275, and they are now regarded as a quintessentially British fruit. They soon became a key ingredient in English country wines, pickles, jellies and jams, and were also used to make sauces for fish, pork, goose and duck, as well sauces for fruit pies and fools. In June, at the beginning of the season, they tend to be rather tart in flavour, but become sweeter towards the end, in August.

Black, red and white currants, originally from Scandinavia, Siberia and North America, have been grown here since the 16th century. Redcurrants were once considered superior in flavour to blackcurrants, but blackcurrants have taken over in popularity since the discovery at the beginning of the 20th century of their extremely high vitamin C content.

Strawberries are the archetypal British forest fruit, the plants once typically collected from woodlands and transplanted to kitchen gardens and domesticated. Wild specimens fruit in June and August and tend to be much smaller than the modern cultivated varieties.

Elderberries, picked in the wild, are black and too acidic to eat raw but can be preserved in a variety of ways – as wine, vinegar, syrup and cordial. The flowers, which blossom in May and June, are also picked to make cordial.

Mushroom ketchup

Nutrients per 15ml tablespoon
- Calories 8
- Carbohydrate 0.2g (of which sugars 0.1g)
- Protein 1g
- Fat 0.3g (of which saturated fat 0g)
- Fibre 0g

PREPARATION TIME: 1 HOUR, PLUS OVERNIGHT SALTING
COOKING TIME: 1 HOUR
MAKES ABOUT 425ML (¾ PINT)

1.8kg (4lb) field mushrooms, wiped with damp kitchen paper
115g (4oz) salt
600ml (1 pint) malt vinegar
4 whole cloves
1 teaspoon allspice berries
1½ teaspoons whole black peppercorns
1½ teaspoons ground ginger
1½ teaspoons ground cinnamon
1 tablespoon brandy (optional)

1 Break the mushrooms into small pieces and place on a plastic tray. Sprinkle with the salt and leave overnight.

2 Put in a large pan, cover with water, then drain several times, to rinse out the salt. Mash the mushrooms lightly with a potato masher, then add all the remaining ingredients except the brandy. Bring to a boil, reduce the heat and simmer for 30 minutes. Remove from the heat and stir in the brandy, if using.

3 Strain and pour into a clean, warmed bottle (see page 266), 2.5cm (1in) from the top. Put the cap on loosely and place the bottle in a deep pan. Fill with hot water up to the level of the ketchup. Bring to a boil, then simmer for 30 minutes. Remove the bottle from the water, tighten the cap and leave to cool. When cold, label and date the bottle. Store in a cool place for up to 3 months.

Delicious for **enriching** meat dishes, mushroom was the **first** ketchup known in **Britain**, appearing in the mid 18th century.

Beetroot and horseradish relish

Nutrients per 15ml tablespoon
- Calories 11
- Carbohydrate 2.5g (of which sugars 2g)
- Protein 0.2g
- Fat 0g
- Fibre 0g

PREPARATION TIME: 1 HOUR
MAKES 900G (2LB)

450g (1lb) cooked beetroot, peeled and coarsely grated
115g (4oz) fresh horseradish, trimmed, peeled and coarsely grated
½ teaspoon salt
115g (4oz) granulated sugar
300ml (½ pint) white wine vinegar

1 Put all the ingredients in a big bowl and stir together until the sugar dissolves.

2 Pack into clean, dry jars and seal with twist-on lids. Label and date, and store in the refrigerator for up to 1 month.

Although vinegar reduces the nutrient content of beetroot, this relish – excellent served with cold meats – is still **rich** in **potassium** and **folate**.

BEETROOT AND HORSERADISH RELISH

Old-English piccalilli

PREPARATION TIME: 2 HOURS,
PLUS OVERNIGHT SALTING
COOKING TIME: 10-15 MINUTES
MAKES 4.5KG (10LB)

2.7kg (6lb) mixture of: cucumber, marrow,
    cauliflower florets, green beans, and
    pickling onions peeled and cut, where
    appropriate, into 1cm (½in) pieces
450g (1lb) salt
1.7 litres (3 pints) white malt vinegar
250g (9oz) granulated sugar
1½ teaspoons ground ginger
20g (¾oz) mustard powder
40g (1½oz) plain white flour
3 teaspoons turmeric powder

Nutrients per 15ml tablespoon
- Calories 6
- Carbohydrate 1g (of which sugars 1g)
- Protein 0.2g
- Fat 0g
- Fibre 0g

Piccalilli was created in the 18th century, by mixing the spices from the East India trade with home-grown vegetables. It is excellent served with a ploughman's lunch, or cold spiced pork (see page 174).

1 Put the prepared vegetables in a large bowl. Sprinkle in the salt and mix with your hands to coat evenly. Cover with a cloth and leave overnight. The next day, drain, then rinse the vegetables well in cold water.

2 Pour all but 300ml (½ pint) of the vinegar into a large pan. Whisk in the sugar, ginger and mustard, then add the vegetables. Simmer over a low heat until cooked but still crisp and holding their shape. Using a slotted spoon, remove the vegetables to a tray.

3 Blend the flour and turmeric powder with the reserved vinegar to form a smooth paste. Stir in some of the hot vinegar to loosen the mixture, then add to the pan. Cook, stirring, for 2-3 minutes until thick. Return the vegetables to the pan. Bring to the boil, then remove from the heat.

4 Spoon into clean, warmed jars (see page 266). Knock each jar gently to remove any air bubbles and leave to cool completely. Seal the jars with lids. Label, date and store in a cool, dry cupboard away from light for up to 3 months.

Tarragon vinegar

PREPARATION TIME: 10 MINUTES,
PLUS 2 WEEKS STANDING
MAKES 1.2 LITRES (2 PINTS)

A handful of fresh tarragon leaves
2.5cm (1in) strip of unwaxed lemon zest
2 cloves
1.2 litres (2 pints) white wine vinegar

1 Put the tarragon loosely into a tall, clean preserving jar. Add the lemon zest and cloves and fill up with the vinegar. Seal the jar tightly.

2 Stand the jar on a window sill for 2 weeks, then strain off and discard the tarragon, lemon zest and cloves. Transfer the vinegar to clean bottles. Seal tightly and label.

Nutrients per 15ml tablespoon
• Calories 1
• Carbohydrate 0g
• Protein 0g
• Fat 0g
• Fibre 0g

Simple herb vinegar

PREPARATION TIME: 10 MINUTES,
PLUS 2-3 WEEKS STANDING
MAKES 600ML (1 PINT)

1 heaped tablespoon fresh herbs, such as chives, chervil, parsley, mint, tarragon, or a mixture
600ml (1 pint) cider or wine vinegar

1 Put the herbs into a clean screw-top jar or bottle, add the vinegar and seal. Leave in a cool place for 2-3 weeks.

2 Strain off and discard the herbs. Pour the vinegar into clean, fresh bottles. Seal and label the bottles.

Nutrients per 15ml tablespoon
• Calories 1
• Carbohydrate 0g
• Protein 0g
• Fat 0g
• Fibre 0g

Herb vinegars are the modern descendants of home-fermented cowslip, dandelion and rhubarb vinegars. They are easy to make and perfect for livening up sauces, dressings and pickles.

Spiced vinegar

PREPARATION TIME: 10 MINUTES,
PLUS 2 HOURS STANDING
COOKING TIME: 5 MINUTES
MAKES 1.2 LITRES (2 PINTS)

1.2 litres (2 pints) vinegar
25g (1oz) whole mixed pickling spices
1 teaspoon granulated sugar

1 Put the vinegar, pickling spices and sugar in a bowl over a saucepan of hot water, so that the bottom of the bowl is clear of the water. Cover the bowl with a plate. Bring the water in the pan to a boil, then remove from the heat.

2 Remove the bowl from the pan and leave to stand for at least 2 hours. Strain and pour the vinegar into a clean bottle. Seal and label.

Nutrients per 15ml tablespoon
• Calories 1
• Carbohydrate 0g
• Protein 0g
• Fat 0g
• Fibre 0g

Elderflower cordial

Pick elderflowers, in late May and June, in areas well away from traffic. They have a wonderful aroma and have long been used in the country to make delicious wines and cordials.

Nutrients per 50ml serving
- Calories 100
- Carbohydrate 30g (of which sugars 30g)
- Protein 0g
- Fat 0g
- Fibre 0g

PREPARATION TIME: 10 MINUTES, PLUS OVERNIGHT SOAKING
MAKES 1 LITRE (1¾ PINTS)

550g (1lb 4oz) caster sugar
25g (1oz) citric acid powder
Grated zest and juice of 1 large unwaxed lemon
600ml (1 pint) boiling water
10-12 large heads of elderflowers, in full bloom and well washed

1 Put the sugar, citric acid and lemon zest and juice in a large heatproof jug or bowl.

2 Pour in the boiling water and stir to dissolve the sugar. Add the elderflower heads, using the stems to push them to the bottom of the syrup. Stir and leave overnight.

3 Strain the cordial through a muslin-lined sieve or a coffee filter. Bottle and seal with a tightly fitting cap. Store in the refrigerator for up to 4 months, or transfer to freezer containers, allowing room for expansion, and freeze. Serve as one part cordial to five parts sparkling mineral water, topped up with ice.

Lemon barley water

Nutrients per 250ml serving
- Calories 35
- Carbohydrate 10g (of which sugars 10g)
- Protein 0g
- Fat 0g
- Fibre 0g

PREPARATION TIME: 10 MINUTES
COOKING TIME: 30 MINUTES, PLUS 2-3 HOURS COOLING
MAKES ABOUT 1 LITRE (1¾ PINTS)

350g (12 oz) pearl barley
1.7 litres (3 pints) water
Finely grated zest and juice of 1½ unwaxed lemons
60g (2¼ oz) caster sugar

1 Put the pearl barley in a saucepan with the water. Bring to the boil, then reduce the heat and simmer gently for 30 minutes. Skim off any scum that forms on the surface.

2 Remove from the heat and stir in the lemon zest and sugar. Cover and leave to cool completely.

3 Strain through a fine sieve, then stir in the lemon juice. Serve chilled, adding more lemon juice or sugar to taste if necessary.

Once used as a soothing drink for feverish patients, but these days more closely associated with Wimbledon tennis, barley water enjoys a long tradition, dating back to the Middle Ages.

Real lemonade is much more refreshing than the fizzy, artificial commercial variety and very easy to make. Look out for thin-skinned lemons, which feel soft and are heavy for their size.

Old-fashioned lemonade

PREPARATION TIME: 30 MINUTES, PLUS OVERNIGHT COOLING
MAKES 1.2 LITRES (2 PINTS)

4 large unwaxed lemons
450g (1lb) caster sugar
25g (1oz) citric acid powder
1.2 litres (2 pints) boiling water

1 Wash and dry the lemons. With a very sharp knife or potato peeler, remove the zest in thin strips. Squeeze the juice from the lemons, strain it through a sieve, cover and chill.

2 Put the strips of zest with the sugar and citric acid in a large jug and pour in the boiling water. Set aside to cool. Stir and prod the rind with a fork occasionally, to help to release its flavour. When cold, cover and leave overnight in a cool place.

3 Strain into a clean jug, stir in the lemon juice and pour into a bottle with a tightly fitting cap. The lemonade will keep in the refrigerator for about 3 months. Serve diluted with mineral or soda water to taste, with plenty of ice.

Note. Citric acid is available in chemists.

Nutrients per 50ml serving
- Calories 74
- Carbohydrate 20g (of which sugars 20g)
- Protein 0g
- Fat 0g
- Fibre 0g

Iced mint tea

PREPARATION TIME: 2 MINUTES,
PLUS 2-3 HOURS COOLING
MAKES 600ML (1 PINT)

2 teaspoons Indian leaf tea
600ml (1 pint) boiling water
2 heaped tablespoons fresh mint leaves,
    plus extra sprigs to serve
Crushed ice and lemon slices to serve

1 Put the tea into a heatproof bowl
and pour in the water. Leave to
infuse for 2 minutes, then strain into a
clean jug. Add the mint, cover and set
aside to cool.

2 Remove the mint and serve chilled
over crushed ice in glass tumblers,
topped with mint sprigs.

VARIATION
For iced lime tea, add 2 tablespoons
freshly squeezed lime juice before
cooling and chilling.

Tea is not only **refreshing**, it also
supplies **bioflavonoids** that may lower
the risk of heart disease and cancer.

Nutrients per 200ml serving
- Calories 1
- Carbohydrate 0g
- Protein 0g
- Fat 0g
- Fibre 0g

Rum and ginger charmer

PREPARATION TIME: 15 MINUTES, PLUS 2-3 HOURS CHILLING
MAKES ABOUT 3 LITRES (5¼ PINTS)

1 litre (1¾ pints) unsweetened pineapple juice
55g (2oz) soft brown sugar
500ml (18fl oz) white rum
350ml (12fl oz) orange juice
Juice of 6 lemons
1 litre (1¾ pints) ginger ale
1 small orange

Nutrients per 200ml serving
- Calories 135
- Carbohydrate 16g (of which sugars 16g)
- Protein 0g
- Fat 0g
- Fibre 0g

Ginger, popular in British cookery since the Middle Ages and an aid to circulation and digestion, adds zing to this fruity summer punch.

1 Heat about a teacup of the pineapple juice until hot, but not boiling. Stir in the sugar until dissolved. Pour into a large punch bowl, then add the remaining pineapple juice, rum, orange juice, lemon juice and ginger ale. Stir well, then chill.

2 Slice the orange finely and add to the punch. Serve chilled in tall glasses, with plenty of ice.

Orange and ginger punch

PREPARATION TIME: 15 MINUTES, PLUS 2-3 HOURS CHILLING
MAKES 2.8 LITRES (5 PINTS)

2 tablespoons caster sugar
600ml (1 pint) weak, hot China tea, strained
300ml (½ pint) pineapple juice, chilled
600ml (1 pint) orange juice, chilled
1.2 litres (2 pints) ginger ale, chilled
Juice of 3 large lemons
2-3 sprigs of lemon balm (optional)
1 small orange, thinly sliced

Nutrients per 200ml serving
- Calories 50
- Carbohydrate 12g (of which sugars 12g)
- Protein 0g
- Fat 0g
- Fibre 0g

Punch – from the Hindi *panch* – came to Britain via the East India Company in the 17th century. Traditionally it includes tea.

1 Stir the sugar into the hot tea until dissolved. Pour into a punch bowl. Stir in the pineapple and orange juices, then the ginger ale and lemon juice.

2 Chop a few lemon balm leaves, if using, and stir into the punch. Float a few orange slices on top, then put a whole lemon balm leaf on each slice. Serve chilled with ice.

St Clement's cup

Nutrients per 200ml serving
- Calories 100
- Carbohydrate 15g
  (of which sugars 15g)
- Protein 0g
- Fat 0g
- Fibre 0g

This hot punch – a **perfect accompaniment** to winter festivities – takes its name from the English nursery rhyme, 'Oranges and lemons say the bells of St Clement's'.

PREPARATION TIME: 15 MINUTES,
PLUS 2 HOURS INFUSING
COOKING TIME: 8 MINUTES
MAKES ABOUT 2.5 LITRES (4½ PINTS)

4 whole cloves
2 cinnamon sticks
2 tablespoons pineapple juice
300ml (½ pint) orange juice
115g (4oz) soft brown sugar
150ml (¼ pint) dry sherry
1.7 litres (3 pints) pale ale
Juice of 3 lemons
Juice of 2 oranges
1 lemon, finely sliced
1 small orange, sliced

1 Put the cloves, cinnamon, pineapple and orange juices and brown sugar in a pan. Bring to the boil, then simmer for 5 minutes. Set aside for 2 hours to infuse.

2 When you are almost ready to serve, pour the sherry and pale ale into a large pan. Strain the spiced fruit juices into this and discard the spices. Add the fresh lemon and orange juice. Heat gently to just below boiling point.

3 Serve the hot punch immediately in warmed glasses, topped with the lemon and orange slices.

Sloe gin

Nutrients per 50ml serving
- Calories 134
- Carbohydrate 6g
  (of which sugars 6g)
- Protein 0g
- Fat 0g
- Fibre 0g

Sloes are the bitter berries of the blackthorn tree. Small and plum-coloured, they **ripen in October**, allowing just the right time for this **delicious** drink to be ready for **Christmas**.

PREPARATION TIME: 10 MINUTE,
PLUS 2 MONTHS MATURING
MAKES 1 LITRE (1¾ PINTS)

225g (8oz) sloe berries
115g (4oz) caster sugar
1 litre (1¾ pints) gin

1 Wash the berries and prick each one with a needle. Put in a tall glass jar, add the sugar, then pour over the gin and stir. Cover with a tightly fitting lid, then leave to stand in a cool, dark place for at least 2 months. Stir or shake once a week.

2 Strain and bottle the bright pink liqueur. Serve neat in small glasses.

Honeyed Kentish cup

PREPARATION TIME: 10 MINUTES
COOKING TIME: 15 MINUTES
MAKES 2 LITRES (3½ PINTS)

2 litres (3½ pints) strong dry cider
4 tablespoons clear honey
1 cinnamon stick, plus extra to serve
½ teaspoon ground cinnamon
½ teaspoon allspice
6 cloves
1 small red apple
1 small lemon

1 Put all the ingredients, except the apple and lemon, into a large pan. Heat slowly until the honey melts, without letting it boil.

2 Just before serving, cut the apple in half, then into thin crescents. Cut the lemon into fine slices.

3 Serve the hot punch in warmed beakers. Top each serving with a slice of apple and lemon and add a cinnamon stick to each.

VARIATION
Stir in a generous dash of Calvados (apple brandy).

Nutrients per 200ml serving
- Calories 90
- Carbohydrate 10g (of which sugars 10g)
- Protein 0g
- Fat 0g
- Fibre 0g

Britain has a long tradition of **cider-making**, especially in apple-growing areas such as Kent. This warming, cider-based punch is ideal for serving on Bonfire Night.

Feasts

and festivals

Highland fling

Hogmanay, the Scottish New Year's Eve, is a night
steeped in tradition and ritual, and offering food to guests
plays an important part in the celebrations. The first person,
or 'first-footer', to cross the threshold after midnight is traditionally a
tall, dark stranger bearing a lump of coal. Scottish households take
turns to provide a meal for guests, with gifts exchanged at midnight

Cock-a-leekie

PREPARATION TIME: 20 MINUTES
PLUS 1 HOUR STANDING TIME
COOKING TIME: 1 HOUR
40 MINUTES
SERVES 6

1 small chicken, about 1.2kg (2lb 10oz)
6-8 thick leeks, slit, washed and roughly
    chopped, keeping green and white
    parts separate
6 black peppercorns
2 fresh bay leaves
12 stoned prunes, roughly chopped
2 tablespoons freshly chopped parsley

1 Put the chicken in a large saucepan. Add the green parts of the leeks, peppercorns, bay leaves and just enough water to cover the chicken.

2 Bring slowly to the boil then cover and simmer for 20-25 minutes. Remove from the heat, cover tightly and leave for about 1 hour, until the chicken is cooked and tender.

3 Remove the chicken carefully and place in a sieve over a bowl and, when cool enough to handle, shred the flesh discarding the skin and bones.

4 Meanwhile, remove and discard the green leeks, peppercorns and bay and add the white leeks to the pan. Simmer until the leeks are tender, adjusting the seasoning.

5 Return the chicken to the pan with the prunes, reheat gently and serve in a warm bowl, sprinkled with parsley. Serve with plenty of oatcakes (see page 240).

Nutrients per serving
- Calories 220
- Carbohydrate 11g (of which sugars 10g)
- Protein 30g
- Fat 6g (of which saturated fat 2g)
- Fibre 4g
- Vitamins A, B_1, B_2, B_6, C, niacin

Haggis

Haggis, traditionally served on Burns Night, is also ideal for Hogmanay. Buy it from a good butcher, or choose vegetarian haggis, which is now widely available. Serve with bashed neeps (mashed swede) and champit tatties (mashed potato).

Cloutie dumpling

PREPARATION TIME: 20 MINUTES
COOKING TIME: 4-4¼ HOURS
SERVES 8

225g (8oz) plain flour, sifted
200g (7oz) golden caster sugar
1 teaspoon ground cinnamon
1 teaspoon mixed spice
115g (4oz) shredded suet
225g (8oz) currants and sultanas, mixed
115g (4oz) stoned dates, finely chopped
1 rounded teaspoon bicarbonate of soda
About 250ml (9fl oz) semi-
    skimmed milk
Plain flour and golden caster sugar
    for sprinkling

1 Put the flour, sugar, cinnamon, mixed spice, suet, dried fruit and bicarbonate of soda in a bowl. Mix, then add the milk until thick but still liquid.

2 Dip a tea towel into a bowl of boiling water, then drain well and lay out flat on a board. Sprinkle with a little flour, then a little sugar.

3 Place the dumpling mixture in the middle of the cloth, then tie the cloth by bringing up the corners and securing with string, allowing some room for the dumpling to expand.

4 Place on a heatproof plate and put the plate into a large saucepan. Top up slowly with just enough boiling water to cover the pudding. Cover tightly and simmer gently for 3½-4 hours. Check the water level from time to time and top up if necessary with boiling water. Meanwhile, heat the oven to 180°C (350°F, gas mark 4).

5 Remove the pudding carefully from the pan and dip briefly into a bowl of cold water, to prevent the cloth sticking. Cut the string and remove the cloth, then invert the dumpling onto an ovenproof plate. Bake in the oven for 10-15 minutes or until the skin feels slightly less sticky.

6 Sprinkle with caster sugar and serve at once, with custard or low-fat crème fraîche.

Nutrients per serving
- Calories 440
- Carbohydrate 80g (of which sugars 57g)
- Protein 5g
- Fat 13g (of which saturated fat 2g)
- Fibre 2g

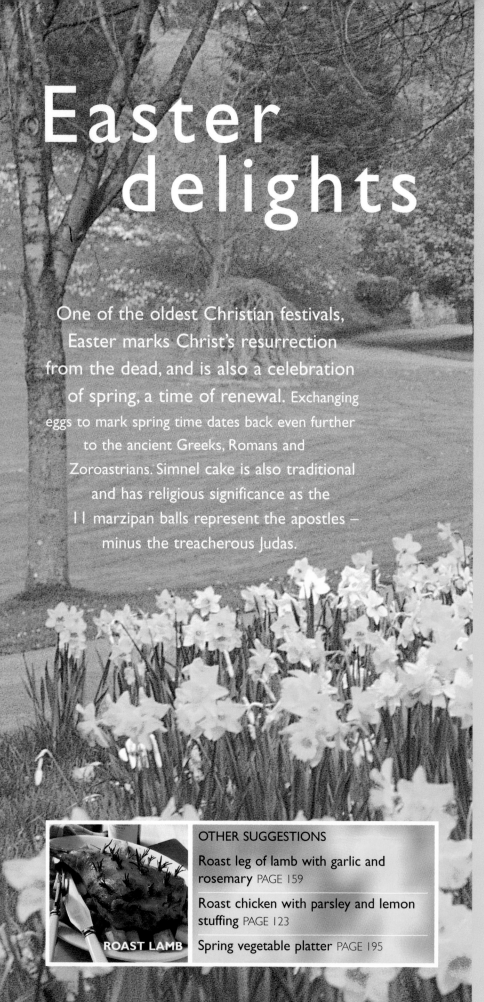

Easter delights

One of the oldest Christian festivals, Easter marks Christ's resurrection from the dead, and is also a celebration of spring, a time of renewal. Exchanging eggs to mark spring time dates back even further to the ancient Greeks, Romans and Zoroastrians. Simnel cake is also traditional and has religious significance as the 11 marzipan balls represent the apostles – minus the treacherous Judas.

OTHER SUGGESTIONS

Roast leg of lamb with garlic and rosemary PAGE 159

Roast chicken with parsley and lemon stuffing PAGE 123

ROAST LAMB

Spring vegetable platter PAGE 195

Simnel cake

PREPARATION TIME:
30 MINUTES
COOKING TIME:
2 HOURS 10 MINS
SERVES 12

600g (1lb 5oz) luxury mixed dried fruit
2 tablespoons cut mixed peel
50g (1¾ oz) light brown muscovado
   sugar
225ml (8fl oz) freshly made strong
   Indian tea
Grated zest and juice of 1 orange
100g (3½ oz) butter, cut into chunks
675g (1lb 8oz) marzipan
100g (3½ oz) flaked almonds
225g (8oz) self-raising flour
2 teaspoons ground cinnamon
1 teaspoon grated nutmeg
3 eggs, beaten

1 Put the dried fruit in a large saucepan. Stir in the mixed peel, sugar, tea, orange zest and juice. Bring to the boil, remove from the heat and stir in the butter until melted. Set aside to cool for 10-15 minutes.

Hot cross-buns

Hot cross-buns are traditionally served on Good Friday. To prepare a batch, simply follow the recipe for Saffron buns on page 257, up to shaping the dough into 12 round buns and placing on an oiled baking tray in step 4. Then, roll out 55g (2oz) shortcrust pastry to about 5mm (¼in) thick and cut it into 24 narrow strips, long enough to lie across the top of a bun. Press 2 strips in the form of a cross on top of each bun. Leave to rise, then bake and glaze as in step 5 of the recipe. Serve warm.

2 Heat the oven to 160°C (325°F, gas mark 3). Line and grease a 20cm (8in) round deep cake tin. Roll out a third of the marzipan on a lightly floured surface to a 20cm (8in) circle.

3 Stir the flaked almonds into the fruit mixture, then sift in the flour, cinnamon and nutmeg. Add the eggs and mix thoroughly until glossy.

4 Pour half the mixture into the tin and top with the circle of marzipan, without pressing it down. Add the remaining mixture and level it out evenly. Bake for 1¾-2 hours, checking after 1½ hours and covering it loosely with foil, if necessary, until risen and cracked on top. Leave to cool in the tin for 15 minutes, then turn it out on to a wire rack and remove the lining paper.

5 Shape 11 small balls from about a third of the remaining marzipan. Roll out the rest into an 18cm (70in) circle between two pieces of cling film. Peel off the top film and pat or trim the edge of the paste neatly, then lift it on the underneath sheet of film and invert it onto the hot cake. Smooth the top of the paste evenly before peeling off the film. Arrange the balls around the edge and leave to cool completely.

6 Heat the grill on the hottest setting. Transfer the cake to a baking sheet and place it under the grill for about 30 seconds to brown the top of the marzipan. Leave to cool before storing in an airtight container. Allow the cake to mature for at least 1 day before serving.

Nutrients per serving
- Calories 600
- Carbohydrate 83g (of which sugars 68g)
- Protein 12g
- Fat 28g (of which saturated fat 7g)
- Fibre 4g
- Vitamins E

Hazelnut truffle eggs

PREPARATION TIME: 1½ HOURS, PLUS 4-5 HOURS CHILLING AND SETTING
MAKES ABOUT 60

150g (5½ oz) blanched hazelnuts
2 tablespoons caster sugar
200ml (7fl oz) double cream
400g (14oz) dark plain chocolate

1 Lightly roast the hazelnuts in a saucepan over a medium heat for 7-10 minutes, shaking the pan frequently. Remove from the heat and sprinkle the sugar over the nuts, then return the pan to the heat and cook for about 30 seconds, until the sugar melts and browns. Scrape the nuts into a bowl, leaving the sugar.

2 Pour half the cream into the pan and bring to the boil, stirring well. Remove from the heat and add half the chocolate, broken into pieces. Stir to melt the chocolate, then remove from the heat and add the remaining cream.

3 Put cold water and some ice cubes into a sink and stand the pan in the water. Grind the sugared nuts to a coarse powder in a food processor or blender and set aside. Swirl the chocolate mixture around the pan to cool, stirring occasionally.

4 When the mixture begins to set, remove the pan from the water and whisk the chocolate until it lightens and forms soft peaks. Stir in the ground nuts and chill for several hours until set.

5 Roll teaspoonfuls of the set mixture into small eggs. Place on a plate and chill. Melt the remaining chocolate in a small bowl over a pan of hot water. Use a fork to dip and quickly roll the eggs in the chocolate, then transfer them to a tray. Leave to set in a cool place for 2-3 hours.

Nutrients per serving
- Calories 70
- Carbohydrate 5g (of which sugars 5g)
- Protein 1g
- Fat 5g (of which saturated fat 2g)
- Fibre 0g

VEGETARIAN SCOTCH EGGS

Picnic fare

The original *pique nique* was a French invention, and in the 17th century described a meal to which each guest brought food. Only in the 1860s did an English picnic become a relaxed outdoor meal. A picnic can be a real feast, not just the odd sandwich and fat-ladened crisps. So many of the pies and flans found in the traditional British culinary repertoire are perfect for outdoor dining. And today, salads will stay crisp and fresh for hours in a cool-bag, and chilled soup is easy to keep cool in a vacuum flask.

Vanilla baskets with summer berries

PREPARATION TIME: 15 MINUTES
COOKING TIME: 13-15 MINUTES
SERVES 4

25g (1oz) butter
40g (1½oz) caster sugar
Grated zest and juice of ½ unwaxed
    lemon
1 teaspoon vanilla extract
25g (1oz) plain flour

For the filling:
200g (7oz) strawberries, hulled and
    halved
200g (7oz) raspberries
100ml (3½fl oz) half-fat crème fraîche

Heat the oven to 190°C (375°F, gas mark 5). Lightly grease two baking sheets. Put the butter, sugar, lemon zest and juice in a small saucepan and heat, stirring until the sugar has dissolved and the butter melted. Remove from the heat, then stir in the vanilla and flour.

Herbed chicken loaf

PREPARATION TIME: 20 MINUTES
COOKING TIME: 1½ HOURS
SERVES 6

Vegetable oil for greasing
4 fresh bay leaves
2 slices of lemon, halved
100g (3½oz) fresh wholemeal
    breadcrumbs
150g (5½oz) lean cooked ham, finely
    chopped
6 spring onions, chopped
½ fennel bulb, finely chopped
8 thyme sprigs, leaves finely chopped
6 large fresh sage leaves, finely chopped
2 tarragon sprigs, leaves finely chopped
Salt and black pepper
6 tablespoons semi-skimmed milk
4 large skinless, boneless chicken breasts,
    about 650g (1lb 7oz) total weight

1 Heat the oven to 180°C (350°F, gas mark 4). Grease a 900g (2lb) loaf tin and arrange the bay leaves and lemon slices in the bottom. Mix the breadcrumbs, ham, spring onions, fennel, thyme, sage and tarragon. Season well, then stir in the milk.

2 Place the chicken breasts one at a time into a large polythene bag and beat them out thinly and evenly with a rolling pin. Lay a chicken breast in the tin, covering the bay and lemon. Top with a third of the stuffing, spreading it evenly. Repeat with the remaining chicken and stuffing, ending with chicken. Cover tightly with foil and bake for 1½ hours.

3 Leave to cool in the tin, then chill for several hours or overnight until firm. Turn the loaf out on to a board or plate and cut into slices. Serve with a mixture of mayonnaise, fromage frais, grated lemon zest, wholegrain mustard and snipped chives, and a mixed leaf salad.

Nutrients per serving
- Calories 200
- Carbohydrate 8g (of which sugars 1.5g)
- Protein 6g
- Fat 6g (of which saturated fat 2g)
- Fibre 1.5g
- Vitamins B_1, B_6, niacin

2 Spoon two separate quarters of the mixture onto each prepared baking sheet, allowing space to spread between them. Cook one batch at a time in the oven for 4-5 minutes, or until the mixture has spread and is pale gold and bubbling.

3 Meanwhile, turn four small bowls upside down. After removing the first batch from the oven, cool on the baking sheet for 30 seconds, or until just firm enough to lift with a palette knife, then drape each biscuit over an upturned bowl. Leave to set. Repeat with the remaining sheet of biscuits to make four baskets.

4 For the picnic, stack the baskets and carry the fruit and crème fraîche in separate containers, so that everyone can help themselves to their own filling.

Nutrients per serving
- Calories 70
- Carbohydrate 6g (of which sugars 6g)
- Protein 2g
- Fat 4g (of which saturated fat 2g)
- Fibre 2g
- Vitamins C

Salad dressings

For a quickly made, light vinaigrette that is easy to transport, put 3 tablespoons olive oil, 1 tablespoon white wine vinegar, 1 tablespoon cold water, 1 crushed garlic clove and 1 teaspoon each of Dijon mustard and runny honey in a screw-top jar. Seal the lid tightly and shake well to mix. Carry to your picnic in the jar, and shake again before adding to your salad. For a herby dressing, mix in 1 tablespoon of finely chopped herbs, such as chives or tarragon. Or for a spicy, oriental touch, use sunflower oil instead of olive oil, add 1 teaspoon grated fresh ginger, 1 finely chopped red chilli and replace the cold water with soy sauce. Season all dressings to taste.

Use yoghurt to make a creamy but low-fat dressing by combining 6 tablespoons half-fat Greek yoghurt, the juice of ½ lemon in a screw-top jar. Season to taste and shake well. Adding 1 tablespoon of finely chopped mint leaves makes a delicious variation. For a tangy dressing, omit the lemon, and add 1 teaspoon wholegrain mustard and a finely chopped 5cm (2in) piece of cucumber.

JERSEY POTATOES WITH SAMPHIRE AND QUAIL'S EGGS

Midsummer barbecue

Until the mid 19th century, it was usual to spit-roast meat over an open fire, both indoors and outside, and ox and pig-roasts were a popular attraction at fairs all over the country. Now barbecues are fast becoming an established part of the British summer. They are such a relaxed, easy way to entertain, with food that is easily prepared in advance and guests often happy to lend a hand with the cooking.

Lamb and rosemary burgers

PREPARATION TIME: 20 MINUTES
COOKING TIME: 20-24 MINUTES
SERVES 4

1 tablespoon olive oil
1 leek, finely chopped
1 large green pepper, seeded and
   finely diced
2 garlic cloves, crushed
2 tablespoons finely chopped fresh
   rosemary
500g (1lb 2oz) minced lamb
1 medium egg yolk
100g (3½oz) fresh wholemeal
   breadcrumbs
Salt and black pepper

1 Heat the oil in a saucepan. Add the leek, pepper and garlic. Stir well and cook for about 10 minutes, stirring occasionally, until tender. Add the rosemary and remove from the heat.

2 Mix the minced lamb, beaten egg yolk and breadcrumbs with pepper and salt to taste. Add the cold vegetables, scraping any juices from the pan and mix with the meat mixture until combined. Divide into eight equal portions.

3 Using wet hands, mould a portion of mixture into a ball before flattening it into a burger about 9cm (3½in) in diameter. Repeat with the remaining mixture to make eight burgers. Transfer to a plate, cover and chill for up to 5 hours.

4 Cook the burgers on a hot barbecue for 5-7 minutes on each side, until well browned and cooked through. Serve in baps with relishes and salad leaves.

Nutrients per serving
- Calories 315
- Carbohydrate 13g (of which sugars 3g)
- Protein 30g
- Fat 16g (of which saturated fat 6g)
- Fibre 2.5g
- Vitamins A, B_6, B_{12}, C, niacin

Hot spiced fruit kebabs

PREPARATION TIME: 15 MINUTES,
PLUS OVERNIGHT SOAKING
COOKING TIME: 6-8 MINUTES
SERVES 6

4 oranges
1 teaspoon grated nutmeg
¼ teaspoon ground cloves
1 tablespoon honey
18 ready-to-eat dried apricots
3 dessert apples
18 large strawberries

1 Grate the zest from 1 orange and squeeze the juice from 2 oranges. Mix with the nutmeg, cloves and honey in a large bowl. Stir in the apricots, cover and set aside to soak overnight.

2 Prepare the remaining fruit no more than 2 hours before cooking the kebabs. Cut each of the remaining oranges into six wedges and add these to the apricots. Cut each apple into eight wedges and cut out the sections of core; hull the strawberries, then add both to the other fruit. Mix well, cover and leave to soak until ready to cook the kebabs.

3 Turn the fruit in the soaking juices before dividing it between six long metal skewers, placing a wedge of orange at each end. Grill over a hot barbecue or under a preheated grill for 6-8 minutes, turning once, until the fruit is browned in places. Serve immediately, with crème fraîche and any remaining juices.

SERVING SUGGESTION
Serve yoghurt or fromage frais with the fruit kebabs. For a more substantial dessert, heat plain waffles on the barbecue or under the grill, then slide the fruit off the skewers on to the waffles. For a completely British twist to barbecue desserts, prepare a creamy rice pudding (see page 232) and chill it overnight. Slide the fruit off the skewers and serve it on bowls of well-chilled creamy rice pudding.

Marinades

Make a quick fruity marinade for poultry by mixing 4 tablespoons orange juice with 2 tablespoons runny honey, 1 tablespoon soy sauce and a little freshly ground black pepper or a dash of cayenne. Marinate meat for at least an hour, basting from time to time while cooking to create a golden glaze.

For delicious fish and shellfish, before cooking, marinate for an hour in 3 tablespoons olive oil, the juice of half a lemon, 1 crushed garlic clove and 1 tablespoon finely chopped oregano leaves, mixed with a little salt and black pepper.

Nutrients per serving
- Calories 100
- Carbohydrate 23g (of which 23g sugars)
- Protein 2g
- Fat 0g
- Fibre 4g
- Vitamins C

Cricket tea

Little could be more English than a lazy summer afternoon watching cricket on the village green. Part of this tradition is the cricket tea, produced by loyal wives and girlfriends to sustain the team and feed supporters during the match. It is a perfect opportunity to show off baking skills, with a huge national repertoire to choose from.

OLD-FASHIONED LEMONADE

Strawberry shortcakes

PREPARATION TIME: 15 MINUTES
COOKING TIME: 7-10 MINUTES
MAKES 6

85g (3oz) butter, diced, plus extra
    for greasing
225g (8oz) self-raising flour
1 teaspoon baking powder
55g (2oz) caster sugar
1 egg, beaten
1 teaspoon vanilla extract
150ml (¼ pint) double cream
Icing sugar to decorate
450g (1lb) strawberries, hulled and
    thickly sliced

1 Heat the oven to 220°C (425°F, gas mark 7) and lightly grease 2 baking sheets. Sift the flour and baking powder into a bowl, then rub in the butter until the mixture resembles fine breadcrumbs. Stir in the caster sugar.

2 Make a well in the middle of the dry ingredients and add the egg and vanilla with 1 tablespoon of the cream. Mix to a soft dough, adding extra cream if necessary. Turn the dough out on to a floured surface and knead lightly until smooth, then roll it out to about 1cm (½in) thick. Use a 7.5cm (3in) diameter round cutter to stamp out 6 rounds, re-rolling the dough as necessary.

3 Place the rounds of dough on the greased baking sheets and cook for 7-10 minutes, until risen and lightly browned on top. Transfer to a wire rack to cool completely.

4 Whisk the remaining cream to soft peaks. Slice the cooled shortcakes into two layers and dredge the tops with icing sugar. Cut the tops across in half. Spread cream on the bottom halves and arrange the strawberries on the cream. Press the sugared tops over the filling, with rounded edges together in the middle.

Nutrients per serving
• Calories 415
• Carbohydrate 42g (of which sugars 14g)
• Protein 6g
• Fat 26g (of which saturated fat 18g)
• Fibre 2g
• Vitamins A, C

Sausage rolls

PREPARATION TIME: 30 MINUTES,
COOKING TIME: 20 MINUTES
MAKES 40

500g (1lb 2oz) packet puff pastry
1 egg, beaten
4 teaspoons English mustard

For the filling:
1 tablespoon sunflower oil
1 large onion, chopped
1 large carrot, chopped or finely diced
1 celery stick, finely diced
10 large fresh sage leaves, chopped
1kg (2lb 4oz) pork sausage meat
Salt and black pepper

1 For the filling, heat the oil in a frying pan and cook the onion, carrot and celery for 5 minutes, stirring frequently. Add the sage, then turn the mixture into a bowl and leave it until it is cold before mixing in the sausage meat and salt and pepper to taste.

2 Heat the oven to 220°C (425°F, gas mark 7). Cut the pastry in half and roll each half out on a lightly floured surface. Trim to a rectangle of about 35 × 23cm (14 × 9in). Spread the mustard thinly on the pastry. Roll the sausage meat mix into four rolls 35cm (14in) long. Place them along the edges of both pastry rectangles.

3 Roll the pastry to enclose the meat and make four long rolls. Cut the pastry and seal. Roll the pastry so that the seal is underneath.

4 Brush with beaten egg and then use large kitchen scissors to snip each roll into 10 pieces. Place on baking trays and make 2-3 snips in the top of each. Chill for 15-20 minutes.

5 Bake for 15-20 minutes until the pastry is puffed and browned. Transfer to a wire rack to cool and serve warm or at room temperature.

Nutrients per serving
• Calories 130
• Carbohydrate 8g (of which sugars 1g)
• Protein 3g
• Fat 10g (of which saturated fat 3g)
• Fibre 0g

Harvest supper

Marking the end of the farming year, harvest feasts were a time for relaxation
and thanksgiving after the crop-gathering and bounty of the harvest.
Today, few of us have such close links with the food we eat, but produce is still
offered at harvest festivals in churches and schools
throughout Britain, and communities still gather
for harvest suppers. In England, these may
occasionally include such traditional
dishes as apple pie and, in Scotland, ale
crowdies made from oatmeal, treacle,
ale and whisky.

Hazelnut meringues

PREPARATION TIME: 20 MINUTES
COOKING TIME: 2½-3 HOURS
SERVES 6

100g (3½oz) blanched hazelnuts
3 egg whites
175g (6oz) caster sugar

For the filling:
50g (1¾oz) caster sugar
300ml (½ pint) dry cider
9 large ripe but firm plums, about 600g
    (1lb 5oz), quartered and stoned
1 tablespoon icing sugar
225g (8oz) curd cheese
2 tablespoons Greek-style yoghurt

LANCASHIRE HOTPOT

OTHER SUGGESTIONS

Lancashire hotpot PAGE 165

Faggots in rich wine gravy PAGE 168

Gammon in cider PAGE 170

Blackberry and apple crumble
PAGE 226

Honeyed Kentish cup PAGE 285

Cidered chicken casserole
with leek and apple dumplings

PREPARATION TIME: 30 MINUTES
COOKING TIME: 1 HOUR
SERVES 4

2 tablespoons vegetable oil
4 skinless, boneless chicken breasts, cut
   into 2.5cm (1in) cubes
2 bay leaves
1 large onion, chopped
2 large carrots, cut into chunks
2 parsnips, cut into chunks
½ swede, cut into large dice
1 celery stick, diced
1 tablespoon wholegrain mustard
700ml (1¼ pints) dry cider
Salt and black pepper

For the dumplings:
1 tablespoon olive oil
1 small leek, finely chopped
1 Cox's apple, peeled and coarsely
   grated
225g (8oz) self-raising flour
115g (4oz) light vegetable suet
150ml (¼ pint) semi-skimmed milk

1 Heat the oil in a large flameproof casserole. Brown the chunks of chicken over a high heat for about 5 minutes, then remove them to a plate.

2 Add the bay leaves, onion, carrots, parsnips, swede and celery. Stir well, cover and cook for 5 minutes. Replace the chicken and stir in the mustard, cider, and salt and pepper to taste. Bring to the boil, then reduce the heat, cover and simmer for 20 minutes.

3 Meanwhile, heat the oil for the dumplings in a saucepan and cook the leek for about 5 minutes, stirring occasionally, until softened. Transfer to a bowl and stir in the apple. Add the flour and suet, then stir in the milk to make a soft dough. Using, floured hands, shape the dough into 16 balls.

4 Arrange the dumplings on top of the casserole and cover. Simmer for a further 25 minutes, until the dumplings are risen, fluffy and shiny on top. Ladle the casserole and dumplings into bowls and serve at once.

Nutrients per serving
- Calories 720
- Carbohydrate 65g (of which sugars 17g)
- Protein 39g
- Fat 33g (of which saturated fat 13g)
- Fibre 7g
- Vitamins A, B_1, B_6, C, niacin

with poached plums

1 Heat the oven to 120°C (250°F, gas mark ½). Line two baking sheets with baking parchment and use a marker pen to draw three 10cm (4in) circles on each. Turn the parchment over and place on the baking sheets, ink side down.

2 Roast the hazelnuts in a small pan over medium heat for 8-10 minutes, until they smell nutty but are not browned. Cool slightly, then grind in a food processor or with a pestle and mortar.

3 Beat the egg whites until stiff. Sprinkle in 1 tablespoon of sugar, whisking. With the whisk still running, add the rest of the sugar gradually, until the mixture is

glossy and forms stiff peaks. Using a metal spoon, gently fold in the ground hazelnuts.

4 Divide the meringue evenly between the circles, mounding it up. Spread it to the edges of the circles and make a hollow in the centre of each one. Bake for 2½-3 hours, until crisp and lightly browned. Remove to a wire rack to cool.

5 For the filling, bring the sugar and cider to the boil in a saucepan, stirring until the sugar dissolves. Reduce the heat and add the quartered plums, then simmer

for 2-3 minutes, or until lightly cooked. Transfer the plums to a bowl, then boil the syrup until reduced by half. Pour the syrup over the plums and leave to cool.

6 Beat the icing sugar into the curd cheese, then stir in the yoghurt. Divide this between the hollows of the meringues. Pile the plums on top and spoon the syrup over.

Nutrients per serving
- Calories 400
- Carbohydrate 54g (of which sugars 53g)
- Protein 7g
- Fat 17g (of which saturated fat 5g)
- Fibre 3g
- Vitamins E

Fiery fun

'Remember, remember, the fifth of November...' The anniversary
of the Gunpowder Plot of 1605 to blow up Parliament is marked
throughout Britain with bonfire and firework parties. Held
outdoors, at a time when winter frosts are starting to bite, it is customary to
serve warming, hearty food, some of it baked in the dying embers of the bonfire.
For some, the fun begins on October 31, Hallowe'en, the night on which the
Celts believed all natural laws were suspended and ghosts and witches ruled

Simple toffee apples

PREPARATION TIME: 15 MINUTES
COOKING TIME: 12-15 MINUTES
MAKES 12

Sunflower oil for brushing
12 wooden dowels or lollipop sticks
12 dessert apples, washed and dried
450g (1lb) light muscovado sugar
6 tablespoons water
2 tablespoons lemon juice
175g (6oz) butter
2 tablespoons golden syrup

1 Cover a baking sheet with lightly oiled baking parchment. Press a wooden dowel or lollipop stick into each apple. Set aside, ready to dip into the toffee.

2 Put the sugar, water, lemon juice, butter and golden syrup in a heavy saucepan, large enough to allow the mixture to rise up during cooking. Heat gently, stirring, until the sugar dissolves. Stop stirring, bring to a boil, and boil rapidly for about 12-15 minutes, until the syrup reaches 142°C (287°F), or a little in cold water forms a slightly pliable lump.

3 Remove the pan from the heat as soon as the right temperature is reached, and working quickly, while the toffee mixture is still bubbling, use the dowels to turn the apples in the toffee until they are thickly and evenly coated. Allow excess to drip off, still turning, then give a final sharp twist to catch any last drips of toffee before placing each apple on the oiled parchment to cool.

Nutrients per serving
- Calories 310
- Carbohydrate 53g (of which sugars 53g)
- Protein 1g
- Fat 12g (of which saturated fat 8g)
- Fibre 1g
- Vitamins C, A

Spiced hot orange juice

PREPARATION TIME: 10 MINUTES
COOKING TIME: 10 MINUTES
SERVES 6

1 large orange
12 cloves
1 cinnamon stick
2 tablespoons honey
1 litre (1¾ pints) orange juice
Orange slices to decorate

1 Cut the ends off the orange, leaving the flesh and, if possible, a little of the pith in place, and stick 6 cloves in each piece, then place in a saucepan. Grate the zest and squeeze the juice from the orange, and add both to the pan with the cinnamon stick and honey.

2 Bring to the boil and add the orange juice. Stir well, cover and simmer gently for about 10 minutes, until the juice is hot, but not boiling. Ladle the juice into heatproof glasses or mugs and decorate with slices of orange.

Nutrients per serving
- Calories 81
- Carbohydrate 20g (of which sugars 20g)
- Protein 1g
- Fat 0g
- Fibre 0.5g
- Vitamins C

Pumpkin soup

PREPARATION TIME: 20 MINUTES
COOKING TIME: 45-50 MINUTES
SERVES 6

25g (1oz) butter
1 large onion, finely chopped
Large wedge of pumpkin, about 1.2kg (2lb 10oz), peeled, seeded and cubed
1 clove garlic, thinly sliced
7cm (2¾in) piece of fresh ginger, peeled and sliced
Pinch of dried chilli flakes
1 litre (1¾ pints) vegetable stock (see page 182)
Salt and black pepper
2 tablespoons half-fat crème fraîche

1 Heat the butter in a saucepan and cook the onion for about 5 minutes, until translucent. Add the pumpkin, garlic, ginger and chilli flakes and cook, stirring, for 10-15 minutes, until the pumpkin begins to soften.

2 Pour in the stock and add pepper and salt. Bring to the boil, then simmer for 20-25 minutes.

3 Transfer to a blender and purée until smooth. Reheat, but do not boil, and serve at once with a swirl of half-fat crème fraîche and a grating of fresh nutmeg.

Nutrients per serving
- Calories 120
- Carbohydrate 18g (of which sugars 10g)
- Protein 3g
- Fat 5g (of which saturated fat 3g)
- Fibre 3g
- Vitamins A, B_6, C

**HONEY ROAST
VEGETABLES**

Christmas-time

In Britain, for more than a thousand years
Christmas has been a time to rest and make merry
with family and friends. Until late Victorian times,
roast goose was the popular centrepiece of a
Christmas dinner, although turkey now reigns supreme.
A rich fruit cake and mince pies are also traditional and ensure a
welcoming treat for chance visitors. The little pies, which originally
included minced meat, have been popular for centuries. Eating
one on each of the twelve days of Christmas was considered
a guarantee of a happy and prosperous twelve
months to come.

Roast turkey with rich fruit stuffing

PREPARATION TIME: 40 MINUTES
COOKING TIME: 6-6¼ HOURS
SERVES 12

2 onions, quartered
1 lemon, quartered
1 orange, quartered
4 bay leaves
5kg (11lb) oven-ready turkey
50g (1¾ oz) butter
Salt and black pepper

For the stuffing:
25g (1oz) butter
2 celery sticks, finely diced
1 onion, chopped
10 large bay leaves
150g (5½ oz) ready-to-eat prunes, chopped
150g (5½ oz) ready-to-eat dried apricots, chopped
150ml (5fl oz) brandy
225g (8oz) rindless streaky bacon, chopped
450g (1lb) pork sausage meat
100g (3½ oz) fresh white breadcrumbs
½ teaspoon ground mace

Nutrients per serving
- Calories 510
- Carbohydrate 17g (of which sugars 10g)
- Protein 41g
- Fat 28g (of which saturated fat 12g)
- Fibre 2g
- Vitamins B₁₂, B₆, niacin

1 Heat the oven to 180°C (350° F, gas mark 4). Put the onions, lemon and orange quarters and bay leaves in the body cavity of the bird. Cut between the skin and breast at the parson's nose end of the bird to separate the skin from the breast, then slide your hand under the skin to loosen it.

2 For the stuffing, melt the butter in a saucepan. Add the celery and onion, cover and cook for 10 minutes, until tender but not browned. Transfer to a large bowl and leave until cold. Then mix in the remaining stuffing ingredients.

3 Put the turkey in a large roasting tin, with the opening between the skin and flesh uppermost. Use a small spoon to push the stuffing into an even layer under the skin. Push a metal skewer through the opening between the skin and flesh to secure. Roll any remaining stuffing into balls.

4 Smear the bird all over with salt and pepper. Cover with foil and roast for 3 hours, basting occasionally. Discard foil and roast for a further 30 minutes until the skin is crisp and golden. Add the stuffing balls as necessary alongside the turkey and cook for the last 30 minutes.

5 Turn the turkey over to breast side up and baste well. Sprinkle with salt and pepper, cover with foil and cook for a further 1¾ hours. Remove the foil, baste and roast for a final 30 minutes, until the skin is crisp and golden and the turkey cooked through — test by inserting a skewer into the thickest part of the leg. Serve with bread sauce, roast potatoes and vegetables.

Bread sauce

PREPARATION TIME: 5 MINUTES
COOKING TIME: 15 MINUTES, PLUS 1 HOUR STANDING
SERVES 10

1 large onion, peeled
6 cloves
3 bay leaves
1 large blade of mace
850ml (1 pint 10fl oz) semi-skimmed milk
200g (7oz) fresh white breadcrumbs
Salt and black pepper
Freshly grated nutmeg

1 Stud the onion with the cloves and put in a saucepan with the bay leaves and mace. Pour in the milk and heat to just below boiling point. Reduce the heat to low and cook gently for 5 minutes. Remove from the heat, cover and leave to stand for 1 hour.

2 Bring the milk back to the boil, then take off the heat and remove the flavourings. Whisk in the breadcrumbs. Return the pan to the heat and bring to the boil, whisking. Simmer gently for 3 minutes, stirring occasionally. Add salt, pepper and nutmeg to taste, then serve with the roast turkey.

Nutrients per serving
- Calories 90
- Carbohydrate 15g (of which sugars 5g)
- Protein 5g
- Fat 2g (including saturated fat 1g)
- Fibre 0.5g

Chestnut and mushroom roast with plum sauce

PREPARATION TIME: 40 MINUTES
COOKING TIME: ABOUT 1¾ HOURS
SERVES 6

50g (1¾ oz) butter, plus extra for greasing
2 bay leaves
3 cloves garlic, crushed
1 onion, finely chopped
1 celery stick, finely chopped
350g (12oz) mushrooms, finely chopped
55g (2oz) ready-to-eat prunes, chopped
Grated zest of 1 unwaxed lemon and
    juice of ½ lemon
Salt and black pepper
3 tablespoons brandy
250g (9oz) can peeled cooked chestnuts,
    finely chopped
1 tablespoon chopped fresh parsley
2 tablespoons chopped fresh thyme
175g (6oz) fresh white breadcrumbs
1 egg
1 leek, finely chopped
1 dessert apple, peeled, cored and
    coarsely grated

For the plum sauce:
Grated zest and juice of 1 orange
4 tablespoons redcurrant jelly
200ml (7fl oz) red wine
6 large, firm red plums, halved, stoned
    and sliced crossways

Nutrients per serving
- Calories 337
- Carbohydrate 48g (of which sugars 21g)
- Protein 7g
- Fat 10g (including saturated fat 5g)
- Fibre 5g
- Vitamins B$_6$

1 Melt half the butter in a large saucepan. Add the bay leaves, garlic, onion and celery. Cover and cook for 5 minutes. Stir in the mushrooms, prunes, lemon zest and juice and seasoning, then cook, uncovered for about 20 minutes, stirring frequently, until the mushrooms are reduced and the mixture is moist.

2 Stir in the brandy and boil for about 30 seconds. Remove from the heat and mix in the chestnuts, parsley, thyme and half the breadcrumbs. Adjust the seasoning, remove the bay leaves, mix in the egg and set aside. Melt the remaining butter in a large saucepan and cook the leek, covered, for 15 minutes, stirring occasionally. Remove from the heat, then add the apple and remaining breadcrumbs.

3 Meanwhile, heat the oven to 180°C (350°F, gas mark 4) and line and grease a 900g (2lb) loaf tin. Place half the mushroom mix in the tin. Put the leek mix on top and add the remaining mushroom mix, pressing each layer down well. Cover with lightly oiled foil and bake for 1 hour, until the mixture is slightly risen and spongy to the touch. Remove the foil for the last 10 minutes. Set aside for 15 minutes.

4 For the sauce, put the orange zest and juice, redcurrant jelly and wine in a small pan and heat, stirring, until the jelly has melted. Boil for 2-3 minutes to reduce by about a third. Reduce to a simmer and add the plums. Cook for 1-2 minutes, until tender, then remove the pan from the heat. Turn the loaf out, cut into slices and serve with the sauce.

Boxing Day turkey soup

PREPARATION TIME: 10 MINUTES
COOKING TIME: 25 MINUTES
SERVES 4

1.2 litres (2 pints) turkey or chicken
    stock (see page 120)
50g (1¾ oz) long-grain rice
50g (1¾ oz) mushrooms, very thinly
    sliced
100g (3½ oz) cooked turkey meat,
    chopped
Salt and black pepper
2 tablespoons chopped parsley

1 Bring the stock to the boil in a large pan, add the rice and cook for about 20 minutes, until almost tender.

2 Add the sliced mushrooms and the turkey meat and cook for a further 2-3 minutes. Adjust the seasoning to taste.

3 Ladle into soup bowls, sprinkle the chopped parsley over and serve.

VARIATION
Use mini pasta shapes or small macaroni (pastina per brodo) instead of rice. For a stronger flavour, use soaked, dried ceps in place of fresh mushrooms. Cook according to times given on the packet.

Nutrients per serving
- Calories 83
- Carbohydrate 11g (of which sugars 0g)
- Protein 8g
- Fat 1g (of which saturated fat 0g)
- Fibre 0g

An ideal Christmas dish for vegetarians, or to serve with cold ham.

Filo mincemeat parcels

PREPARATION TIME: 30 MINUTES
COOKING TIME: 15 MINUTES
MAKES 20

4 tablespoons sunflower oil
40 sheets filo pastry, each measuring
   19 x 15cm (7½ x 6in)
450g (1lb) mincemeat
Icing sugar for dusting

1 Heat the oven to 200°C (400°F, gas mark 6) and lightly oil two baking sheets. Keep all but the filo pastry you are using covered with cling film.

2 Lay a piece of filo on a board, brush lightly with oil, then add another sheet. Brush again with oil, then place a large teaspoonful of mincemeat in the middle. Scrunch the pastry together to enclose the mincemeat. Place on the baking sheet and repeat with the remaining pastry and mincemeat.

3 Bake for about 12-15 minutes, until crisp and browned. Transfer to a wire rack to cool. Dust with icing sugar and serve.

Nutrients per serving
- Calories 111
- Carbohydrate 20g (of which sugars 15g)
- Protein 1g
- Fat 3.5g (of which saturated fat 1g)
- Fibre 0g

Dressing up the Christmas cake

Transform the Dundee cake on page 250 into a Christmas cake by omitting the nut topping and following these easy decorating ideas to create a stunning, eye-catching result.

Gilded holly. Cover the top and sides of the cake in marzipan, then lay alternate, 2.5cm (1in) wide strips of red and green roll-out icing across the top, making sure they butt closely together. Trim the ends to fit neatly around the edge of the cake. Roll out and fix a band of red or green icing around the sides. Wash and dry several small holly sprigs. Paint them gold, leave to dry, then arrange around the top edge of the cake. Tie a gold ribbon around the sides, finishing in a large bow.

Chocolate trees. Cover the cake with marzipan, then white roll-out icing. On non-stick paper, draw three tree shapes, sized to fit together on top of the cake. Lay a cocktail stick 'trunk' down the centre of each. Melt some white chocolate, colour it green with food colouring and thickly coat the tree shapes with it. Fork up roughly, dot with gold and silver sugar balls and leave to set. Melt more chocolate and colour it red. Spread this in a tub shape under each tree – leave enough cocktail stick uncovered to stab down into the cake. Allow to set. Arrange the 'trees' on top of the cake and scatter sweets around them. Tie a red ribbon around the sides.

menu planner

STRAWBERRY JAM

WINTER SALAD OF BATAVIA
WITH POMEGRANATE

Creating meals that offer the right nutritional balance along with an appetising mix of tastes and textures can be tricky. But following the menus here will ensure success on any occasion, and may help to inspire some ideas of your own.

weekend brunch

Kedgeree PAGE 29

Winter salad of batavia with pomegranate PAGE 60

Cottage cheese pancakes with berry fruit compote PAGE 28

Creamy, lightly spiced kedgeree gives a satisfying, energy-packed start to the day, and the salad and fruity pancakes make a refreshing contrast. Serve with herbal tea, as a healthier alternative to coffee.

Total nutrients per person
- Calories 765
- Carbohydrate 78g (of which sugars 26g)
- Protein 44g
- Fat 32g (of which saturated fat 7g)
- Fibre 32g
- Vitamins B_1, B_2, niacin, B_6, B_{12}, C

Mixed grain muesli with dried fruit salad PAGE 26

Asparagus with anchovy eggs PAGE 45

Potato scones PAGE 246

Give this fibre and protein-rich spread a sharp, zingy lift by serving it with chilled glasses of elderflower cordial (page 280).

Total nutrients per person
- Calories 575
- Carbohydrate 70g (of which sugars 13g)
- Protein 24g
- Fat 22.5g (of which saturated fat 7g)
- Fibre 8.5g
- Vitamins B_1, B_6, C

high tea

Warm potted shrimps on shredded lettuce PAGE 46

White or wholemeal bread PAGE 260

Curd tart with glazed gooseberries and grapes PAGE 216

Sweet and salty flavours, crunchy and creamy textures, all are found in this healthy classic selection.

Total nutrients per person
- Calories 684
- Carbohydrate 67g (of which sugars 32.5g)
- Protein 23g
- Fat 36.05g (of which saturated fat 15g)
- Fibre 5.5g
- Vitamins A, C, B_{12}, B_1, B_6

Smoked salmon on horseradish potato farls PAGE 47

White or walnut bread PAGE 260

Strawberry jam PAGE 267

Lemon meringue pie PAGE 217

Making your own bread and jam allows you to use the best ingredients as well as enabling you to control the sugar and fat content.

Total nutrients per person
- Calories 660
- Carbohydrate 105g (of which sugars 35.5g)
- Protein 31g
- Fat 19.05g (of which saturated fat 9g)
- Fibre 4.7g
- Vitamins B_6, B_1, B_{12}

ASPARAGUS WITH ANCHOVY EGGS

APPLE BATTER PUDDING

family supper

Fish supper with swede patties
PAGE 90

Apple batter pudding PAGE 220

Packed with vitamins and fibre, this combination of dishes makes a hearty, warming main meal, ideal for winter.

Total nutrients per person
- Calories 380
- Carbohydrate 107g (of which sugars 53g)
- Protein 39g
- Fat 59g (of which saturated fat 12g)
- Fibre 14g
- Vitamins A, B_6, B_{12}, C, niacin

Turkey likkey pie PAGE 126

Berry jellies PAGE 208

The fresh tangy jellies make the perfect foil to the richly flavoured turkey pie, an old West Country dish that has been cleverly adapted by reducing the fat.

Total nutrients per person
- Calories 482
- Carbohydrate 55g (of which sugars 25g)
- Protein 31.5g
- Fat 16g (of which saturated fat 7g)
- Fibre 3.5g
- Vitamins C, B_1, B_6, B_{12}, niacin

Sunday lunch

Grated courgette and potato soup PAGE 50

Roast beef with a mustard crust and Yorkshire pudding PAGE 149

Deep custard tart with caramelised plums PAGE 226

A quickly prepared soup and a dessert that can be made in advance make this a great menu for a leisurely family meal. It also offers a superb balance of tastes, textures and health-giving nutrients.

Total nutrients per person
- Calories 906
- Carbohydrate 89g (of which sugars 33g)
- Protein 69g
- Fat 31g (of which saturated fat 13g)
- Fibre 6g
- Vitamins B_6, B_{12}, niacin

SMOKED SALMON AND MELON

Smoked salmon and melon
PAGE 32

Country rabbit with caramelised apples PAGE 138

Chocolate mousse PAGE 232

Rabbit is a wonderful meat for the health-conscious cook, as it is low in fat and high in protein, iron and B vitamins. It is also delicious as the hearty central focus of a lunch that features a cold, refreshing starter and rich but light finish.

Total nutrients per person
- Calories 975
- Carbohydrate 72g (of which sugars 51g)
- Protein 84g
- Fat 38g (of which saturated fat 13g)
- Fibre 5g
- Vitamins B_2, B_{12}, B_1, B_6, C, A

BERRY JELLIES

TURKEY LIKKEY PIE

low-calorie lunchbox

Crowdie eggs PAGE 70

Oatcakes PAGE 240

Shrewsbury biscuits PAGE 240

Creamy, soft Crowdie eggs contrast well with the crumbly, nuttiness of oatcakes. Try to include a piece of fresh fruit and a refreshing low-calorie drink, such as lemon barley water (page 280).

Total nutrients per person
- Calories 341
- Carbohydrate 34.5g (of which sugars 7.5g)
- Protein 9g
- Fat 14g (of which saturated fat 5.5g)
- Fibre 2g
- Vitamins B$_{12}$

Parsley-coated smoked mackerel pâté PAGE 46

Wholemeal bread PAGE 260

Cornish fairings PAGE 238

Rich in omega-3 fatty acids, mackerel pâté will help to protect against heart disease as well as making a tasty, filling lunch. For an extra boost of vitamins, follow up with a delicious fresh fruit salad packed in a box.

Total nutrients per person
- Calories 413
- Carbohydrate 29g (of which sugars 5.5g)
- Protein 19g
- Fat 25.05g (of which saturated fat 6g)
- Fibre 3.5g
- Vitamins B$_6$, B$_{12}$, C, B$_1$, niacin

CROWDIE EGGS

PAN-FRIED SCALLOPS WITH RIBBON VEGETABLES

suppers for slimmers

Pan-fried scallops with ribbon vegetables PAGE 114

Summer pudding PAGE 214

It will take hardly any time to produce this low-fat, vitamin-rich meal. Scallops cook quickly and summer pudding can be made well in advance. Steamed rice will go well with the scallops.

Total nutrients per person
- Calories 440
- Carbohydrate 49g (of which sugars 23g)
- Protein 23g
- Fat 16g (of which saturated fat 4g)
- Fibre 6g
- Vitamins C, A, B$_{12}$

SUMMER PUDDING

Old English stewed rosemary chicken PAGE 121

Rose-strawberry yoghurt ice PAGE 213

Chicken and rosemary create a stunning blend of flavours in a casserole that is filling and tasty, yet still low in fat. The rose and strawberry yoghurt ice is a great low-calorie alternative to ice cream, and a bright, refreshing finale.

Total nutrients per person
- Calories 540
- Carbohydrate 30g (of which sugars 23g)
- Protein 48g
- Fat 25g (of which saturated fat 7g)
- Fibre 0.05g
- Vitamins niacin, C

BUTTERNUT, BLUE CHEESE AND WALNUT SALAD

entertaining

Butternut, blue cheese and walnut salad PAGE 59

Duck with glazed turnips PAGE 129

Ginger syllabub with ginger wafers PAGE 212

High on flavour and low on fat, Blue Vinney cheese zips up the unusual starter salad, while a ginger dessert provides a warming glow that nicely completes this varied meal.

Total nutrients per person
- Calories 959
- Carbohydrate 39g (of which sugars 18g)
- Protein 38g
- Fat 66g (of which saturated fat 23g)
- Fibre 6g
- Vitamins B_6, B_1, B_{12}, niacin, A

Minted pea soup with prawns and chives PAGE 52

Foil-baked salmon trout with gooseberry and elderflower sauce PAGE 102

Cherry charlotte PAGE 223

From the fresh-tasting soup to the piquant sauce that accompanies the moist, mineral-rich fish, and the juicy cherry pudding, this entire meal is one that will leave your taste buds feeling really refreshed.

Total nutrients per person
- Calories 975
- Carbohydrate 79g (of which sugars 31g)
- Protein 82g
- Fat 34g (of which saturated fat 10.5g)
- Fibre 19.5g
- Vitamins B_1, C, B_6, B_{12}

vegetarian choices

Winter vegetable soup PAGE 56

Spinach, cheese and egg filo pie PAGE 83

Elderflower sorbet PAGE 212

Here is proof that a menu without a shred of meat or fish can offer a wide spectrum of tastes and textures, as well as a good healthy balance of nutrients, including generous doses of vitamins and minerals.

Total nutrients per person
- Calories 775
- Carbohydrate 72g (of which sugars 42g)
- Protein 29g
- Fat 42g (of which saturated fat 16g)
- Fibre 8g
- Vitamins C, B_{12}, B_6, A, B_2

Beetroot salad with mint dressing PAGE 61

Irish soda bread PAGE 261

Celeriac and Stilton soufflé PAGE 80

Blackcurrant fool with almond shorties PAGE 210

This delicious menu offers a mix of sharp and creamy taste sensations and is also a great way to pack in healthy vitamins and minerals.

Total nutrients per person
- Calories 839
- Carbohydrate 95.5g (of which 29g)
- Protein 40g
- Fat 36.5g (of which saturated fat 14g)
- Fibre 15.5g
- Vitamins B_6, B_1, B_{12}, C

MINTED PEA SOUP WITH PRAWNS

BEETROOT SALAD WITH MINT DRESSING

index

a

313

Picture credits

t=top, tl=top left, tr=top right, r=right, l=left, c=centre, ca=centre above, b=bottom, bc=bottom centre, bl=bottom left, br=bottom right

6/7 (c) Getty Images (b) David Murray; **7** Chris Gasgoigne/View Pictures; **9** (b) Jacqui Hurst; **10** (t) Hulton-Deutsch Collection/Corbis (l) Topham Picturepoint; **11** (t) Paul Felix; (inset) Belhaven Brewery; (ca) Mary Evans Picture Library; (c) Tara Fisher; (b) Collections/Robert Estall; **30** (t) Anthony Blake Photo Library/Mark Turner (c) Collections/Philip Craven; **31** (tl) Jacqui Hurst (c) Restaurant magazine/ Laurie Fletcher (r) Anthony Blake Photo Library /Mark Turner (bl) Collections/Gerry Gavigan Rural History Centre The University of Reading; **40–1** (b) Ed Young/Corbis **54** (tl) Debbie Patterson (tr) Derek St Romaine/garden, Congham Hall (bl) Anthony Blake Photo Library (br) David Murray; **55** (tl) David Murray (c) Collections/Roger Scruton (r) Jacqui Hurst (c) Mary Evans (bl) Andrew Lawson (r) Derek St Romaine; **60–1** (t) Jacqui Hurst; **74** (tl) Collections/Michael St Maur Sheil (tr) Rural History Centre, The University of Reading (bl) Anthony Blake Photo Library/David Marsden (br) Anthony Blake Photo Library/RDL; **75** (tl) Anthony Blake Photo Library/Tim Macpherson (c) Steve Davey/La Belle Aurore (tr) Debbie Patterson (bl) Jacqui Hurst (br) Steve Davey/La Belle Aurore; **100** (t) Anthony Blake Photo Library (c) Debbie Patterson (bl) Hutchison Library (br) Hutchison/Library/Peter Rippon; **101** (tl) Jacqui Hurst (tr) Hutchison Library/Edward Parker (c) Tara Fisher (bl) Collections/Michael St Maur Sheil (br) Steve Davey/La Belle Aurore; **132** (tl) Anthony Blake Photo Library/Maximilian Stock (tr) Hutchison Library/Leslie Woodhead

(c) Mary Evans Picture Library (bl) John Darling/Cephas (br) Travel Ink/Terry Whitakker; **133** (tl) Hutchison Library (tr) Hutchison Library/JG Fuller; (c) Mary Evans Picture Library (b) Getty Images (br) Mary Evans Picture Library; **160** (tl) Steve Davey/La Belle Aurore (tr) Topham Picturepoint (bl) Hulton Getty (br) Collections/George Wright; **161** (tl) Tara Fisher (tr) Anthony Blake Photo Library/John Sims (c) Mary Evans Picture Library (bl) Hulton Getty (br) Steve Davey/La Belle Aurore; **190** (tl) Adam Woolfitt/Corbis (c) Tara Fisher (tr) Derek St Romaine/Cleve West (bl, br) Tara Fisher; **191** (tl) Eye Ubiquitous/E L Neil (tr) Hulton Getty (c) Mary Evans Picture Library (bl) Tara Fisher (br) Debbie Patterson; **218** (tl) Lamontagne/Garden Picture Library (r) Rachel Spivey (bl, bc, br) Anthony Blake Photo Library/J Topps; **219** (tl) Hutchison/Robert Francis (r) James Ravilious for Common Ground (c) Clifford Harper for Common Ground (bl) Jacqui Hurst/Garden Picture Library (r) Rachel Spivey; **248** (t) Collections/Liz Stares (bl) Ab/Ming Tang-Evans (c) Anthony Blake Photo Library (br) Mary Evans Picture Library; **249** (tl) Collections/Ray Roberts (tr) Anthony Blake Photo Library/Georgia Glynn Smith (c) Topham Picturepoint (bl, br) Paul Felix; **274** (t) Anthony Blake Photo Library (bl) Tara Fisher (r) Hulton Getty; **275** (tr) Travel Ink/David Toase (c) Mary Evans Picture Library (bl) Derek St Romaine (br) Jacqui Hurst; **288** Anthony Blake Photo Library; **290** Pictures of Britain; **298** Robert Estell/Corbis; **300** Anthony Blake Photo Library; **302** Pictures Colour Library

Acknowledgments

Great British Dishes the Healthy Way
was published by the Reader's Digest Association Limited, London

First edition Copyright © 2002
The Reader's Digest Association Limited, 11 Westferry Circus,
Canary Wharf, London E14 4HE

We are committed to both the quality of our products and the service
we provide to our customers.
We value your comments, so please feel free to contact us on
08705 113366 or via our web site at: www.readersdigest.co.uk
If you have any comments or suggestions about the content of our books,
email us at: gbeditorial@readersdigest.co.uk

Copyright © 2002 Reader's Digest Association Far East Limited
Philippines Copyright © 2002 Reader's Digest Association Far East Limited

For Reader's Digest, London
Project Editor **Rachel Warren Chadd**
Art Editor **Joanna Walker**

Reader's Digest, General Books, London
Editorial Director **Cortina Butler**
Art Director **Nick Clark**
Executive Editor **Julian Browne**
Development Editor **Ruth Binney**
Managing Editor **Alastair Holmes**
Picture Resource Manager **Martin Smith**
Style Editor **Ron Pankhurst**

Reader's Digest Production
Book Production Manager **Fiona McIntosh**
Pre-press Account Manager **Penelope Grose**
Senior Production Controller **Sarah Fox**

Origination **Colour Systems Limited, London**
Printing and Binding **Partenaires Fabrication, France**

Great British Dishes the Healthy Way
was edited and produced by
Carroll & Brown Limited,
20 Lonsdale Road, London, NW6 6RD,
for the Reader's Digest Association Limited

Art Director **Chrissie Lloyd**
Managing Editor **Antonia Cunningham**
Project Editor **Sally Somers**
Art Editor **Jacqueline Duncan**
Design Assistant **Justin Ford**

Photographers **Ken Field, David Murray,**
   Jules Selmes
Food Stylists **Virginia Alcock, Lorna Brash,**
   Lizzie Harris, Lucy Knox, Clare Lewis,
   Louise Mackaness, Kathy Man,
   Annie Nichols

Stylists **Claire Carter, Jo Cox, Lucy Pearse**
Production Director **Karol Davies**
Production Manager **Nigel Reed**
IT Manager **Paul Stradling**
Picture Research **Sandra Schneider**

Contributors
Hilaire Walden Breakfasts, snacks and savouries
Rosemary Stark Starters, soups and salads
Caroline Marson Eggs and cheese
Jenni Muir Fish and shellfish, features
Christine France Poultry and game
Lyn Hall Beef, lamb and pork
Chrissie Ingram Vegetable dishes
Bridget Jones Puddings
Sue Lawrence Baking
Grace Mulligan Preserves and drinks

Nutritionist **Fiona Hunter**
Recipe Testers **Anna Brandenburger,**
   Sarah Lowman

Carroll & Brown would also like to thank:
Laura Hicks for the index, **Roy Butcher** for
proofreading, **Cécile Landau** and **Carla Masson**
for editorial help, **Evie Loizides-Graham** and
Gilda Pacitti for design assistance and **David**
Yems for studio assistance.

ISBN 0 276 42698 3
BOOK CODE 400-013
CONCEPT CODE UK1245/L